T.
bo
be
la
ad

-6.

15.

90

31.

A book
to the li
you shou
numbers

KLARA'S VISITORS

KLARA'S VISITORS

A NOVEL

by

WESSEL EBERSOHN

LONDON
VICTOR GOLLANCZ LTD
1987

First published in Great Britain 1987
by Victor Gollancz Ltd,
14 Henrietta Street, London WC2E 8QJ

© Wessel Ebersohn 1987

British Library Cataloguing in Publication Data
Ebersohn, Wessel
 Klara's visitors.
 I. Title
 823[F]   PR9369.3.E/

ISBN 0-575-03946-9

Printed in Great Britain by
St Edmundsbury Press Ltd, Bury St Edmunds, Suffolk

Long, long ago, but not far away, there was born to Klara Hitler a child of unusual beauty. His eyes were a shining blue and possessed a gentle mystical quality that drew admiration from all who saw him.

So comely was the child that on the night of his birth the good fairy appeared to the mother in a dazzling glow of light that swept away the darkness in the room. "Because of your child's beauty," the fairy said, "as a man he shall rule all Europe and under his rule all Germans will be good, all Germans will be clever and all Germans will be National Socialists."

As suddenly as she had come the good fairy disappeared, leaving the room again in darkness. Klara was just falling asleep when she was awakened by another voice, calling her name. From the deepest shadow in a corner of the room a second vision appeared, gathering the darkness around her like a cloak. It was the bad fairy."It shall be as my fair rival says," she told Klara. "Your son shall indeed rule all Europe, excepting that under his rule all Germans shall possess only two of the qualities that she promised."

So it came to pass that when the boy reached manhood he was lord of all Europe, but under his rule there were Germans who were National Socialists and were also good, and there were Germans who were National Socialists and also clever, and there were Germans who were good and clever, but they were not National Socialists.

– German folk-tale.

This book is dedicated to the memory of Adolf, the Alois's senior and junior, Klara, Angela, Martha, Gustl, Reinhold, Harrer, Drexler, Ernst, Alfred, Joseph, Ludendorff, Heinrich, Emil, Hermann, Putzi, Hélène, Rudolf, Geli, Schmundt, Kirdof, Eva, Hans, William Patrick, Leni, Junger and my uncle Abdool.

They are always with us.

PROLOGUE

WE DID NOT did not normally acknowledge Uncle Abdool Ebersohn. When race classification first came along his branch of the family fell on the wrong side of the line and had to move to the Cape Flats. What could you expect with a name like Abdool?

Some of us were a bit dark. There was a story at the time that some of the cousins had to bribe an officer in the Department of the Interior to get the right sort of identity documents.

My uncle was a broad old man with a skin the colour of copper and a long nose with a gentle concave slope, just the opposite sort of curve that a Malay nose should have had. But his eyes were the feature that you remembered. They were narrow and they crinkled into a thin line when he smiled. They had a knowing, winning look that gave you the feeling that in any conversation or transaction with him he would be coming out of it stronger than you would. They imparted the air of a man who was well satisfied with the way life had treated him, race classification or no race classification. I have always known that of the men I have met Uncle Abdool had made love to more beautiful women, backed more winners, won more bets and suffered fewest insults.

In the years immediately after the war, before he and his family were moved, we would visit him at his big old house above the military hospital in Wynberg. In those days there were still horse-drawn cabs at Wynberg station. Travelling in them, their iron rimmed wheels clattering over the cobbles in the older streets, the entire coach swaying precariously from side to side, and hearing the cries of the driver, I would watch the traffic thin, the shops and office buildings drop away, and the old houses with chickens and ducks in the yard appear alongside the road. It is my clearest childhood memory.

The house was on a large piece of ground near a stream that flowed through Wynberg park. On winter days Uncle Abdool would sit in the kitchen, at a big wooden table near to the coal stove, drinking a cheap sour wine called Oom Tass and playing chess with anyone who dared to take him on. I would sit next to my mother at the table for a while, responding awkwardly to his questions, showing respect as I had been taught to. Then when the chance came I would slip outside to play cricket or catch tadpoles with my Muslim cousins. There were many of them. I cannot remember how many.

After they were moved we never saw Uncle Abdool for more than a few hours at Christmas. More than that seemed a bad risk. We might all have found ourselves living in sub-economic housing on the Flats.

I left Cape Town as an apprentice telephone technician in the Post Office in 1958, never returning for more than a brief visit and seeing Uncle Abdool little more than once every five or six years. By that time he was living in a tiny cottage built to precisely the same plan as another ten thousand surrounding it. It always angered me to see him sitting in front of a single-bar electric heater in a living room barely big enough for a gathering of three or four. I never asked him if he thought back about the big old house and the coal stove. He seemed to have shrunk a little with the shrinking of his property.

The new neighbourhood was known for its lawlessness. My cousins told me with pride that no policeman ever patrolled the area alone. They walked in pairs. That was more than twenty years ago. Since then it has become tougher still. Today they go six at a time in armoured cars. On the last of these visits, some three years ago, Uncle Abdool drew me aside and told me that when he died there would be a surprise for me. "You an' me," he said, "are the same kind of people."

"Sure we are," I said.

"Don't humour me, Wessel," he said. "You an' me, we have the same blood in our veins, the same blood. You know that?"

"Perhaps you could keep that to yourself," I suggested.

"We got the same spirit too. That's why when I die you're getting a little surprise."

I was about to say that perhaps whatever there was to leave should be left to his children, when the thought arose that perhaps that would be hasty and I might be well advised to see it first. "It's not worth much," Uncle Abdool said. "But I think you'll find it very interesting."

I thought no more of it until I received the parcel in the post four months ago. Apparently Uncle Abdool had died and his family had buried him quietly, with dignity and without informing the white relatives. Maybe we deserved that.

The parcel contained a letter from him to me, written five years before, and seven worn and yellowed notebooks. The writing in the books was the work of a fountain pen, but very faded now. I turned to the letter. It was in Uncle Abdool's characteristic handwriting, a large bold script without unnecessary flourishes. *Dear Wessel*, it said.

I was glad when you became a writer. I always wanted to be one myself, you know, but like so many things in life it was postponed to a later date. I think my problem has been that I have always had other activities that I needed to attend to. There was one more horse to back, one more skirt to track down, card game to play or bottle to empty to have had much time for work.

For this reason having you become a novelist is a great pleasure to me. I would like to think that by passing this stuff to you I am helping your career in some way. I know that this is just an old man's fancy. I mean old Adolf lost the war and no one is interested in a loser. I just like to think that in some way they might be of help.

I suppose it could be something of a surprise that your old Uncle Abdool should be in possession of this stuff, so let me tell you how it happened. You know that during the war I was in North Africa with the Cape Corps. They let us bear arms in those days, even if they were waiting at the docks to take the rifles away the moment the boys stepped off the boat. Well, I was taken prisoner at Tobruk. Your old man was down the road at Hamra with Dan Pienaar's mob. One of their staff officers sent us a message that said, "You are an example to us all. South Africa will remember your sacrifice." From that moment we knew we were finished and it seemed a better idea to be a German prisoner than a South African casualty. They kept us in Egypt for a few weeks, then they moved us to Italy and eventually to Germany. We did not know exactly where we were, but we did know that it was somewhere in the south.

In August '43 I broke out over the wire during a power failure, and about a mile from the camp I hopped onto a German army truck loaded with antique furniture (I swear it) and the damned thing travelled all night, stopping only at check points. I did not know where we were going, how far, or in what direction. It was mid-morning of the next day when we finally stopped and by this time I had worked out that we had travelled north, deeper into Germany.

3

We stopped in a narrow street bordered by old buidings, those with a lot of woodwork on the front. At the time I thought that nothing worse could have happened. Remember that I was wearing my old ragged South African army uniform. I did not think that I was going to last two minutes outside of the truck. On the other hand it was clear that, having brought the furniture to Berlin, they would soon be off-loading, so the right thing to do would be to get myself off-loaded first.

There was no chance of the street being completely empty of people. There was an old toppie sweeping the streets, a white man. I could hardly believe it. And a couple of women with shawls and baskets. They could have been straight from the Cape Flats except that they were also white.

I waited until I thought no one was looking at the truck then I made for the nearest door. I was inside in a second, maybe two. It was a passage and from inside there was music coming, this nice gemütliche German music they sing while they drink beer. They know how to sing and they know how to drink, those Germans, but if they come to the Cape for a visit we'll teach them something about both.

A window half-way along the passage had heavy velvet curtains that reached down to the floor. There were big pictures with heavy frames on the wall and a nice carpet on the floor. From the outside it had looked like a slum, but inside it was quite a classy place.

Whoever the house belonged to I felt safer there than in the street. I was tip-toeing along the passage whence, through the archway at the end of the passage from where the music was coming, two German officers stumbled. I say, stumbled, because the pair of them were blind drunk. Nevertheless, drunk or not, you can imagine that I did not want to get into conversation with them. I turned back to the door, but before I reached it, it opened half-way and I could see more German officers on the outside. They had stopped and were talking among themselves before actually coming in, but these all looked sober.

The choice being between drunk German officers and sober ones, I settled on the drunk ones. I suppose the debate inside me lasted about a quarter of a second. Without a glance in their direction I marched past the two drunk officers and stepped in behind the curtains. I stayed there all day and almost all night. The damned place was like a railway station during rush hour until past four o'clock in the morning, streams of German uniforms coming and going past my curtain. Except for the sounds of music and laughter and female voices I would have thought that I was in German military headquarters.

The sun was coming up and I had not heard a sound for perhaps half an hour when I thought for the first time that it was safe to try the window. It was one of those wooden frame types that slide up and down, and spend half the time stuck fast. This one was stuck.

I slipped away from the window, looking for some other way out of the back of the house. I was not yet even thinking about how I was going to reach Switzerland.

I had found another window and this one was just starting to slide open when a woman spoke behind me. "Und du?" she said.

The sound of her voice spun me round as if I was a top on the end of a piece of string. She was standing in the middle of the room, a kind of a sitting room, like a hotel lounge. Martha was a woman of about fifty then, but let me tell you something, women like her, at any age, are one in a million, maybe ten million, maybe more. And this comes from a man who has devoted a lot of his life to women.

She was standing in the centre of the room like a great actress who had just made an entrance. She had long black hair, dense and hanging in curls down her naked shoulders onto her bosom, and such a bosom, but things being as they are, me being your uncle, I mean, I should not go into this in much detail. Nor should you be interested. It is a matter of respect. Let me just say that she was wearing a crimson gown that fell down to the ground, like a red waterfall, spreading on the floor at her feet, while her shoulders and most of her bosom were naked. Her skin was white, so white that it seemed ... but never mind.

She was standing there in the centre of the room like a queen and I was standing with my back to the partly open window, wearing the ragged remains of my army drill and probably looking like a burglar in enemy uniform. She looked amused, just a little, as if she had known me before that moment and expected this of me. She also looked a little tired. I only knew about ten words of German, but I had understood her words to mean, "And you?" So I said the first thing that came to mind. Remember I had not been near a women for a couple of years. "Ich liebe dich," I said.

The expression on her face did not change for a moment, then she chuckled, a deep sound, full of pleasure, and came slowly up to me. She touched my cheek with the tips of her fingers. "What a lovely colour," she said in English. "You're like a brass jug. If I shine you, will you glow?"

5

"If you keep standing so close, I'll glow without any shining," I told her.

At this she chuckled again. Her eyes were dark, wide and round and they seemed to see through me and my miserable foolish profession of love. What she saw was the cause of her amusement. "And what are you?" she asked. "You aren't English."

"I'm South African," I said, as if admitting that I was an enemy soldier was the most natural thing in the world.

"Ah," she said. "I thought Africans were darker." She slid a finger-tip between two of my shirt buttons. "Are you the same colour everywhere?"

Looking back, the conversation seems a bit strange now, but at the time it was a simple exchange between a man and a woman. It had nothing to do with nations at war or any such nonsense. I told her that I was the same colour everywhere that I could see.

"And so, my African, what are you doing in Berlin?"

"Looking for a way to go home," I said.

"Home?" Her eyebrows were raised high. "This might not be so simple."

Before I could answer she took me by the hand and led me up a staircase, down a passage and into her bedroom. By this time I had finally worked out what sort of place I was in. But if I was in a Berlin brothel, I asked myself, why did it have to be one that was used by practically the entire German officer corps?

Up to that time I had never seen a bedroom anything like Martha's. I had never seen any room like it. There were wood carvings, and furniture made out of either marble or glass or finely carved wood like the furniture on the truck that had brought me. Lace curtains and velvet curtains and ankle deep carpets: it could have been a picture in a magazine. And the bed: the bed was big enough to enable her staff to lay the entire High Command, all at the same time. I'll tell you something about the wages of sin, Wessel, sometimes they are not so bad.

Well, Martha said I had better explain my presence. So I told her God's truth, exactly as it happened. And when I had finished she told me her name and what sort of place I was in and that she was the madame.

By and by I asked her what she was doing awake after a hard night's work and she told me that she could not sleep and it was the girls who were doing the work, not her. She said that she always struggled to fall asleep. Now you and I both know that there is one dead certain way of

6

putting a woman to sleep and obviously she needed sleep. So I did it. I put her to sleep.

And that is where I spent the rest of the war, in that room with Martha locking me in and bringing me food. She got me ordinary clothes and a few times in the two years that I was there we went for walks after dark. We were stopped by soldiers once and questioned, and were only released because she offered the Captain a free pass to her house. Martha always said that she was a humanist. She said that what she was doing for Germany was obvious and I was her gesture of goodwill to the other side.

Surviving the war in Berlin was no laughing matter. The allied bombers flattened all the buildings around us without doing more than smash a few of our windows. Martha said it was because Winston Churchill knew her well and had ordered them to miss us. Martha's only failing was that she loved to rub shoulders, and not just shoulders either, with the great. She was a terrible name dropper. If one of the heads of the army or navy came in, Martha would service him herself. And the strange thing is that they seemed to feel that it was an honour to be singled out by Germany's most famous madame. At least Martha always insisted that she was the most famous name in the business.

I became very fond of her. I mean she saved my life. This was the toughest part of the war for me, sitting squashed up in Martha's wardrobe, watching through the keyhole while she laid Germany's top brass. She said I was foolish to carry on so. She said that it was a professional matter and I should see it in that light. Would I expect Picasso to stop painting, Tauber to stop singing or Field Marshall Rommel to become a pacifist? Birds must fly, she said.

She would always tell me exactly what she had done to get the best response from Göring, Goebbels or Sigmund Freud. She had lived in Vienna but I did not believe about that last one. She thought Freud was an opera singer. And there was old Adolf himself. She always claimed to be the only one with whom he managed it, but who can tell? I did not believe about Winston Churchill either.

At the end of the war when the Russians reached Berlin we were not so lucky though. Their shelling was not as discerning as the allied bombing had been. More than half the house got blown to bits, fortunately not the half that I was living in. Clearly old Joe Stalin had never been one of Martha's clients.

But the Russians needed Martha's place as badly as the Germans had *(the Americans were more generous than the Russians, but there were not as many of them), and her house remained a little island of peace and prosperity in the middle of shattered Berlin. She used to say that it was a place where all the nations met and found that they had something in common. If they had made her place the United Nations headquarters world peace would have been assured.*

The stuff in the parcel came into my possession while the Russian shells were falling around us and the members of the German High Command were all dashing across for a last quick one before they ended up in allied custody for the next twenty years. I think they were reckoning on a long period of celibacy when that happened.

I was lying down on the bed (I did a lot of that) when Martha came rushing into the room, grabbed me by the arm and all but dragged me into the wardrobe. Before she closed the door she whispered softly to me. "I'm sorry to do this to you, Albert," she said, "but this is one I have to do myself. It's a question of patriotism and loyalty, also sentimentality. Don't watch."

Watching was very difficult. The keyhole was low and I had to get down on my hands and knees to see out. To further complicate matters the bed was high and I could never get a clear view of what was happening on it. I watched. The first view of him that I got was from behind. He was wearing a uniform like a bus conductor wears, peaked cap and all, and was stooping forward a bit, holding something in his hands. One of the girls had let him in and Martha was lying down spread across the bed like a bloody tart. She struck these poses as a matter of habit. She got up and walked slowly over to him like a cat fraternizing with a mouse, then she took his cap off and threw it onto the bed. "Hello, lover," she said.

"M-M-Mar-th-tha," he said, her name coming out in little pieces. I think he himself was just little pieces at that time, held together loosely by sheer insanity. "Martha, I have something important here. I don't think the Russians will disturb you, so I want you to look after these for me." He turned halfway, enabling me to see his face, and I recognized old Adolf, little moustache and all. His face was twitching as if he had an army of ants under the outer layer of his skin. "I want you to look after them for me," he said, "and when all is finished give them into the keeping of someone who can be trusted." He was holding a brown paper parcel in both hands.

"I know just the man," she said, taking the parcel from him. "His

8

name is Albert. He'll look after them well."

"They are my writings," he said. "They are my legacy to civilization. This Albert, he is a historian?"

"In a manner of speaking. He is also a survivor."

"Ah," Adolf said, "a survivor. This is very important. Survival is everything." He stopped speaking suddenly. Now that he had handed over the parcel he did not seem to know what to do with his hands. Only by clenching them tightly together could he keep their shaking within manageable limits.

"Anything else?" Martha said. The question was accompanied by a sidelong look that could have burnt the hide off an elephant. I could have got right out of that cupboard and killed her. Only the likelihood of a couple of SS guards, waiting outside the door, stopped me.

"Well . . . perhaps," he said. "Perhaps . . ." He was pleading with her. "Perhaps . . . one little thing."

She put down the books on the foot of the bed and placed a hand on his shoulder. "Oh, Adolf, you just weren't a success, were you? You should have stuck to art."

The idea triggered off a worse bout of shaking. "We . . . we . . . all m-make mistakes."

"Was it you alone who was mad? Or were we all crazy?" Martha was looking into his face in such a soft and loving way, I think she really fancied the old bastard.

He seemed not to have understood her question though. "Perhaps . . . one little thing?" He pleaded again.

"Why not?" Martha asked.

What I saw in the next half hour explained a lot about politics to me. Let me tell you, Hitler's invasion of Poland had little to do with lebensraum and much to do with other things that he could not do too well. Martha worked on him like no woman has ever worked on a man. She did enough to raise the anger, so to speak, of at least a hundred men, but old Adolf seemed to sort of freeze and get a funny look on his face as if he was not even present, but in some other place, listening to his own music.

Well, eventually, desperately perhaps, he seemed to sort of manage something. I could not see clearly because of the keyhole being low and the bed so high and she having him stretched out on his back, like a corpse. She got up and shook herself like a duck that's just been laid straightening out her feathers. Her tits . . . no, I won't tell you about

9

that. You should have a little respect for your uncle. You shouldn't want to know that sort of thing. "My God, Adolf," she said. "You don't improve with age." Then she sat down next to him and, putting a hand on his chest, gave him a little shake. "You'd better get up. I don't suppose you'll want the Russians to find you like this." Her face suddenly became puzzled and she leant closer to him.

I lost sight of her as she got off the bed. A moment later I rolled out of the cupboard and onto the carpet. She had unlocked the cupboard door. "Albert," she said, her voice sounding indignant, "you were watching." She always called me Albert in those days. She said that Albert must be the German form of Abdool.

I put a finger to my lips and started creeping towards the door. With old Adolf on the bed and the thought of what he might do to me if he knew that I had been in the cupboard, it seemed sensible to leave while I could. To further complicate matters there was this Aryan thing, you know. One look at me and I would have been on my way to the forced labour camps, if they still existed.

Martha took my arm. There was a strange sound to her voice, like I'd never heard before. "Albert, I think he's dead."

That was the truth of it. It was no wonder that he looked like a corpse. He was flat on his back and his mouth was hanging open, as if his last action had been to gasp for air.

Well, I had to get back into the cupboard while Martha sent a couple of the girls out, carrying a white flag, to look for someone who might want the body. It turned out there had been no SS guards at the door. By the time they got back the Russian artillery had stopped, but there were sounds of machine gun fire from the direction of the Brandenburg gate, but closer by. The girls were coming up the stairs when a burst of machine gun fire smashed the window in Martha's room and tore a string of holes in Adolf's pants that were hanging over a chair. Martha and I were near the door and the bullets hit the wall opposite us.

By the time the girls came into the room, bringing with them an SS colonel, Martha and I had got a pair of tartan pants that she had bought me onto Adolf's backside and she had locked me into the cupboard again. The SS man looked a lot less confident now than his breed had a few months before. As soon as he saw the body the expression of his face became suspicious. "The Führer, Adam Humps's Führer, does not wear such trousers."

"Who is Adam Humps?" Martha asked.

"I, I am Humps. And Humps's Führer does not ..."

"Look at his face, you big moron," Martha suggested.

He leant towards the body, suddenly snapping erect like a jack-in-the-box. "Heil Hitler," he yelled. It was a good day for learning things. I had just learnt about politics, now I had the finest demonstration of the conditioned reflex I have ever seen.

"At ease, Colonel," Martha said. "He's not going to return your salute."

"Enemies of the State," the SS colonel yelled, more loudly than before. "This is the work of enemies of the State." He was a big man, tall and broad in the shoulder, and his voice was as big as the rest of him. Wearing his black uniform and shouting about enemies of the State, he was not a man to argue with.

But Martha was different. She grabbed him by an arm and tried to shake him. "State," she yelled. "Where is the State? What is left of the State? What is left of the Führer for that matter?"

The SS man was not one to be deviated by reason from his line of thinking. He threw Martha off, whipped out his side arm and took a step back, glancing around the room as if expecting to find enemies of the State everywhere. The step backward was a mistake though. This is the thing about backward steps. You never know where they are going to take you.

One of his feet got entangled in old Adolf's perforated pants that were lying on the floor by now, and he fell over backwards. The gun went off and the bullet entered the open mouth of the corpse, doing substantial damage to the top of the skull before lodging in one of the bedposts. The colonel scrambled to his feet and saw what had happened. "God in heaven," he said. "Merciful saviour. Lord above." All of which clearly shows that despite their pagan ideology the Nazis knew who to call on when they were in trouble. "I have shot the Führer," he said. "A mortal wound. What will Germany say? What will history say?"

He raised the pistol to his own temple but Martha, grabbed his arm, hanging onto it like a monkey hanging from a tree branch. "Listen, you maniac, the man's dead. He was dead before you shot him."

"The Führer, I shot the Führer." His face had turned the colour of a sheet, an ordinary white sheet, not pink or lilac or crimson like Martha's sheets. "He's dead," he kept saying.

At this point Martha got the idea of releasing me from the cupboard. I came hobbling out with cramps in both hamstrings. She introduced me

11

to the SS man as Admiral Hirihoto of the Japanese fleet. "Heil, ally," I said in German.

"I shot the Führer," he told me.

"Nonsense," I said. "I saw the whole thing. It was suicide. He shot himself. Your bullet went straight out of the window."

I could see that Martha liked this version of events. She pointed to the window the Russians had destroyed, as if to lend weight to the idea. By this time I was trying to wrap Hitler's dead fingers around the handle of the gun. I thought they might sort of freeeze in that position and then there'd be no doubt at all, but let me tell you dead fingers don't easily wrap round the handle of a gun. In fact they don't at all. I had to be satisfied with one finger threaded between the trigger and the little whatsit that makes a sort of frame round it. You know the thing I mean.

The SS man was still in a state of shock, but this turned out to be an advantage. Martha, using her most authoritarian voice (she always used to say that in her position she outranked a colonel in the Waffen SS and a brigadier in the regular army), said to him, "The Führer has committed suicide. This is a tragic day for Germany. Go now and return with two men to take him back to his headquarters with dignity." She had scarcely finished speaking when another burst of machine gun fire had us all down on our knees.

They carried old Adolf down the stairs and we watched two soldiers picking their way furtively through the rubble of the city, one holding his feet and the other his arms, my tartan trousers flashing against the grey of the surroundings like a lit-up sign.

A few hours later the house was swarming with Russians. During the first two days three girls had to be treated for dislocated vertebrae, four for friction burns on the inside of their thighs, and almost all of them for various swellings, inflamations and so on. That was how long it took Martha to reach the top brass of the Red army. As soon as she explained it to them they declared her premises off-limits to anyone below the rank of major. A few days later the Americans arrived in Berlin with plenty of money and a clear idea of how they wanted to spend it, and Martha became the start of the German economic miracle.

I stayed on in Berlin for four years after the war. At home I was reported missing, presumed dead. But in time the longing for the Cape became too much for me and I felt bad about the old girl thinking I was dead. I told Martha I had to go. So I took old Adolf's parcel, Martha gave me my ticket and a few bob, well more than a few bob, and I came home. I never bothered to change the missing, presumed dead thing. My reasoning was that dead men are not required to pay income tax.

All these years I have looked after old Adolf's notes. Every now and then I would take them out and have a read. It kept my German in condition and it reminded me of the sort of trouble a man can get into if he's not satisfied with the simple things in life.

So look after them for me. Maybe you can straighten them out a bit, work on the plot or something, you know. If the story was speeded up a bit it could be pretty good reading. Introduce a few interesting characters, see what you can do. Maybe you can set the action at home, give it a bit of authenticity.

If you get any royalties from it, buy yourself a bottle of Scotch, go down to Plumstead cemetery and have a snort over my grave. You might consider spilling a few drops.

All this from your favourite uncle, Abdool.

Cape Town
January 1980.

Today: Frau Nawrotski have a big face. She have a big red face and hairs come out her nose. Red hairs and grey come out. She say, Adolf, why, why, why? I say, Of course I want to taste.

But wine? She say. The grey hairs and the red hairs shake when air come out her nose. Little boys not have wine, she say.

Of course I want, I say.

Not argue, not never argue, Frau Nawrotski say. Come to kichen. I clean.

Frau Nawrotski take hand. I try to make loose, but her big hand hold me. Come, she say.

Frau Nawrotski take off shirt with wine on. She take off pants with wine on. She wipe with dish cloth. Her big red face get more red and her grey hairs and her red hairs stick out by the holes from her nose. That better, she say. That much more better, she say. She clean legs and tummy and everywhere.

Then she say, only one, Adolf?

Leave me, I say.

But only one, Adolf? Why only one?

Leave me, I say. Everybody have only one Hochstetter.

Her big face is more red. Hochstetter is only one, she say. Why only one peanut?

Leave me, I say. Leave me.

Not leave, Frau Nawrotski say. Must clean, she say. Must also have two peanuts. Perhaps one is hiding. Here? Or here?

Frau Nawrotski feel. Only one? she say. Why only one, Adolf? Must be two, must always be two.

Leave me, leave, I say.

This day I six, my birthday. Frau Nawrotski is stupid and she have hair come out her nose. One peanut is good. One peanut, one Hochstetter. Nuthing is wrong.

Tomorrow, next day: Klaus bird Irma make a seed. Take Irma seed to show Angela, also Mama. Seed birst in pocket. Not small bird inside, just mess inside. Mama clean pants. She say, not let Papa see.

Tomorrow, next next day: I say to Klaus, how many peanut?

Klaus say, what is peanut?

Hochstetter in front, I say. Peanut behind.

Two, Klaus say.

I see, I say.

Two, Klaus say. He say, he two, Wilhelm two, Helmuth two, everybody two. He also two, he say.

I see, I tell Klaus.

Klaus take off pants. Klaus got two. Klaus say, I take off pants.

No, I say. Klaus is a fool.

Next next next day: Alois say, I don't know how Adolf say such funny stuff. I don't know how he think such funny stuff.

Quiet, Mama say.

How he think such funny stuff? Alois say.

Quiet, not talk, Mama say.

Leave our sweet Adolfus, Angela say.

He have rotten inside his head, Alois say.

You have empty inside head, I say.

Alois hit. I fall. Stop, Alois, Mama say.

I tell Papa, Angela say. Alois run away. My sweet Adolfus, Angela say.

More next day: Papa get Herr Kauffman's wagon. Wagon got too wheels, got too horses, got wip. Papa like wagon. Like wip. Like to hit.

We go to Herr Lochner. Herr Lochner by Lambach. Papa say, I know the way. Papa say, always I know the way. Papa say, I go there and I go there. I know the way. Mama say nothing. Angela say, Papa clever, Papa know the way. I say nothing.

We lost. Papa lost.

I ride and ride two hours and I not find Herr Lochner, Papa say.

Five hours, I say.

Two hours, Papa say. I not find Her Lochner.

Six hours, I say. We explore the whole Lambach.

Two hours, Papa scream.

16

Seven hours, I tell Papa.
I kill you, Adolf, Papa shout.
Quiet, dear, Mama say.
Quiet, little Adolfus, Angela say.
Shut up, Alois say.

Today: Angela not give me of her cayk. I put Angela's cat in box and kick. Twenty-five kicks.

More day: Say sorry for sister, Papa say.
  Not kick sister. Kick cat.
  Sorry, sorry, Papa scream.
  Kick cat. Not kick sister.
  Papa hit. Sorry, sorry, sorry, Papa scream.
  Sorry, fat face, I say for Angela.
  Papa hit. Angela cry.
  Tomorrow I catch cat more. Thirty-five kicks next time.

Day: Papa hit Alois. Alois a fool.

More day: Papa hit Alois with belt. Papa say, where is horse wip? But horse wip by Herr Kauffman. Else Papa hit with horse wip. Belt make red lines on Alois. Papa not have horse wip. Horse wip make blue marks. And blood. And scabs. But Papa not have. Only belt.

Today: Mama put mirir in room. I want to look, but Alois in room all the time. I hayt Alois.

More: Mama see Angela sitting with legs wide. Close legs, Angela, Mama say. Angela close legs, smack. Why, Mama? Angela say.
  Because you a girl, Mama say. Girls not have wide legs, Mama say.
  Why not? Angela say. Adolf sit with wide legs. Alois sit with wide legs. When Edmund gets big he sit with wide legs. I sit with wide legs.
  No, Mama say, not girls. Adolf sit with wide legs. He learning to be a man. He sit with wide legs like Papa. Alois also. But not girls. Girls sit with close legs. I sit with close legs, Angela. You also sit with close legs.
  Why can boys have wide legs? Angela say.
  Because is better, I say. Poor girl, I say.

17

Shut up, Angela say. He getting just like Alois, Mama. Papa will have to smack every day.

All right, dear, Mama say.

I want to look in new mirir in room. Alois still there. No time to see in mirir.

Tomorrow: Klaus find worms. Klaus keep worms in box. I say, we see inside.

Klaus say, no. Klaus say, see inside, worms finished.

I say, see inside.

Klaus say, no.

I see inside. Worms green inside.

Klaus say, just one, just one, just one.

All worms green inside. Worms from Klaus finished.

Day: Teacher say story about Napolen, king of France. Papa fix fence by river. I talk to Papa. If there come a war, Papa, will you kill Frenchmen?

We not have war with France, Papa say.

But if we have a war, will you kill Frenchmen?

But there is not war, Papa say.

But if, I say, if, if, if, I say, will you kill Frenchmen?

Not war, not war, Papa scream.

I think if comes a war Papa not kill Frenchmen. If comes a war and I am big I kill Frenchmen and Frenchmen and Frenchmen.

Wensday: Alois by Gertrude. I look in mirir. I look front. I look side. I look other side. Hochstetter is one. Peanut and Hochstetter is two. Two is good.

Alois come home from Gertrude. I give Alois clean panties. I tell Alois, Mama say must put on. I hide under bed. Alois put on clean panties. One Hochstetter, two peanuts. Three.

Three is bad. Two is better. I hayt Alois.

Friday: Frau Lochner come. Mama in bed. Mama cry. All night Mama cry. Frau Lochner in kitchen, say to Papa, this is bad one.

Adolf go to own room, Papa scream. Alois you also. I go. Papa talk softly to Angela. Must help Frau Lochner, he say.

One day I kill him, Alois say. He do to Mama.

18

You have two, you fool, I say.

Alois hit. I cry in bed. Alois say, shut up. Papa come kill.

Alois a fool. Not cry for Alois hit. Cry for Mama sick. Cry for Frau Lochner say is a bad one. Why Angela help? Why not I help? Why not Mama's little Adolfus? Why is bad one? When is good one?

Morning: Frau Lochner is tired. Papa is drunk. Alois is a fool. Mama? I want to see Mama.

Come, dear little Adolfus, Angela say. She hold my hand.

Mama? I say.

Come see Mama, Angela say. She tayck in room. I also go. Mama very much tired. More tired than Frau Lochner, much more tired than Frau Lochner. Small bayby with Mama.

Is Frau Lochner's bayby, Mama? I say.

Is our little Paula, Mama say. Mama's voice is old and creak like Herr Kauffman's wagon.

Is Frau Lochner give it to us, Mama? I say.

Frau Lochner help Mama, Mama say.

Is Mama's bayby, not Frau Lochner's bayby, silly Adolfus, Angela say.

Now I know. If a Mama get sick, then bayby comes. That why we have doctors. Else too many baybies. Now I know.

Tewsday: Papa hit Alois. Alois a fool. Only belt. Only red lines, no blue. No scabs. No blood.

Wensday: Alois in kitchen. Alois cry. Mama holding Alois. Want to push Alois, but Mama holding. And Alois hit if I push. I stay by door.

Mama, mama, Alois cry. I hayt him. I hayt Adolf also.

Quiet, my dear, quiet, Mama say, not cry.

They not cry Alois say. Alois cry. They not cry. They not can cry. They not can love. They not can feel.

Quiet, my dear, Mama say, not say such things. Of course Papa and Adolf can love.

Not love, not love, Alois say. Alois a fool. Also not kill Frenchmen if comes a war. They need you, Alois say, not love. They not feel anything, whole life they never feel anything, Papa and Adolf, he say. You can have many babies for him, Papa will go. You can look after

19

Adolf, Adolf will go. Not love.
Not talk, not talk, Mama say.
Alois cry, Mama talk softly, hold him. Alois a fool.

Friday: Teacher say Kaiser Wilhelm got thousand letters in a week. I never get one letter in whole time, whole life.

Friday: Papa call me, call Alois. Get coal from Herr Kauffman, Papa say, not let Herr Kauffman see. It cold tonight. Get much coal.
Come, Adolf, Alois say.
Not let Herr Kauffman see, Papa shout.
We go.
Not do it, Adolf, Alois say.
Papa hit, I say.
Poor sweet Adolfus, Alois say, not want Papa to hit.
Poor sweet Alois is a big fool, I say.
I kill you, Adolf, Alois say.
I look up him. I look down him. You not leader, I say. I leader. One day I punish you.
Alois say, you mad, little sweet Adolfus. I steal Herr Kauffman's coal today, then I run away. I not steal for him again. I not get hiding from him again.
Just belt, I say, not horse whip.

Munsday: Alois gone. Alois bed empty. No Alois. I hear Mama cry. Mama say, poor Alois. Alois is not happy. Alois cry. Poor Alois.
Papa say, I find him I kill him. I hit him with horse whip.
Blue lines, I think. Also blud and small scabs.
I kill him, Papa say. He owe me sumthing, Papa say. He owe me.

Friday: Alois still gone. Good, I think. Alois a fool. Two peanuts not help Alois, I think. One is better. Hochstetter work better with one.

Friday: We gone to Lambach now. Farm was much better, but Papa say Lambach is better. Papa say farm is lonely. Papa say no one to talk with. Mama look sad when Papa say. When Papa go Mama say, who are we? No one I suppose?
Third floor, Gasthof Leingartner. We stay there.

20

Munday: (Teacher say Munsday not right) 1896: Papa not here tonight. Papa at Gasthaus, drinking beer and touching barmaids, Mama say. Papa name is Alois, like Alois. Also got two like Alois, I think. Not one like me.

Tuesday, 1896: Paint picture in class. Colour for trees, colour for grass get confused. Colour for trees go into colour for grass. Colour for grass go into colour for trees. Teacher say, Adolf, you clever boy, you have real talent.

Very clever teacher. Now I go to be a painter. Not painter, artyst.

More, 1896: Not write more. Writing is for girls. Now I am man of deeds. Boy of deeds. Man of deeds.

1897: Man of culture must write. I am a man of deeds and culture. Father Gustave says I have a good voice. I must sing in the choir. Mama is making clothes for sing in the choir.

Father Gustave preaches. He stands in front and he says, thus saith the Lord. And, dearly beloved brethren. And, repent ye sinners.

An artist is not so good. I will be a Father. I will stand in church and say, thou shalt not. I will say, the day is at hand. I will shout in a strong voice, prepare ye the way.

I will be a bishop, a cardinal. I will be a pope.

1897: I am long. I am longer than Sigmund. I am longer than Otto. I am longer than anyone in the class, just Ulrich and Karl and Walter and Kurt are longer than me. But I am growing faster.

1897: The monastry have a badge, a nice badge with a cross, and the legs of the cross, they all bend. I will make my own badge when I am pope. I will put in the cross with the bent legs.

19 January 1899: Now I do the date correct. I also write correct. Before I did not know. Now I know. Now I play chess with Papa. Sometimes I let Papa win. Papa is like Alois. Alois is like Papa. Alois is gone.

20 January 1899: Mama is with Edmund all the time.

April 1899: Papa says Angela has nice cherries. Last year she only had cherry pits. Where is Angela's cherries. I ask her for one, but she says, Adolf, you fool.

April 1899: Today I play chess with Papa. I think better than him. I always think better than him. I say, I am attacking your soldiers now, Papa. I am killing them. I am Bismarck, Papa, I say. You are Napoleon III. I am taking back Alsace-Lorraine.

Shut up and play chess, Papa says.

But I am thinking better and better. Now I have thrusted you nicely, I say to Papa. My soldiers have made a ring around you. You cannot get out. I am Bismarck, I tell Papa.

How can I concentrate, Klara? Papa screams at Mama, with Edmund and Paula crying all the time.

Do you know why I am doing this move? I ask Papa.

Adolf, do you remember that hiding you got yesterday? Papa screams. Do you remember how you cried?

I never cry again, I say.

We'll see. We'll see, Papa screams. He hits me with his belt. I do not cry.

June 1899: I am taking back Austria, Bismarck says.

Watch out, says Napoleon III. I will overrun Prussia.

I am taking back Austria, also Alsace-Lorraine, says Bismarck.

You will grovel at my feet, Napoleon III screams. He has whiskers like Papa.

I think not, says Bismarck, I think not.

1 June 1899: Ohm Bernhardt Kelpere and Ohm Walter Ulricht played for town champion. Chess, they played. Ohm Ulricht won.

When they die I will be champion.

June 1899: Papa wants to play chess again. I think better than Papa again. I think Papa is at the Gasthaus too much. I think the beer is too much. I think one Alois is like another Alois.

I am the champion chess player, I tell Papa. I am like Bismarck, beating the French, killing Frenchmen.

Quiet, Adolf, Papa says. Do you remember last time we played chess?

Very well, I say. I am the champion in the house.

Adolf, Papa screams.

Not so much noise and play, I tell Papa.

I kill you, Adolf, Papa screams.

I stand up next to the table. I think not, I tell Papa.

Papa jumps up. He looks at me. His face is red like Frau Nawrotski and his whiskers shake like the hairs in Frau Nawrotski's nose. He looks at me and his eyes open and close quickly. Then he kicks the chess board and all the men are on the floor. Stupid game, he screams. Stupid game. But he does not hit me. I am Bismarck. He is a dead Frenchman.

July, 1899: We are in Leonding. There is the cemetery. If you go outside the cemetery is there. All the people who died in Leonding, fighting Napoleon III. Papa likes Leonding better than Lambach or the farm. Leonding has more Gasthausen, also more barmaids.

August, 1899: Horst and Otto want to steal apples from Herr Adendorff's garden. I say, no, a leader does not steal, a leader takes.

Herr Adendorff is hiding in the shed. I have blue lines with small scabs. Also Horst. Otto got away.

October, 1899: Angela always gets an egg. I know you will understand, little Adolfus, she says. But you can have a small piece of my egg, Angela says. I am bigger than you. But you can have a small piece.

Mama is with Edmund. I got no egg, I say to Mama.

Shame on you, Angela, Mama says.

Mama, it is not true, Angela says, he nearly got half.

I got nothing, I tell Mama. I got no yellow.

You did. You got a big piece of yellow. Angela told a lie to Mama.

Me? Yellow? I got no yellow.

Adolf is a liar, Angela screams to Mama.

I am a leader, I say.

Leader? Angela's face looks ugly. Who do you lead?

I am a leader. I am going to be an artist or I am going to be a pope.

That shows how much you know, Angela says. You cannot be a pope. You can only be the Pope.

Then I will be the Pope or I will be the artist. I say.

You are mad, Angela say.
I think not, I say to Angela.

October, 1899: Herr Bergmann was here. He says the English are having a war. He says they are fighting the Boers. The Boers are in Africa. He says a hundred Boers are beating a thousand English. He says the Boers have a General called De La Rey. He beats the English every time with a hundred Boers. The Boers fight on horses.

That is why Bismarck beat Napoleon III. We had more horses. In Lambach and Leonding are many horses.

October, 1899: How many? I ask Otto.

Two, of course, Otto says.

One Hochstetter, one peanut? I ask Otto.

What do you mean? Otto asks. One Hochstetter, two peanuts. One in front, two behind the one in front. Everybody is the same. What do you mean?

Nothing, I say to Otto.

October, 1899: She behaves like a stupid virgin, I hear Papa say to Herr Bergmann. What is a stupid virgin?

I ask Papa who is the stupid virgin?

You are heading for the gallows, he says. Also Syphilis.

Who is Syphilis?

Friday, October, 1899: I tell Mama Frau Bergmann is a stupid virgin. Oh, Adolf, she says, how can you say that? But she laughs, then she makes her face straight again. What a terrible thing . . . she says. But she laughs again. You will get into serious trouble, she says.

The gallows? I ask.

Perhaps not the gallows, she says.

What about Syphilis? I ask.

Adolf, Adolf, Adolf, she says.

October, 1899: What are virgins? I ask Otto.

Virgins are girls who have never done that thing with a boy, Otto says.

What thing? I ask Otto.

That thing that you have to do to make babies, Hermann says.

24

What is that thing?

I do not know, Otto says. My cousin knows but he will not tell me, Otto says.

Angela is a stupid virgin, I say to Otto.

How do you know? Otto says.

I know everything.

Except that thing you have to do to make babies, Otto says.

Munday, October 1899: Adolf, I want to talk, Papa says. I want to talk about your future, my son, he says. I want you to think what you will do when you are a man.

I do, I say to Papa.

Quiet and listen, Papa says. Do not think while I am talking. Listen. A boy must consider what he must be when he is a man. Now is a good time for you to think, little Adolfus. Now is a good time for you to use your head and think, after listening to me. Now when you grow up if you work hard at school you can be a customs officer like me and wear a nice uniform and everyone will say, good day, Herr Hitler, and you will have respect.

No thank you, Papa, I say.

Quiet and listen, Papa says. His face is starting to get red and his whiskers are shaking. You see how your Papa has respect in the town. People say, how do you do, Herr Hitler? And, are you well, Herr Hitler? Jawohl, Herr Hitler, sofort, Herr Hitler. And, your good health, Herr Hitler. And you have a uniform and the ladies look at you in your uniform and blush. And everyone wants to know you because you are the customs officer and you are in the service of the Fatherland.

No, thank you, Papa, I say.

What do you mean, no thank you, Papa screams. Are you listening to what I say?

Yes, Papa, I am listening, I say to Papa. I do not want to be a customs officer and I do not want to have a customs officer's uniform. And Austria is not the Fatherland, Germany is. And I do not want people to say, how are you, Herr Hitler. I want them to salute and say, Heil Hitler.

Heil Hitler, Papa screams, who do you think you are? What do you think you are going to be? The country's Führer?

No, I am going to be the Pope, Papa, I say

25

Really now? And what will you tell the world when you are the Pope?

Repent ye, I say.

You are mad, Papa screams.

I think not, Papa, I say. And while I have your attention, could you tell me what is this thing to do so that girls are not virgins any longer?

Out, Papa screams, out, out, out.

November 1899: Angela says that if you wear . . . no, if a girl wears a white frilly night dress and she sits in front of the mirror, combing her hair, she will see her husband. Angela is nearly as stupid as the fool, Alois.

November Monday (this time it is right) *1899:* Today Heinz brought a letter from Leo for Angela. I take the letter and run to my room. Close the door before Angela can get in. Please, please Adolf, Angela say. That letter is very important to me.

What will you do for me? I say.

Anything, Adolf anything. Please my sweet darling little Adolfus. I will do anything for you.

I can see through the tiny opening in the door and my foot is in the way so she cannot get in. No, not good enough, I say.

Please, darling sweet Adolfus, please, she says.

Say Heil Adolf, I say.

Heil Adolf, she says. Please, Adolf, open the door.

Say Heil Adolf and salute, I say.

Adolf, I will kill you. Give me that letter. Angela pushes on the door and I slip. I am on the floor, rolling and she is in the room. I run but she has me on the bed. The letter, Adolf, she says. Her voice is sharp like a needle. I hold the letter behind me.

Heil Adolf Hitler, I say.

She grabs me. She grabs my peanut. Give, Adolf, she screams.

No, no, let go. It's just one, I scream.

I know it's just one. I'll tear it off, Angela screams.

No, Angela. Please, Angela. I give her the letter.

Thank you, she says and walks away with the letter. Next time I'll tear it off and put it in the mince meat, then you'll be a choir boy for the rest of your life, not the Pope. She goes into the kitchen to read the letter.

I look in the mirror. It looks red, but it is still there. I will not fight with Angela again. She fights too terrible.

Mince meat?

1900: I am in the Realschule. Doctor Leopold is very good. He teaches us about Bismarck and Napoleon. What would you do, he asks me, if you invaded Russia like Napoleon?

Only a fool invades Russia, I tell Doctor Leopold. Doctor Leopold likes me. I am impressing him. I am impressing everyone at the Realschule.

Edmund is dead. Mama and Angela are there.

1900: Today I say to Mama I cannot go to school. My shoelace is gone.

Here is a piece of string, Papa says.

May I have one of your shoelaces Papa? I ask.

Here is a piece of string, he says.

I don't want a piece of string.

It's better than nothing, Papa says.

But can I have one of your shoelaces? I ask.

And what will I have? Papa asks.

You have the piece of string, I say.

I do not want a piece of string, Papa screams.

It is better than nothing, I tell him.

I go to school. Why are you having a piece of string for a shoelace, Adolf, Doctor Leopold asks.

Doctor Leopold says that I failed. I cannot believe it. I ask Doctor Leopold how it can be that I fail when I know exactly what Napoleon should have done in Russia. How could it be?

Doctor Leopold says that I do not know facts. I only have opinions. I can see I was wrong about Doctor Leopold. Not wrong, mistaken. Not mistaken either, I never really thought he was clever.

Friday: Papa wants to know why I failed. I will not be a customs officer, I say.

Customs officer be damned, Papa screams. What about the Pope? Do you think the Pope failed his examinations?

It depends on if he had fools marking the examinations, I say. In any case, I tell him, I will not be the Pope. I will be the Artist. To be the Artist you do not need Doctor Leopold.

The Artist, he screams. He will be the Artist.

Then he walks away to the Gasthaus, talking to himself. As he goes I hear he says, one in jail and the other mad.

Is Alois in jail, I ask Mama.

Quiet, Child. Do not talk about it, Mama says.

Alois is in jail. I am sure of that.

Today I made a speech. The Artist shall be able to make a good speech.

In the audience was Heinz and Otto and Horst and Friedrich and Alfred. I tell them that the future of Germany depends on having commandoes with horses like the Boers. In this way one hundred Germans can beat one thousand English. Also French or Russians. We are going to have money and buy a horse for our first commando. The leader will have the first horse. Otto said we should vote on who will be the leader. But I said the leader is the leader and no voting is needed. I am the leader.

I said that only those with blue eyes are true Germans. Otto asked if he can be in in the commando. I said, yes, but not an officer. Otto has brown eyes.

What about green eyes? Friedrich asked. Better than brown, I said, but blue is best. They are lucky to have me here to explain.

Papa has brown eyes.

October: I have not been able to write much this year because I have been attending to the important matter of my career as an artist. My drawing is almost perfect now. Also I am doing well at school. But this takes no effort. Doctor Leopold says I will certainly pass. I should think so, I said in reply.

1901: A boy at the Realschule, a dirty boy with brown eyes and dark hair, told me what this thing is to make babies and to make girls no longer be virgins.

It is a lie.

Otto believes it. Horst also. I, fortunately, know better.

This boy, the dirty boy with brown eyes, said that for this thing the peanuts are used.

What about one? I said.

Both, he said.

August: Horst's mother is going to have a baby. Hah, your mother, I said to him.

It is nothing, he said, all mothers do it.

Liar, I said. You will not be in the commando.

Wednesday: Horst admitted his mistake. I agreed to allow him back into the commando. Perhaps next year there will be a horse.

Saturday: I told Mama that I know of this thing ladies have to do to have a baby.

Quiet, Adolf, she said.

I said that it is all right that I know of this because I realize also that it is many years since she last did this because that brat, Paula, is five. Therefore she obviously is not the sort of women...

At this point she picked up her knitting and walked quickly to her bedroom. As she was walking she said, Adolf, please speak no more of this. You know nothing of this matter, she said.

I know everything, I said.

Friday: But do all ladies do it? I asked Mama.

Adolf!

But do they?

Adolf, I will not speak of this.

Even married ladies?

Adolf, I am ashamed.

Old ladies? What about Tante Hilda? What about my grandmother?

Adolf, how can you?

She would not answer any of my questions. Now I also believe it.

Friday (same day): The peanut, I asked Mama, is it used?

One is enough, Mama said, if used in moderation.

Friday (again): You and Papa should have separate beds, I told Mama.

Adolf, if you don't stop I will speak to your father.

It would be better though, I said.

November: "Today! I have learnt something useful at school!":-
(Punctuation!) This is very important; all manner of expressing
yourself, being possible??!" To accentuate something: (whatever you
want is 'possible' — with punctuation!").

Monday: The language professor marked my essay. "Too much
punctuation also is possible," he said!

4 January 1903: Papa is dead. He died at the Gasthaus of much beer. I
wanted to go and watch him die, but he was dead already. After he
died I cried for him because Mama and Angela and Paula cried. Alois
came. He is not in jail now. But he did not cry. I will always cry. If
Mama cries I will cry.

   Mama said that it is not necessary to cry for him all the time. Just
sometimes think about him a little.

VOLUME II

June 1903. Mathematics! Why do I need mathematics? The man of destiny, the artist, the statesman, the general, the great man of action: he does not need mathematics. The year must be repeated unless mathematics is passed in the autumn. This is humiliation upon humiliation. I ask myself how these teachers will feel when my paintings are on view in the State Museum. How great will be their shame?

July 1903. We are at the farm, after coming all the way from Weitra in Uncle Anton's ox wagon. At least I am away from those imbecilic teachers for a while.

7 July. There is a girl here, Martha. She milks the cows and looks after the chickens. Her hair is dark, but she has blue eyes. This is what the true German women should be like. Blue eyes, simple and hard working. She has to work and Uncle Anton has to give the food. Also the bed and dresses.

She is very developed in her front.

I heard Mama say that she is Uncle Anton's virgin. How does Uncle Anton know that this thing has not been done to her?

8 July. I am working at my painting. Uncle Anton does not understand. He says I should come with him and work in the field, but Mama said that this was impossible. My work is too important, she said. He said nothing, just his eyebrows went up and then down.

9 July. Today Martha was hanging washing near my window. I drew a picture of her standing on her toes, hanging the washing. She wears a big skirt, but when she reaches up I can see her legs to above the ankle. If she has been working she takes deep breaths and her chest goes up and down like Uncle Anton's eyebrows.

11 July. The children are bothering me, throwing things against the window or knocking on the door and running away, even creeping into the room while I am working. Did Michelangelo have to suffer? Did Rembrandt?

12 July. Today I got Uncle Anton alone. He was at the field, digging in the water furrow. "Ah, have you come to help, Adolf? A little work out of doors is good for a growing boy."

"A question," I said. "This Martha, the virgin, how do you know?"

"How do I know what?"

"That she is a virgin."

Uncle Anton looked puzzled. He is a man of slow understanding. "You have seen her?"

"Yes," I said eagerly, hoping to gain the knowledge of how it is possible to see this in a person, a person of the female type.

"Well, if you have seen her, I do not think she can be easily mistaken for a boy, do you?"

"No," I said.

"So, what else is there. Pick up that spade and get down here."

I will ask him no more questions.

13 July. My drawing of Martha: I took it out today to look. It is perfect. Her head is a little to one side and her skirts are lifting.

While I was looking it came to me what it would be like to see Martha in her true self. Using my first drawing as a master, I drew her again without her skirts, also her blouse. Naturally I have never seen her like that, but the artist is the artist and no secrets are hidden.

First I lightly sketched the general form, capturing the fine lines of the body, curves and sweeps like a great cathedral. After that I filled in the details. My pencil moved faster and faster as I sketched the forbidden sacred parts. She is perfect, like a goddess, an angel, a great triumphal arch. As I worked a certain condition ensued in the Hochstetter. This is a point of embarrasment. Also some pleasure.

I was absorbed by my work. I was captured and captivated by my art. Because of this I did not hear Angela come in. The first time I became aware of her was when she said, "It's Martha."

Turning slowly I spoke in a deliberately calm and controlled voice. "How do you dare to come into my room and interfere with

32

my work?"

"Stop screaming at me, Adolf," she said. "It's Martha," she said again.

Again I was careful to show self-control. Self-control is a historic virtue that should be taught in all German schools. I spoke very quietly to her. "I am an artist," I said. "Haven't you seen works of the great artists?"

"If you don't stop screaming everyone is going to be here to see your picture of Martha," she said. "Yes, I have seen the pictures you're talking about, but they appear more innocent."

"What do you know about art?" I said, so quietly you could hardly hear my voice. The certain condition I mentioned in the region of the Hochstetter had faded away utterly.

"If you scream once more I'm going to tell Mama about this picture," Angela said.

Then I heard the children, Maria and Paula, running down the passage like a herd of cows coming for the feed tray. "Why is Adolf screaming?" The voice of that little brat, Paula, was making most of the noise.

I rushed to the door and locked it. "It's your fault," I said to Angela. "They heard you."

On most days Angela is a clever person, but today she was a fool. She had her arms crossed over her stomach, holding her sides, and she was laughing with great vigour and stupidity. I looked at her fiercely in silence and I could sense that the power of my stare had an effect on her. After a certain time she stopped laughing. When she spoke again her voice was weak, as if exhausted. "You have obviously never seen her in that position Adolf," she said. "She is a girl, not a cow." And then she started laughing again. I have never seen such foolish behaviour on the part of someone like Angela.

And all the time Paula and Maria were hammering on the door. "We want to see. We want to see."

14 July. Today I was unable to work. How long will we have to stay at this farm where I am tortured every day by Martha coming past my window, where Uncle Anton keeps staring at me (every evening at dinner he makes a speech about time-wasting loafers) and where the children throw stones against my window and run off? The little brat Paula is becoming even worse here than she was at home.

33

And Martha, what exquisite pain. It is part of her exquisite beauty. And the exquisite nature of my passion for her.

I found exquisite in a book yesterday. It means of supreme beauty.

15 July. Again I cannot work. I have been meditating and the power of my meditation has left me weak. I have been meditating on the thing that men do to women and the state the Hochstetter must be in and whether or not there is something to be done by the peanut, or peanuts, as the case may be.

There are times when I wake up in the morning and the Hochstetter is in a suitable condition, but with just one peanut is the condition enough? Will there be stamina? I have discovered that it goes away quickly. How long is it needed to last? If there is a woman, will the condition be gone before the woman is gone?

I have heard other boys speak. I know there is a thing they do to themselves, a sinful thing.

16 July. I did the sinful thing this morning in bed. When I woke up the condition was correct.

At first I resisted as one would expect of someone of my character. I stood firm, but the condition was firmer still. Then I made the mistake of touching it with my finger tips.

Doing the thing exhausted me. My whole soul came out of me in a flood, like a volcano or a tidal wave, and spewed upon the sheet. For an hour I could not move. The peanut had contracted into a tight little ball, a tight shivering little ball, churning round and round in bewilderment.

I took the sheet from the bed and washed it myself. I scarcely had the strength to complete the task. The terrible deed had drained away the power of my spirit.

Angela is always the one. She saw what I was doing but still she asked. "What are you doing, my sweet Adolfus?"

"The sheet needs to be washed," I said.

"Why?" she asked.

"It needs it," I said.

"What of Martha?" she said.

"What of Martha? What of Martha? What of Martha?" I cast the fierceness of my spirit upon her.

"No need to scream," she said. "Why can't Martha wash the sheet?"

"The work of the hands is dignified," I explained to her.

"I know that," she said. "I am surprised to hear that you know it though."

I was still busy with the sheet when Uncle Anton came past. He looked at me and he looked at the sheet and he smiled, a crooked evil smile. He is nothing but a common farmer. He can dig his own watering furrows.

Paula also was there. "Why are you working, Adolfus?"

Also Mama. "Martha can do that. You have such important things to do, Adolf."

And Martha. She took the sheet away from me. "I'll hang it for you," she said. As she lifted it from the water, she brushed against me, the strong smooth flank of German womanhood against my anguished body. She smelt like the milk from the cows and the hay in the barn and another smell I do not know. After she was gone I was weak from the smell. Also from the deed of the morning.

17 July. I will never do such a thing again. The artist must be a man of complete moral character.

18 July. My resolution stands firm.

19 July. A leader of the German people must have a strong will.

20 July. I did another drawing of Martha. The drawing was so realistic in its splendour that the condition was achieved. It stayed for one hundred counts.

21 July. I hate this farm. Terrible things happen here. Mama says she is enjoying herself and Angela says she is enjoying herself, but they are only simple women. They do not understand the deeper currents of life.

Today the worst thing of all happened, the worst of my life, of many lives perhaps. I was at my window where I had been trying to draw, trying to concentrate, trying to ignore the deep roots of my pain when Martha walked past the window and looked at me. She looked out of the side of her eyes without turning her head, a long look with a little smile, a crooked sort of smile like the smile Uncle Anton gave me when I was washing the sheets. It was not a virtuous smile. I could see no good moral character in it.

35

Of what happened then I will be ashamed all my life. I will never repeat it except in these sanctified pages.

The condition ensued like a stone. It lasted all the time while she walked past my window and to the barn and then for another one hundred and seventy-six counts. Then the peanut must have become tired because it went away.

22 July. At dinner table Uncle Anton spoke. If I had such thoughts as he I would never say a word in public. I would keep total silence. "Austria is going to the dogs," he said. "There are too many loafers among our young men. Young men who sit around and have evil thoughts instead of doing an honest day's work." He looked at me all the time while he was speaking.

"Quite true, Anton," Mama said. "I'm so glad we have no one like that in the family."

Uncle Anton made a snorting sound in his nose and looked from Mama to me. "Now, take Martha," he said. "There's a good little virgin who works hard for a living. Now, if our young men could be more like that . . ."

"Adolf works very hard at his painting," Mama said.

"Especially figure work," Angela said.

"I am very proud of him," Mama said, looking straight at Uncle Anton.

"He is a patriot," Angela said. "He loves the German form."

Uncle Anton snorted again, but he said nothing more.

23 July. Martha did it again today. Can it be that she plans deliberately to walk past my window? I was wrong about the smile. It was not a crooked smile like Uncle Anton's smile. I could clearly see moral character in it today. The first time must have been a deceptive shadow. The condition ensued again.

If she comes past tomorrow I will follow her to the barn. The great artist must have experience of all things.

24 July. I sat at the window all morning, then all afternoon, and she stayed away. My work was ruined. I could not get the pencil to even touch the paper, still less to draw a figure on it. All great artists have to go through the refining fire to cleanse their souls.

After dinner I asked Angela where Martha was. She looked at me

36

for a long time before she answered. "Do you want to do a few studies from the real thing?" she asked.

I turned and strode purposefully to my room. The day will come when I will not allow anyone to speak to me in this way. No one will dare when I am the great artist. Angela came running after me. "Wait, Adolfus," she cried out to me. She held onto my arm. At first I did not want to stop, but she pleaded and I am by nature a merciful person. "Please, my little Adolfus," she said. "I did not mean to impute evil thoughts . . ." she said.

"How could you think such a thing of me?"

"I'm sorry, my sweet Adolfus. Martha has her day off today. That's all."

"Where did she go?"

"To Weitra, I think. She got a lift in a wagon with that boy from the farm down the road."

"What boy?"

"Keep your voice down, Adolf. You don't need to shout. Just the boy down the road." We were inside my room and she had her head right next to my ear. "She just got a lift, Adolf. That's all."

Throughout dinner I looked down at my plate. I did not want to see Angela. She has no business searching my mind. She has no business thinking of the things that I am thinking.

Tomorrow, if Martha comes back, I will follow her.

25 July. She is here. I saw her at work in the kitchen. But she never came past the window. I cannot draw. I cannot paint. I am lost. I shall never be able to work again. My life is over, my mighty spirit entangled in a web of noble passion.

26 July. Today the urgency was upon me to do the sinful thing again. I woke up in the condition and I tried not to think of Martha. If I thought of her for only a moment the thing might have been too strong for even my immense power of will. Then I thought of washing the sheet again and Uncle Anton giving me the crooked smile again and Mama and Angela and Paula observing the washing of the sheet. I also thought of all the energy going out of me until there is nothing left and my one poor peanut is exhausted. When I thought of all this the condition passed.

"Moderation," Mama said. "If there is moderation, one is enough."

27 July. Today the worst thing of all happened. Even worse than the shameful things that have tortured me in this place before today.

Martha came past the window again. And she smiled again. And again the smile seemed crooked and evil, not the smile of a true woman of the German soil, and now I know it was not the light because I followed her to the barn and I know what happened.

I would not normally tell this, even in these pages, but perhaps it should be shown how the man of quality can be deflected from the path of his true destiny, if only for a short time. Also suffering. The man of quality can also participate in the act of suffering, much suffering.

When I reached the barn Martha was bending over, doing something to one of her shoes. I came up behind her and put my arms around her waist. Oh, the softness of her stomach, as soft as the Alpine snow, but not cold like the snow.

She made a little cry of surprise and jumped up, turning her head to see who had hold of her. For a moment, less than a moment, less than an instant, a flash, that I still remember as clearly as if it had taken hours, her face was a centimetre from mine, a millimetre even, less. Then we had fallen into a heap of hay. How that happened I do not know. I do not remember tripping or falling or moving at all. I just remember that I was in the hay on my back and she was on top of me. "Herr Hitler," she said, "you surprise me."

But who was the one who was surprised? She or I?

I could scarcely breathe. Nose and mouth were smothered in the great tangle of dark curls. Her face was again almost touching mine and her bosom: her bosom was a great feather cushion, a great heaving feather cushion, pressed against my chest, my neck almost. I tried to say, "No, Martha, it is you who surprise me," but I only got as far as "No, Martha . . ." when she interrupted me with "You are so bold, Herr Hitler."

I was choking for air. Her lips, even softer than her bosom or her stomach, were blocking my breathing in a way that was even worse than the curls. Her tongue was doing something, first against my lips and then within my mouth. It was a very large tongue, like a huge earthworm, swollen and writhing in agony, filling up my mouth until I felt that I was going to suffocate, or if not suffocate, at least vomit.

At least she had called me Herr Hitler, which was more fitting than Adolf or my little Adolfus. But now the condition was needed. I was the victim of a vulgar carnal assault. Her tongue was twisting and turning inside my head like a boneless creature that had gone out of its mind. The condition would not appear.

It would not even begin to think of appearing, not even begin to struggle to appear. The Hochstetter lay limp, like a caterpillar that has been trampled on, a poor lifeless worm.

I tried to concentrate on the condition, closing my eyes and pressing the power of my thoughts downwards to the area where they were most needed. I shut my mind completely from Martha who I had so severely misjudged and concentrated with complete intensity. To the man of purpose such a thing should be possible. But there was nothing, no condition, only a weak unhappy thing like one of the sausages Mama used to make when we had the farm, such a sausage before cooking.

I was still concentrating when I noticed that Martha was no longer on top of me. The feeling of suffocation was gone. My mouth was empty. I opened my eyes and she was standing above me, hands on hips. "Is something wrong, lover?" she asked. I looked up at her and tried to speak. "Did I misunderstand something?" she asked further. "Speak, my prince." She had a smile on her face that I still remember. How could she sneer at an artist such as myself? Suddenly she turned away and left the barn. Over her shoulder she said, "Go back to Mama, liebchen."

Profuse is an excellent word. I learnt it yesterday. It means many of, or plenty. I learn many new words every day — from reading.

28 July. Today I kept the curtains of the room closed. I hate her.

29 July. I am having my meals in the room so that I do not have to see her. I hate her.

30 July. How long do we have to stay on this farm? I hate her.

31 July. I left the room today for the first time since it happened and only got as far as the kitchen. She was there, talking to Angela. I stopped in the passage and I could hear what they were saying. Martha was talking. "Are you sure?" she asked Angela. "I have heard of boys who do not want girls. They want other boys. I have never met one and I have met quite a few boys. But I have heard there are such boys."

"Not Adolf," Angela said.

"Well, I have heard that you get such boys. When I was twelve the boys of my age used to look at me already. And how old is your Adolf? Fifteen?"

"Fourteen," Angela said.

"You see. That's what I mean. I was right on top of him in the hay, in the hay inside the barn. And there was nothing. I had my leg pressing there to feel when it would start to happen, but there was nothing."

"Martha, you are a bad girl," Angela said, but she laughed when she said it.

Martha laughed too. "I am a bad girl, but your brother is a funny little boy."

I went quietly back to the room and closed the door and locked it. I will stay here until we go home. Also I will keep the curtains closed.

22 September 1903. I always thought Angela was a sensible person, but she has shown otherwise. She has married that fool Leo. "Art," he says. "What is art? How many people does it feed? How many battles does it win?"

"It wins the battles of the soul," I said to him. "It feeds the hunger of the spirit," I said.

"No need to shout, Adolf," Angela said.

October. Paula needs discipline. I shall have to exercise it. Today she asked Mama at what age a girl may start drinking wine. She is seven years old, this Paula, seven years old.

"There is no need for ladies to drink wine," Mama told her.

"But we have to start drinking wine some time," Paula said.

"I don't understand, my little Paula," Mama said. "A lady does not have to start drinking wine at all."

"But we have to sometime," Paula said.

I could not control the power of my spirit any longer. I fixed my strongest, most penetrating gaze upon Paula and said, "You do not have to start drinking. You do not ever have to start drinking, not a lady," I said.

"All right, Adolf dear, try to keep your voice down," Mama said. Why do they always speak to me this way? They don't tell Angela to

40

keep her voice down. Or Paula. It's always me.

"Now you turn on me, Adolf," Paula said.

"I? How did I turn on you? I have your best interests at heart."

"No need to shout, Adolf dear," Mama said. "Paula," she said, "Adolf is quite right."

"Oh, yes, Adolf never does anything wrong. He's always perfect." I could see the malice in her ugly little face. How can one child have so many good qualities while the other has none. I suppose Paula was unfortunate to be born after me. All Mama's fine qualities of spirit passed to me and nothing was left for that miserable child. She has inherited only the qualities of poor old Alois.

19 March 1905. Frau Sekira likes me. "So many candles, Adolf? How can you use so many candles?" She always asks. "Ever since you have been staying with me you have used up so many candles."

"Gnadige Tante, it is for studying and for painting," I tell her. "To be a great artist takes much study and practice." She is a kind lady and I want to make her happy so I tell her that one day she will be able to make a lot of money by showing people the room where I once stayed. I could see by her face how pleasant was this news.

April 1905. "Why always *sie, sie, sie,* Adolf," Frau Sekira asks me. "The others say, *du* and *du* and *du,* but Adolf only says, *sie.* Why so formal, Adolf? Why can't we be friends?"

"It is in keeping with my rank in life," I explained to her. She is a clever lady. She nodded right away and I did not have to explain further.

11 May. Frau Sekira is a good lady, but I will be glad when the Realschule is over and I can go home to my own dear sweet Mama, my soft and gentle Mama who loves me so. I did a few drawings of Martha from memory. I sold each one for a pfennig to boys at school. Now I am a professional artist.

12 May. Professor Bruckstein searched Otto's case today and found one of the pictures. That coward Otto told him who drew it. Professor Bruckstein looked straight at me and said, "Adolf, I will see you after school."

But I am not to be intimidated by these abnormal professors of ours. I am much too strong of mind for that, also too senior. Last month I even had to shave my moustache for the first time. Soon I will let it grow. I will have a long dense moustache that reaches out on either side of my head, curling at the points.

I stood next to my desk and looked straight into his eye. "I shall certainly be there, Herr Professor," I said.

After school he was waiting for me. I stood at attention in front of his desk, my shoulders square, my arms at my side and my head held high, a picture of Prussian nobility. In the soul I am purest Prussia. What is Austrian frivolity by comparison.

"Is this your work," the Herr Professor barked at me.

"Certainly, Herr Professor," I said.

"What do you mean by producing such a thing?"

"I am going to be a great artist, Herr Professor," I said.

"A great artist? A great pornographer is more likely."

"I do not understand that word, Herr Professor. But I do not think that is what I am to become. I think artist is right. Perhaps you would explain if that other thing is some kind of artist."

"Certainly," he said. "It is a kind of artist." He looked at me with one eyebrow raised. "How long have you been busy with this form of art?"

"Since the beginning of the year, Herr Professor," I said. I was showing him that I could not be cowed easily, not at all, in fact.

"Hmmm." He was holding the picture up and looking at it. "You have a facile imagination, young Hitler. Also a steady hand. Could you do one of these in colour?"

"Water colour, Herr Professor?"

"Water colour would do very well."

15 May. Professor Bruckstein gave me one krone for the picture. Professor Langendorff has also placed an order. I am going to be rich.

17 May. They want more poses and different poses. The one with the head between the legs is very popular, but each one wants his picture to be different. How will I explain to Mama where the money comes from?

20 May. I have received orders from Professors Adendorff, Zimmerman,

Pfaff and Lochner, also one from Inspector of schools Prinze. Where will it end? I cannot think of more poses. Fortunately Inspector of schools Prinze suggested one of his own. I told him that it is impossible for a girl to leap into the air with her legs in that position, but he told me not to bother about such technicalities. Also he would give me two kronen.

22 May. I work till late every night. Naturally I keep my door locked. I cannot have Frau Sekira coming into the room. The inspiration would be affected. I heard her speaking to Herr Sekira. "Adolf is working very hard," she said. "He is going to do very well in his examinations."

I have been considering that. I have the realization that the Herr Professors Bruckstein, Langendorff, Adendorff, Zimmerman, Pfaff and Lochner, and also Inspector of schools Prinze will have to think carefully regarding the consequences of an unfavourable aggregate of marks.

27 May. Today I explained the problem of possible poor marks to Professor Pfaff. I explained about how late I had to work each night on my art.

He looked at me over the top of his spectacles. "Art?" he said. I think it was a question.

"Yes, my art," I explained to him. I also explained how little time was left for studies and also that the Herr Professors all have wives. When I spoke about the wives Herr Professor Pfaff immediately understood my problem. I think we have come to an agreement.

June. "This girl?" Professor Pfaff asked. "The drawings all seem to be of the same girl. This girl? Where can one find such a girl? One who is not unduly the slave of convention?"

I explained about Uncle Anton's farm and also that my name was not to be mentioned and the information would cost two kronen. After all, the man of art has to live and to care for his mother. Professor Pfaff looked a little pale when I told him the price, but he is a man of understanding. He paid me. I am keeping all my money in a box with my only picture of Mama.

7 June. Herr Professor Herzstein called me to him in the school grounds. He took me on a walk to the far end near the trees so that we could not be overheard. First he congratulated me on the excellence of my drawing. I thanked him in my most dignified manner, saying that praise from such as he was praise indeed. He nodded and said that one with a talent such as mine should use it as widely as possible, explore as many new areas as possible. I told him that I had not understood his deep interest in art and that I am trying to explore new areas and that I was very interested in this, also that I was sure that my genius would open avenues that had never been trodden by the foot (swept by the brush) of man before. He nodded in deep understanding, saying that the one area in which I was limiting myself was in the painting of girls only. Why not boys too?

"Boys?" I asked.

"Certainly," he said. "Have you seen Michelangelo's David?"

"A picture," I told him. "I have seen a picture."

"A work of genius," Professor Herzstein said, "but not of the female figure, never of the female figure. I will pay three kronen," he said.

"For three kronen we have an arrangement, Herr Professor."

"I would like you to pay attention to a certain point while painting it, Adolf," he said.

"Just tell me the point, Herr Professor, and I will execute it."

The Herr Professor looked back over his shoulder towards the school buildings before answering. "As you know the male anatomy has certain states," he said.

"States, Herr Professor?"

"Certainly, states of greater and lesser stature, as it were. States of greater and lesser firmness, in a manner of speaking."

I looked keenly at Professor Herzstein, but he was not looking at me. "The condition?" I asked. "You want the figure to possess the condition?"

"The condition, exactly," the Professor said. "Also of reasonable size. Let us not have to look through a microscope. Of fair size."

"Even great size?" I asked the Professor.

"In a manner of speaking," Professor Herzstein said, "even great size would be acceptable, most acceptable, as it were."

"Three kronen?"

"Three," the Herr Professor said. He was still looking towards the building, but no one was coming from that side.

44

9 June. "The condition is excellent," the Herr Professor said, "but the peanut appears to be only one."

"It is the angle," I said.

"Ah, the angle," the Professor murmured softly. He looked very carefully at the picture. "I like the colour," he said, "very realistic."

"Three kronen," I told the Professor.

11 July. I have persuaded Mama not to go to the farm this year. Uncle Anton wrote that we were to come, but I said that my health was not good enough for me to go. I told her that the pain in my lungs was frightening. I said that I suspected a haemorrhage was imminent.

"Poor brave Adolf," she said. "You must see Doctor Bloch."

"Imminent," I told Mama, "not yet active."

"Does imminent not mean now?" Mama asked. "I thought it meant now."

"Not at all, Mama. Not the same at all." I always speak patiently to Mama when there is something she does not understand.

12 July. Angela and that fool Leo were here today. "Why not go to the farm, Adolf?" she asked me. "It will be good for your chest complaint."

"Perhaps it will, Adolfus my sweet," Mama said. Mama is very easily led.

"It will make things worse," I said. "Even a haemorrhage is possible, more than possible, even likely."

"Country air is good for you," Angela said, "and the pleasant company. Let us not forget the pleasant company. That too is good for you." And all the time she was looking at me with big round eyes as if she was really concerned for my health. "Also your painting," she said. "Your painting came along wonderfully last year when we were at Uncle Anton's."

"Oh, Adolf, and I haven't seen any of those paintings," Mama said.

"Painting is a pastime for layabouts and vagabonds," that fool Leo said. His lip was curling over like a dog's.

But Angela was not yet finished. She should have been finished. A person with any sort of decency would have been, but she was not. A person with decency would not have conducted such a conversation to begin with. But she did. "I think you judge Adolf too soon," she

45

told that fool Leo. "I think you would have appreciated those paintings."

"I would like to see these paintings that I would appreciate," the fool said.

"Perhaps Adolf will show you a few." Angela smiled at me with the big round eyes of the hypocrite.

"I was not happy with them. I destroyed them," I said.

"They will improve with experience," she said. "The more experience you have, the better you know your subject, the more intimate your knowledge: so much your work will improve. But such knowledge must be of an intimate nature."

"I will listen to no more of this," I said and rose quickly. It was a dramatic moment. The manner in which I did it made it so.

"Oh don't go, Adolf," Mama said. "It sounds like good advice."

I went to my room. Afterwards Angela came to the door. She knocked softly, but I would not open. "I'm sorry, Adolf," she whispered, so softly I could just hear her. "Open the door, Adolf. I am truly sorry and I do admire you so." It was a weakness and I would not tell it except that only my own eyes will ever read these words. But even the man of genius, the natural leader of men, has moments of weakness. I am using up my moments of weakness now while I am young so that afterwards when I am the Artist there will be none, and the admiration of the mass will not be hindered by blemishes. I opened the door. "Oh, Adolf," she said, coming into the room and putting her arms around my neck. "I'm sorry. I'll never make fun of you again."

One moment I was hard and resolute, a natural Prussian officer, a second Bismarck; the next I felt soft arms around me and her softness against me and I was not hard, nor resolute and not even fit to be Bismarck's valet.

I started to cry. "Oh, Adolf," I heard her say. "Oh, Adolf, you're such a fine person, so gentle and easily hurt. You're going to bring so much happiness into people's lives. I'm sorry for what I did. I'll never do it again."

13 September. Just a few days, then I am finished with Realschule forever. There is a problem though. I thought that everything was in order. The Herr Professors had agreed to everything. They have the pictures and I was to have had a satisfactory report. I am a

46

reasonable person. I did not insist on a brilliant report, only a satisfactory one. But now there are problems.

A new professor, Herr Professor Whal, is the professor of the examination. I went to speak to him today so that there would be no mistake or any misunderstanding. "I have the agreement," I explained to him.

"Oh yes, young Hitler." He had the same sort of expression, lip-curving and stupid, as that fool Leo. "What sort of agreement do you have?"

"I have the agreement, regarding the examination."

The lip curled further than before. I realized that I should not be speaking to this fool, but I had said too much. To stop would have been dishonourable. "Oh really, young Hitler, so you have the agreement regarding the examination. With whom do you have such an agreement?"

"With the Herr Professors, Herr Professor."

"Surely not all the Professors?"

"Not all, Herr Professor. Only Professors Bruckstein, Langendorff, Adendorff, Zimmerman, Pfaff, Lochner and Inspector of schools Prinze, oh yes, and Professor Herzstein, especially Professor Herzstein."

"All those Professors and Inspector of schools Prinze have an examination agreement with you? I do not believe it. What sort of agreement?"

"That I should pass, Herr Professor."

"That you should pass, Herr Professor? Why, Herr Hitler, should they do this?" The lip was no longer curling. I believe the shock in the Herr Professor was too great.

"It has to do with paintings, Herr Professor." I was standing erect, my elbows close to my sides, my chest pushed out, my heels together and my head high, my pride and breeding being visible; breeding on my mother's side. Clearly I have inherited very little from old Alois.

"Because of paintings there is an agreement?"

"That is so, Herr Professor."

"These paintings are the result of your labour?"

"Quite so, Herr Professor."

"And the subject of these paintings?"

"Figures, Herr Professor." My voice was sharp and precise, almost military, no, altogether military.

"Ah, figures. Human figures?"

"Exactly so, Herr Professor."

"You may leave, young Hitler."

"Herr Professor?"

"You may leave. You may go."

"But, Herr Professor, my agreement?"

"Go. Go now. Get out of my classroom." The words were spoken in a vulgar, discourteous manner, not the manner of a man of breeding, such as I.

14 September. Only two days to the final examination and Herr Professor Wahl is still the Professor of the examination. I have passed him in the corridor, but he looks away from me. So does Herr Professor Pfaff and also Bruckstein and Lochner.

15 September. They still did not want to speak to me today. The matter is serious. Tomorrow is the examination and I know that I cannot spend another year in this place. I can feel the illness in my lungs. If I fail I shall have a haemorrhage. Then they will not laugh. They will see then how serious was my illness. The Professors also will not laugh, not even a brief chuckle. There is a matter of wives, also reputations, to be considered. And while I am a person of restraint and compassion, certain things must be done.

Because they would not speak to me at school I followed Herr Professor Adendorff after classes were over. My intention was to catch up to him when we were a certain distance from the Realschule.

He walked very fast, never looking back and not going in the direction of his home. I let two corners, then three corners pass before I felt we were far enough and it was surely time to catch up to him. But before I had put my thoughts into action he had slipped into a narrow lane between two houses, almost avoiding me in this way. I passed the opening of the lane to find that he had disappeared from sight. Cunning though the Herr Professor is, I am equally cunning, in fact more so.

I dashed back to the lane in time to see him pass round the corner at the far end.

Around three more corners, across two squares, down one alley, in the front door of the museum and out the other side, and through the park I followed. Finally he entered an old and grey building where the brick walls were dirty and drying washing hung out of the windows. He entered quickly, glancing over his shoulder in a manner to suggest guilt, or perhaps just fear of discovery.

The stairs were dark, but I went quietly up, staying close to the wall, my bearing erect despite the circumstances. I reached the second floor in time to see a door closing behind the Herr Professor. Immediately there were sounds of laughter, loud and prolonged and fat laughter, and also, to my astonishment, there was the laughter of women. Or was it just one woman? And had I not heard that voice before?

And was it not . . .? But, no, it could not be . . . or could it be?

I approached the door quietly, seized the handle (the true man of action does not hesitate) and threw it open. I did not notice the room, nor the furnishings, and it was only in passing that I noticed the Herr Professors, all of them. Apart from Professor Adendorff, the Professors Bruckstein, Zimmerman, Pfaff and Langendorff were all looking at me with horror in their plump faces. Professor Herzstein was not present. But I barely saw the Herr Professors. I noticed only the girl sitting cross-legged in the centre of the table, her bosom bulging over the top of her corset like two wild creatures trying to escape imprisonment. It was Martha, Uncle Anton's virgin.

I stood and stared in silence and surprise and they stared back in a silence that was equal to mine in every way, also surprise.

16 September. I passed the examination. Realschule is over forever. There was talk of an Oberrealschule, but I told Mama that I would have none of it. I am tired of suffering under the authority of those who are my natural subordinates. I shall never suffer it again. At sixteen years of age, it is enough.

October. My moustache is developing. My upper lip has almost more hair than skin. I can only see skin here and there. Soon it will be dense and long. I think nothing of small carefully trimmed moustaches. For me a man's moustache shows his character. And a small neat moustache shows a small character, a person who is subject to the severest boundaries, not a man whose horizons have no limits, like me.

I shall have the biggest and broadest moustache in Germany.

I cannot wait.

17 October. I have met an interesting person. His name is Gustl Kubizek. He is obviously someone of great intelligence. When I speak he always listens very carefully to what I say, never interrupting. And when he does ask a question it is always phrased with sufficient respect to allow our relationship to have a deep meaning for him. I think that already our conversations have taught him a great deal about the destiny of nations and men.

6 November. Gustl has made me a present of a cane, jet black with a handle of ivory. Of an evening when we stroll to the opera or down Landstrasse or to the bridge to stand for a few minutes watching the river moving majestically towards its own destiny: on all such occasions the cane goes with me now, the handle fitting my gloved hand as if the two were part of each other.

And if we walk it flicks out ahead of me, making sharp little click-clack sounds on the paving stones. It will be interesting for those who come afterwards to know that Adolf Hitler once passed this way, that a great artist spent the years of his waiting for the call of destiny in these humble surroundings. I told Gustl this and although he said nothing I could see the admiration in his eyes.

7 February 1906. I do not understand Gustl. Today he asked me why I do not find employment. I answered with a single word and a meaningful glance.

"I?" I asked. I cannot believe that Gustl will ever again ask such a question.

22 February. All day I sat in my room. Gustl called but I would not see him. Mama knocked on the door twice, but I did not answer her. These rooms are quite unsatisfactory. To have Mama and Paula, sleeping in the living room, right next to my bedroom, so that I have to go past them coming in or going out, is quite impossible.

I sat in my room all day, looking out of the window. I should have been painting or meditating, but I was doing neither.

I have tried not to allow her to trouble my mind and I have tried not to go near that dreaded apartment, but I am able to think about nothing else. Since that day last September, the day before my final Realschule examination, I have tried vainly to concentrate on important matters. Gustl has been an important diversion, but even his wise and admiring presence has not been able to clear my mind of this intolerable subject.

I will try to sleep tonight. Perhaps in my sleep I will be free of this terrible obsession. It is undignified that one such as I should be plagued in this way.

28 February. Gustl has been pleading outside my door on each of the last four days. I must do something. Destiny must be taken hold of and shaken as a dog shakes a rabbit.

4 March. I went. I stood inside the door of the building for fifteen minutes before mounting the stairs. It was dark in the crumbling corridor, darker than it had been the first time. I climbed slowly, holding my breath.

The passage outside her door was almost as dark as the stairs had been, and the door was closed, as I had expected. The door of such an apartment would never stand open. I reached it and knocked. I wanted it to be a soft and discreet knock, but it sounded like cannon fire, echoing along the passages and up and down the stairs. For a moment the impulse to turn and run seized me, but I withstood it. At that moment I realized that no peril, no matter how great, will ever again cause me to flee. There was a sound inside the door, again I almost ran, but again my strength of character prevailed.

The door opened and she stood before me. Gone was the farm apron, the long plaits in her hair, the high collar and the wooden shoes. Her hair hung around her naked shoulders in huge dark waves. She was again wearing the dress that revealed almost her entire bosom. I averted my eyes, looking over the top of her head, but the strain of not being able to see her face was too great. I let my eyes fall just far enough to look into hers. She was smiling. "Hello, lover," she said. "What would Uncle Anton have said now?"

"Good afternoon, Fraulein," I said.

"Good afternoon then, Herr Hitler. I'm surprised at your coming to see me again. Your last visit was so brief . . . but, of course, I did have company at the time."

"I . . ." Talking to her was very difficult. For one such as I to have the need to visit one such as she is the most humiliating part of the entire matter. I should be able to send for such a one. I should be able to issue a summons, saying, appear immediately. Or, present yourself

51

at my apartment. Or, the Artist requires your company, do not be late. I should issue such orders ... but on an orphan's pension, and with the small allowance my mother gives me, orders are not possible. It will not always be so. When I am the great Artist things will be different. "I ..." The other words were caught in a constriction of undeniable intensity in my throat. "I ..."

"You want to come in, lover?"

I went in. "Don't call me that," I said.

"No, I suppose it doesn't suit you. I see that you passed your examination."

"Of course," I said. The force of my personality was asserting itself. She was rocking slowly back and forth in front of me, her weight resting first on one heel then on the other, her skirt swaying and bosom rolling in a majestic turbulent rhythm.

"Of course," she said, "under the circumstances."

"What are you doing here, Martha?" My voice held the demand of someone who had the right to know.

"It's much pleasanter than milking cows. Also it has better prospects. Fringe benefits too."

"But. . . " The words again stuck fast in the knots that had formed in my throat. I would soon have regained control, but she spoke first.

"That nice Herr Professor Pfaff came to see me on the farm. He made me a wonderful offer."

"The other Herr Professors . . .?" The words squeezed past the knot.

"They have a co-operative, you might say. But tell me, you seem to have had something to do with it. What did you tell them about me?"

"I ..." The knot was even bigger and tighter than before.

"It's all right. I don't mind. I'm just curious. Whatever it was, you can tell me."

"I ... " The usual tone of command returned to my voice. "I told them you were a true woman of the German soil."

She looked at me as if she had not fully understood the words. Then she fell onto a small couch, her face turned away from me and her body shaking as if she had been seized by a fit of weeping. It seemed that my words had struck some deep chord of remorse within her. I sat next to her on the couch and lay one hand gently on her shoulder. My naturally deep compassion stirred as I felt her body shaken and wracked by the intensity of her emotion.

She raised her head and looked at me. Tears were running down her cheeks in streams, but she was not crying. The intensity of her spasms was caused by laughter. Her voice was a shrill hysterical squeak when she tried to speak. "You must have told them a little more than that."

"You are a woman of no moral character," a voice called out. It was a harsh voice, but cracking as the voices of young men do.

I looked round to see who was in the room with us, but she was speaking and her voice had calmed. "It's all right, lover. It's all right. I didn't mean to make fun of you." She had moved towards me and had taken hold of one of my arms with both hands. Her bosom was a great precarious overhang, threatening to break away from the cliff to which it was attached and crash to the valley below. "I just wonder at the scene though. You told them I was a true woman of the German soil so they came running to Spital with such a proposition? You must admit it seems unlikely. Nevertheless, it is more pleasing than being your Uncle Anton's virgin." She moved still closer and drew my arm towards her until my forearm pressed against her bosom. There was a sensation of tingling at the point of contact. For a moment I was incapable of admitting anything, only for the moment though. I would soon have recovered. But she was babbling on. "Never mind," she said. "Tell me what brings you here today? What do you want from me?"

I was still troubled by the man's voice I had heard a few moments before, but her question needed to be answered. What did I want from her? Why had I come? Who can answer such questions? One does not question destiny when you are within its grip. "I . . ." I said and again the knot was in my throat, throttling anything I might choose to say.

"You've said that before, liebchen," she said. "You have beautiful eyes. Such a lovely blue and such a dreamy look, do you know this? You have the eyes of a mystic. Perhaps you would like to continue where we left off in the barn?"

"No," I said, but immediately I changed it to "Perhaps." The reason was not hard to understand. The condition had commenced. This was the first time since September last year when I had followed the Herr Professors to Martha's apartment. But it was there, solid as an Alpine peak and pointing in the same direction.

"Ah, perhaps," she said. "Why not? Why should a poor student not have something that the rich Herr Professors have to pay for? Kiss me, Adolf."

"The tongue," I said.

"With the tongue I will explore the insides of your mouth. I will find the warm dark damp places."

"No," I said. I remembered clearly the experience of the barn. "Keep the tongue in your mouth."

"All right, lover. Anything else you want covered up?"

"Just the tongue," I said.

I put my lips against hers. They were soft like the belly of one of Uncle Anton's pigs, but more pleasant to the touch. After a few moments she withdrew her lips a fraction and murmured, "You are sure about the tongue?"

"I'm certain."

"All right, but it seems unnatural to me."

I pressed my lips against hers again, keeping them tightly closed in case she should forget. Then I felt her hand. It was pressing down the inside of my thigh, pressing and holding, squeezing and rubbing. There was a contact, a fiery red-hot contact, and the condition was a stone, a piece of granite, a thing of such hardness that it might easily shatter and burst.

Suddenly she drew away, turning her back on me. "Help me with the buttons," she said. They were down the back and I started at the top. The first one was threaded through a hole too small for its size and only after a struggle did I get it through. The second was almost touching the first and the third touching the second and so on, down Martha's back, button next to button, dozens of them. I struggled with the second and the third, and slowly her back was appearing, white, the colour of snow or the milk she used to take from the cows. The fourth and fifth buttons were freed with equal slowness and difficulty, and the front of her dress was dropping, her bosom bulging over the top in extravagant fashion. The sixth, seventh and eighth buttons, and one half of her bosom slipped out of the dress, round but pointed and shivering. I stopped.

The condition was fading. Granite had become a branch of the willow and the willow branch was becoming old leather, and I knew soon the old leather would be jelly or even the whipped cream dressing. Martha turned her head to look at me. There was a question and some part of a warning in her face.

"Lover," she asked, "you aren't doing this to me again, are you?"

"I . . . I . . . I . . ." The knot was back but worse than before.

"Will you stop your I . . . I . . . I . . . What's wrong with you?" The half of the bosom that had slipped out, had poured over the edge and was pointing, bulge-like towards the soil of the Fatherland.

"I . . . I . . . I must go," I said.

"Go then, go," she screamed. "And don't ever come back, Adolf Hitler."

16 June. I have returned from a visit to Vienna. Mama paid. She understands how important it is for me to further my knowledge. It is a small sacrifice for her when weighed against the greater good of Germany. Gustl is jealous.

7 July. Ah, the sweet voice of destiny. Always attuned to it, my ear never fails to receive the smallest signal. Today it spoke to me more clearly than ever before. It said, "take a ticket in the lottery." This is how my fortune is to begin. The state lottery will provide me with the initial impetus, the push that will lead on to glory.

Ten kronen was my only problem and Gustl was my most likely solution. "It was my idea," I told Gustl, "and we will share the winnings equally, therefore it is only fair that you pay the ten kronen."

For once Gustl was unreasonable, saying that I should be part of the financial risk. I tried to explain that there was no risk, but he would not listen to rational argument. Eventually I agreed to pay two of the ten kronen and we purchased a ticket. I placed it carefully in the back of my drawer. Of such frail substance is the future of art.

10 July. Paula overheard Gustl and me planning the manor house we are to buy when the winning lottery ticket is drawn. She laughed and told Mama. The little brat does not believe that we are going to win. I cannot comprehend such immaturity in a ten-year-old.

11 July. The day draws closer. Gustl and I have decided the style of the manor house. I have completed the drawings. Also a carriage and six horses, and a lady to keep house and cater to all our needs will be required. Our house will be the headquarters of German art, its study and execution. The young will come to learn, the old to wonder.

14 July. Only two days before the state lottery is drawn. I have bought new clothing for receiving the prize. Gustl says he will wait a while. He will be sorry when I appear more splendid than he.

Mama was a little reluctant to give me the money for my new clothes.

15 July. Just one day.

16 July. Today is the day. I will dress in my new coat. Mama is polishing my shoes. I am wearing a cravat Gustl lent me. I have also prepared a short speech of acceptance, ending with the words, "I receive this bequest in the name of the German people and to the glory of our Greater Germany."

17 July. We did not win. I have appealed to the Commissioner of Police to investigate the manner in which this lottery was conducted. I explained that obviously something was amiss, perhaps even a serious misdemeanor.

He wanted to know why I thought so and I explained that we should have won, and he wanted to know why we should have won and I explained to him the true meaning of destiny, so he said, "All right, Herr Hitler, if I come across anything I'll let you know."

I have a thought it was not seriously meant, though. There is much corruption among those in authority.

19 July. How can ordinary mortals contrive to divert the path of fate? The organisers of the state lottery have much to answer for.

20 July. My life is over, the grand dream ended, the beauty fled. Gustl says it was just bad luck. How can an ordinary youth like him be expected to understand?

21 July. The vision of German art is reduced to ashes, scattered in the dust. I will make them pay for cheating me in this way.

October. I have been mistaken all along. Last night I saw Wagner's great opera *Rienzi* and as I watched the pageant unfold and experienced the great wall of sound that flooded the opera house I knew my true destiny. I am to follow in the footsteps of Wagner. Germany's greatest composer will live again.

I confided the news to Mama and, even though she was very tired at the time, I could see how it thrilled her. "Will it be very expensive?" she asked.

"A grand piano is needed," I told her.

13 October. I have commenced piano lessons on the grand piano Mama purchased from the Jew, Rosenkowitz. A worthy instrument.

Composition will soon follow. German musical history is about to be rewritten.

20 October. Rather too many finger exercises for the serious future composer.

1 November. Finger exercises, finger exercises, finger exercises! Where is the glory, the beauty, the grandeur? Must the sensitive life of the soul be buried under an avalanche of finger exercises?

28 December. Today I confronted the Herr Professor of music about the finger exercises, also the unnecessary technicalities. Is this the path of Wagner? I asked him. Of Mozart? Of Bach? Immediately I had mentioned Bach I was sorry that I had. There can be no greatness, not even any thought of greatness in the sentimental religious nonsense of those such as Bach. Did Wagner have to do finger exercise? I asked. The great Wagner? Did he? What of the technicalities? I demanded. Where is the glory amidst the technicalities?

I could see that he had no answer to my questions. When confronted with the truth lesser men are left speechless.

He stood before me, struggling for words, for perhaps a minute. At length he repeated the sort of thing that has no relevance at all. "Young Hitler," he said, "if you are too lazy to practice you had better give up piano lessons. Leave Wagner to those with talent."

15 January 1907. Mama is sick. Doctor Bloch told us that she might die. It is an unhappy thing that we cannot have a German doctor to tend her. It is impossible to tell what primitive inspirations might grip this alien physician.

16 January. This thing of Mama is terrible. Where will I go if she dies?

57

How can one survive on nothing more than an orphan's pension? There is no provision made in Germany for the young artist. The capitalists should be made to support the men of genius. What is needed is a socialist state, a German socialist state, perhaps a National Socialist state. I shall bear this thought in mind in the years of my fame. Perhaps something can be done.

17 January. They are to operate on Mama. Part of her is to be removed. I have explained to the doctor performing the operation how serious the matter is. I wanted him to understand that one of my temperament cannot be left without support. I only wanted them to proceed with more than usual care. To my surprise he pointed me to the door and said in a loud voice, "Excuse me, Herr Hitler, I have important matters to attend." Even one such as Doctor Bloch is better than he.

3 February. The world of music is not yet ready for the storm of genius with which I intended to flood it. I shall concentrate on my drawings and writings instead.

21 December. She is dead. I am alone. Gustl cannot be compared to her. Paula is just a little ruffian. Angela is married to that fool Leo. And Alois, the younger? Of what sense is the life of Alois?

She is gone. She was the one who understood and supported me. No one else comprehends my genius or my importance. It is a happy thought that she will be remembered in history. Soon all will know that she was Klara Hitler, the mother of Adolf Hitler.

She should not have died so young. Somewhere there is a responsibility for her death. This Doctor Bloch, I never felt that he should have been trusted. The dark of his eyes, the colour of his skin, too yellow for the peace of mind of the true German; these tell their own story.

Doctor Urban too is a man whose work should be examined carefully. And old Alois himself, some of the responsibility must be his. His treatment of her must be partly responsible. And Alois, the younger, and Angela. They have caused her much suffering. Let the guilt be apportioned to those who have earned it. They have wronged me and I shall not forget.

She is dead. If only she could have lived to see the triumph of my will.

VOLUME III

April 30th, 1908. There is something in the bearing, perhaps in the eye, certainly in the presence of the man of purpose. It is not my black ivory-headed cane, not my elegant black coat, or the gleam to my boots. It is not even my moustache (which is progressing excellently). It is far more profound than any of these tangible marks of quality.

The man of purpose carries his mark of quality within himself. It is a matter of the soul, the brain, the spirit, and it is there for all to recognize. Only the most hopeless fools fail to see it. That Leo Raubal, who my sister Angela was foolish enough to marry, is an example, also Alois. Gustl never had any doubt, nor did Mama, sweet, sweet Mama.

Ah, Vienna. I should have come before. The opera house, the cathedrals, the churches, the woods, the river, the library, the art galleries: I should have been here all my life. Only Gustl is a nuisance. He had been here two days when he passed the entrance examination to the Music Academy. As for me, it is not true that I was not allowed to sit for the academy's entrance examination. There was a certain misunderstanding, but that is all.

Gustl of course, passed. It seems that bourgeois mediocrity is its own reward.

May 3rd, 1908. Of course. Of course. I have been mistaken. This time the Herr Professor at the Academy was correct. My future lies in architecture, not art. A mere canvas is too small for my nature. Far more is needed to contain the potency of my spirit. Granite, marble, steel: these are the components with which I am able to express myself. How could a canvas or a sheet of paper ever be sufficient?

May 28th. Gustl wanted to spend Sunday on the river again, but I refused. "Girls," I said to him. "It is only to see girls that you want to go. The river has nothing to do with it." I could see that my accusation struck at the very core of his dishonesty. Immediately he agreed that we would not go. I could see how ashamed he was. "Purity of mind and body," I told him, "should always be the German ideal." Gustl's shame was pitiful to see.

June 6th. To speak with an impressive voice is needful. It is not possible for a leader to possess a truly dominating presence, if he has a tenor voice. Even worse would be a thin piping male alto. A baritone would be better, but what a leader truly needs is a deep rich basso profundo. I must work on it.

June 7th. I exercised my voice for two hours today after I saw Frau Zakreys go out. The tone was coming along well, also the power and the dramatic intensity, when there was a banging on the door. Herr Schumann from down the passage was there. "You cannot behave this way," he said. "I shall report it to Frau Zakreys this evening. Shouting at each other all afternoon, it is impossible." I did not argue with him. I have learnt that to argue with such as he is a great foolishness.

June 8th. I met Frau Zakreys on the stairs and greeted her in my most courteous manner. "What is wrong with your voice, Adolf?" she asked. "You must have a doctor look at your tonsils. My nephew's voice sounded just like yours. They took his tonsils out and everything was normal."

June 9th. Gustl wants to practise on the piano while I am busy with my voice exercises. He says he cannot concentrate if I make such a noise. He says that your voice is your voice and cannot be changed.
Perhaps all this time I have been overestimating him.

June 10th. Something I have never thought of before is my hand-grip Someone such as I should have a hand-grip of great power. It is to be expected that thousands will want to shake my hand and what a trial it will be if my hand is not strong enough. Also, those shaking hands with me should be able to sense the iron in my will through the grip of my hand.

June 11th. I have acquired a board of the right width and thickness on which to practise my hand-grip. I calculate that if I practise for an hour each day I will soon have a grip that will be the envy of all I meet, at least all that shake hands with me.

June 12th. I exercised on my board for two hours today while Gustl tinkled meaninglessly on his piano. He asked what I was doing, but I did not answer. Let him continue his trivial pastimes.

June 13th. Today I asked Gustl to shake hands with me. "Of course, Adolf," he said. "I am glad that we can be friends again." I grasped his hand firmly with my new grip. He tried not to show pain, but I could detect a sign in his eyes, the smallest of signs, but it did not escape me. He tried hard to smile and he said, "I am so glad that we're friends again."

June 16th. They are plaguing me more sorely than they have at any time. I woke up this morning with many bite marks.

June 20th. Most of the city needs to be rebuilt.

Even the Opera is not what it should be. As for the buildings on the Stumpergasse where I am unfortunate enough to live, disgusting! And the Ringstrasse, even worse. I will set about the task of new plans immediately. When completed I will submit them as a bequest, no a gift, to the city. The new structures will be of a magnitude that will leave the city fathers gasping in awe and wonder. Tonight. I must begin tonight.

June 25th. Gustl says rubbing olive oil on the bites helps. I have tried it, but I might have known better.

July 15th. Gustl has gone home. He says he will be back in November. But November is far away. What sort of friend is it that goes away for four months? Just because that stupid academy of his is closed is no reason for him to leave. Whenever I spoke about it all he could say was parents, parents, parents. I cannot believe Gustl's values are so shallow. Surely he must know that I have need of him.

August 30th. I am alone. Frau Zakreys asked me if she could wash my clothes for me. You would think she had nothing better to do. Cleanliness and Godliness are the brother and sister of wisdom she

61

said. She said a person cannot live on nothing more than bread and milk. I explained to her about the mind of the artist. "The stomach of the artist is what I am talking about," she said.

"What about the bed bugs?" I asked her.

"Bed bugs are like the poor," she replied. "We will always have them with us. In any case I am talking about food. Bed bugs are beside the point."

September 7th. So Gustl was successful in his examinations. Then he goes home and leaves me alone. And the other money is gone. Only the orphan's pension remains. Soon I will not even be able to afford this place amongst the bed bugs and rotting wood.

October 1st. Frau Zakreys says my hair is long. She says my moustache should be trimmed, my coat needs patching. She says I am pale. Obviously I am not eating enough. Obviously I am not getting enough fresh air. Obviously exercise is needed. Much is obvious to Frau Zakreys.

October 4th. Today I took the offensive in my relationship with Frau Zakreys. Before she could say anthing to me I spoke about the bed bugs.

"What do you suggest, Herr Hitler? To get rid of the bed bugs, we would have to burn down the building."

October 6th. Such examinations as those which Gustl passed are of no interest in the greater purpose of things.

October 7th. I have not been to the Opera for more than a month now. Even living off bread and milk does not leave me with money for a ticket. It is even longer since I worked on the drawings and the plans.

I wrote to Gustl yesterday, telling him how hard I am working. He will believe it. Of me, he will believe it.

The condition has been absent since before Gustl left. It would come at night to plague me, rising up out of the depths of wanton desire, tearing down my self-discipline, but not altogether. I have never done the sinful thing since that morning at Uncle Anton's farm. My body is weak, but my resolution is steel.

October 15th. I will not go.

October 16th. Never, never, never.

October 17th. My will is indomitable.

October 18th. But perhaps it is necessary. Perhaps the man who is a figure of destiny should see all things for himself. Perhaps I should at least know of the women of sin.

October 19th. I went to the Spitelberggasse tonight. I passed through slowly. In almost every house the lights were on and you could see them inside. There were no curtains. Lean and heavy, pretty and ugly, some on the pavements, resting against the walls of the build-ings, some sitting inside on couches, waiting; and men were coming, all sorts of men. They could have been shopkeepers, members of an orchestra, clerks, civil servants; who can tell?

The dresses of the women were like the dresses of Martha, their bosoms bulging for all to see, an advertisement. They were talking to each other, red lips moving in pale faces. Occasionally one saw me and waved or called out.

The men were coming down the streets and going into the houses. Do they really do this thing with these women in the back rooms of the Spitelberggasse's old houses, then just go away, walk away like a man who has gone to the Opera or to a concert?

But I, in me the flame within burns pure and clean. I turned my back and walked away, this time looking neither to the left nor the right. At the entrance to the alley I was accosted by another sort of voice, also the voice of a woman, but without the crude sexual character of the prostitute. It was a plaintive begging voice. "Please, some money, sir. Please, sir. I have not eaten for three days."

I looked in the direction from which it was coming. The woman was frail and she had thin blonde hair that might not have been washed for a year. Frau Zakrey would have had something to say to her. Even at the most difficult times I have not neglected to give my hair its regular monthly wash. Frau Zakrey is aware of this, and I am sure she appreciates it.

The woman was holding out her hands to me, both hands, the palms cupped. The fingers were long, the joints prominent, like knots

63

in a piece of chopped wood. The bones of her cheeks and forehead also were large, leaving cheeks, temples and eyes in shadow. "Money please, sir. A gratuity. I have not eaten in three days." There was a smell from her, a strong and ugly smell which I have never before known.

I turned away in disgust. How could such a person accost someone like me on the street. If there had been a policeman I would have had her arrested immediately. As it was I turned my back and started purposefully away. But behind me I heard her voice. "Poor devil," she said. "He probably is no better off than I am."

I stopped. It was unthinkable that I should allow her to compare me to herself. I felt in my pocket and drew out a one krone piece, my last one. Half turning so that I would not have to look directly at her, with a gesture that was both generous and royal I tossed the coin in her direction. It landed halfway between us and rolled across the narrow road, tinkling on the cobbles until it stopped in the gutter on the other side. The wretched scarecrow of a woman scurried after it, crouching so low that it looked as if she was running on both hands and feet. Her filthy coat flapped around her, dragging on the road and making her look like a great brown beetle. She examined the coin quickly by the light of a nearby gas lamp.

I turned and continued on my way home, but I heard her voice behind me. "A krone," she said. "A krone." It seemed that she could not believe her wonderfully good fortune. But then it is not every day that such a person meets someone like me. And I am a person of great compassion.

I had only taken a few paces though when she caught up to me and took hold of my sleeve. "Please, sir, where do you stay? I must show my gratitude. Please, sir."

I paused to look down at her. The fawning gratitude was pitiable. "Stumpergasse," I said. I gave the address of Frau Zakreys's establishment and walked on. It is impossible for such as she to repay such as I.

October 20th. I have seen no sign of her yet.

October 21st. There is no food at all now until the pension for orphans is due. I must do a painting. Unless I sell a painting I will certainly starve.

Still no sign of her.

October 22nd. I have done a painting of Martha. I remembered my success at school. Tonight as soon as it is dark I will go out to sell it.

A person like that cannot be trusted. It is three days since I gave her the krone. Gratitude. Pah!

October 24th. It is art. I explained to them that it is art. What right have they to arrest me for selling a work of art? They said that if it happens again I will not spend only two days in jail.

This cannot be real. Did Michelangelo go to jail for painting? Did Rembrandt? At least there was food in prison.

I have completely forgotten that wretched bag of fleas and her promise of gratitude. The incident is removed from my mind.

October 25th. She came tonight. She looked cleaner and the smell of her was not as strong as before. She knocked on my door and asked if she could come in. She was wearing the same dirty brown coat, but through the holes I could see that her cotton dress was clean. Also her hair had been washed since I had last seen her.

I stepped aside in gentlemanly fashion to allow her to enter. Her behaviour was soon to show that this was a mistake. I have learnt that a certain class of person easily misuses the generosity of their superiors.

She was no sooner in the room than she told me that she had been very lucky recently. She said that she had collected two kronen today and nearly one krone yesterday. Then she said that she had some sausage and a piece of bread that she had bought with yesterday's money, and would I like to share it with her?

I deliberated a moment, then very thoughtfully I said that I would do her the honour. Immediately I could see how this pleased her. She sat down on the chair and I sat on the bed. I was sorry to see that the food came out of a pocket in her coat. It was wrapped in a piece of newspaper through which the grease of the sausage was soaking. She broke the bread and sausage in half. I waited for her to start her half before I started mine. That is a rule of etiquette. There are also other rules of etiquette. This is cultural behaviour. My knowledge in matters of this sort is very thorough.

"I said that I would come to show my gratitude," she said. Her face was very thin, the hollows still deep in cheeks and temples despite the almost three kronen she had collected in the last two days.

"You are a person of honour," I said. I could see that even in a beggar woman the spirit of greater Germany was triumphant.

She did not seem to understand what I had said. She looked at me curiously for a few seconds, her head tilted first to one side, then to the other. When she did speak she said something that did not seem to be related to what had gone before. "If you turn around I will not be long."

Now it was I who looked at her curiously. Was this some sort of a game? Apparently I had to turn around while she did something for me. I was still pondering her strange behaviour, wondering if perhaps she was an insane person, when she stood up suddenly and took off her coat. "It doesn't matter," she said. "You don't have to." She folded the coat as if it was a fine garment, instead of the rag that it was, and put it down on the chair. I would have been afraid of her infecting the chair with bed bugs, except that the chair was already infected.

I was surprised, shocked even, at the familiarity of her behaviour. The dress that was now revealed was of a material that was adorned with a pattern of tiny roses. The roses had once been red, but now they were a faded pink, almost white and there were little holes along the seam down the side of the dress. In front I saw that four or five large buttons held the pathetic decaying rag around her body. Some of the button-holes were torn and the buttons hung loosely in them. I was still pondering her ragged clothes when I realized that I was seeing her petticoat, even more frayed and torn than her dress, with holes through which the small pieces of white flesh showed, like the dead flesh of a hen or fish at the market on Saturday mornings. She was undoing the buttons, removing her clothing.

A voice spoke, a harsh voice, but possessing a certain power. I had heard it before somewhere. It said, "What are you doing, witch?"

The woman stopped and stared at me as if it was I who had spoken. "Bitte," she said. Her voice was thin and shaking. "I wanted to show my gratitude."

I looked around the room to see who had spoken, but there was no one.

"Bitte," she said. "Please, gratitude."

I was still chewing the sausage she had brought with her. I had to move it to the side of my mouth before speaking. "Go," I said quietly.

She had her dress over one arm. It hung there like a rag for cleaning the floor. "Bitte," she kept saying, "I came to show you gratitude. You were kind to me. Bitte." Through the holes in her petticoat her navel showed. It looked like the dent made in a pool of mud if a stone is dropped there, except that it had ragged-looking wrinkles running from it in every direction and its colour was white, white with yellow patches like the edges of very old paper. Through another hole in her petticoat a knee showed, a square and angular thing, a strange and unnatural growth.

I looked at her. My eyes were like spears of fire. I could see nothing but her pale ugly figure. Around her everything had become black. "Gratitude," she said again, "gratitude." She had moved further from me, down a passage or a tube. Around her the darkness was complete.

"Go!" It was this alien voice speaking, not I. It possessed a terrible harshness to the ear.

"Bitte . . ." She was trying to say something, the ragged dress hanging across her arm and shaking like a leaf in the wind. How can she come to me this way, offering her sort of gratitude? Gratitude? And bringing it to one like myself who has eaten almost nothing for two weeks.

The condition would have been an unlikelihood with my stomach empty and faced by that creature of horrors with her yellow skin and her fleshless limbs. An unlikelihood? It would have been an impossibility.

I followed her to the stairs, then watched her from the window as she scurried across the courtyard, still trying to pull on her dress and coat. Her thin blonde hair was standing in every direction, her broken shoes scuffing on the cobbles, a disgrace to German womanhood.

October 27th. I have found a way to get them. I turn down the lamp, then I hang my coat on the chair in front of it to darken the room. I sit quietly on the bed and count to ten, no more and no less. Then with one swift movement I throw off my coat and turn up the lamp. This evening I did it three times. The first time I caught four, the second time three and the third time seven. Seven at one stroke, what an achievement.

Each time after capturing them I place them in my saucer, then ceremoniously I drop them into the flame of the lamp. Those that are already full of blood pop loudly and sometimes a few drops of blood are sprayed against the inside of the lamp's glass.

October 28th. I am deeply disturbed. Last night I spent the whole night hunting the bed bugs. I had killed forty-three by the time dawn came. Then I slept. When I awoke at midday I had sixty-seven bites on my legs, five on my arms and sixteen in my arm pits. How many of these disgusting creatures are there?

October 29th. Last night I caught only two and they are still biting me. And the bites on my legs are higher than before. No longer are they satisfied with biting the calves, or even the knees and lower thighs. Some have chosen to bite me closer to the hip than the knee, also on the inside of the leg. I would mind them less if reasonable boundaries were respected.

October 30th. I caught none and they are still biting. I shall have to create a new plan while I still have blood.

November 3rd. Nothing works. Who can credit a bed bug with intelligence to challenge my own? The idea is ridiculous. Nevertheless, they are avoiding me.

I shall work on a new device. Who are they to resist my genius? I shall show them an ability to destroy that they have not yet seen. I shall triumph in the end. Let the world listen.

November 4th. Traps, lures, stalking, decoys: nothing works. There must be a way. One bit me just below the place where the power of the soul has its source. They show no respect.

November 5th. There is no way. Oh, defeat. Oh, misery. Oh, nameless loss. Also seventy-two bites.

November 7th. Today I remembered what Frau Zakreys said about the bed bugs. To get rid of them you would have to burn down the building. This is what she said.

November 8th. If that is the only way then that is the way it shall be.

Tomorrow night when the last light is out I shall start a fire in the store-room at the back. Frau Zakrey's wood pile will soon set the whole building ablaze.

These disgusting creatures will learn what it is to show respect for a superior being. This old building, rotten and decaying as it is, is a small sacrifice. Unless action is taken I shall have no blood left at all.

January 7th, 1909. "But why fire, Herr Hitler?" Doctor Silberman keeps asking. They say they will not let me out of this place until I answer the questions and until Doctor Silberman is happy with the answers. Why should Doctor Silberman be happy with the answers? I am happy with the answers. I even told this Silberman: "Herr Doctor," I said. "Herr Doctor, I was killing the bed bugs in the building. They were a problem. They had infested everything. It was necessary."

But do you think he showed interest. Instead he asks only questions of a completely different sort. "Do you hear voices?" he asks. "Have you ever done that thing with a woman? Do you ever want to?"

He expects me to answer such questions, and he says that, if I do not answer, then we have plenty of time.

January 10th, 1909. "A boy," this Doctor Silberman asks, "do you ever have fantasies regarding a boy?" I looked at him with disdain, not stooping to answer such a question.

January 11th. "What of the sinful thing?" he asks. "How often? And do you enjoy? Is there guilt?"

January 15th. "Why such questions?" I asked today. "I have explained about the bed bugs, but you ask about the Hochstetter. What do the bed bugs have in common with the Hochstetter?"

He smiled. It was a stupid supercilious expression. It was an expression that suggested to me that he knew all and I knew nothing. I looked at this expression for a long time, the manner in which the mouth curved, and also the moustache, the teeth that showed behind the lips with little spaces between them, and stained yellow, and the beard, the fuzzy crinkly dark beard. "The bed bugs have nothing in common with the Hochstetter," he said. "The fire and the Hochstetter, they have much in common."

"The fire and the bed bugs," I said.

"The fire and the Hochstetter," he said.

January 16th. "What equips you?" I asked him. "What is it that equips you to ask the questions?"

"I have studied. I have studied problems like yours."

"I have no problem," I said.

"I have studied problems like yours," he continued, pretending that he had not heard me. "I have studied such problems and I know where to find the cause."

"The Hochstetter," I said.

"Precisely," he said.

"Now I know it too," I said, "so perhaps I may ask the questions now."

"There is more that must be learnt," he said and the stupid supercilious smile of yesterday returned. "It is called psycho-analysis. It is a new science."

"And the name of the inventor?" I asked.

"Herr Doctor Freud," he said. "I have studied under Herr Doctor Freud himself. In person," he said.

"Herr Doctor Freud? Is this a German name?"

"This is a Jewish name."

A Jewish name? I am being treated by an invention of a Jewish doctor, and by another Jewish doctor? And they search for the trouble at the Hochstetter? My memory of Doctor Bloch is clear.

January 20th. "What about your father?" he says. "What about your mother? What about the sinful thing? Why not answer?" I have explained in detail, but they choose not to understand.

January 30th. Today I told him. He had asked so many times that today I told him. "The sinful thing is impossible. The peanut exhausts itself."

"The peanut? One peanut?" His eyes were wet with joy, like those of a prospector who has discovered gold.

"One peanut." Then he wanted to see it, but there are demands that cannot be, and humiliations beyond bearing. I marched from his office in a way that left him in no doubt as to the manner of man with whom he was dealing.

"Show me," he had said, "show me." A man with the name Silberman. And what is the connection between the fire and the peanut?

February 7th. "It is for your own good," Herr Doctor Bleyer said today. "How can Doctor Silberman help you, if you will not allow him to examine you? It is not a big thing."

"It is of reasonable size," I interrupted him.

"Of course, Herr Hitler, but surely it is a small matter. You have been examined by doctors before. We have examined hundreds of people. Nothing surprises us. Let Doctor Silberman examine you. Or if you like I will. And let us not have more nonsense about bed bugs. Please, Herr Hitler, do not say anything. Let us conduct the examination. It is for your own good."

February 10th. There are times when things must be done. There are moments in the march of destiny which it is not possible to change. There is much that can be and much that cannot be.

I allowed them to examine me. They looked for a long time, also they felt. "Well, well, well," Herr Doctor Bleyer said, "only one."

February 13th. "It is a small matter," Doctor Silberman said, "a thing of no consequence. One is sufficient."

I have tried to be patient with this man. I have tried to show appreciation of his intellectual inadequacies. "The fire," I said. I was speaking slowly with emphasis on every word. "The fire is not of the Hochstetter."

Doctor Silberman smiled and raised a finger towards the ceiling. "Ah," he said, "I agree on that. It is not the Hochstetter that has to do with the fire. It is the peanut. Not even the peanut, it is the absence of the peanut."

"Bed bugs," I said, "bed bugs. I have explained concerning the bed bugs."

"Perhaps, if you would co-operate, Herr Hitler . . ."

"Co-operate!" I said, my voice calm and subordinate to my iron control. "Co-operate!"

"Also shouting will not help," he said.

"Do not accuse me of shouting," I said. "Do not accuse me . . ."

71

Herr Doctor Silberman's face was stern and unfriendly. "Keep your voice down, Herr Hitler. You will disturb the other patients. Some are seriously ill, you know."

February 14th. "This Doctor Freud," I asked, "he is Jewish?"

"As a matter of fact, he is." I could see that this Silberman was troubled by my question. "But what is good for the goose is good for the gander. What is the root of the trouble for the Jew is the root of the trouble for the gentile, if you get my meaning."

"And the root is always the same?"

"Without fail," Herr Doctor Silberman said.

"And these are the words of the Jewish Doctor Freud?" In his face I could see the disturbance within and I felt strong at the sight of it.

"These are the words of Doctor Freud, yes," he said.

I shall remember this Doctor Freud.

October 15th. I sold my coat today. It is four days since my last meal, a bowl of soup from the convent. I have eaten there every day for two months and I would have gone back, except that they insulted me. I might normally have overlooked it, but the way in which it was done was unforgiveable.

I was singled out. Everyone else was allowed to take their soup and drink it, but when I took mine I had taken not even two steps when the nun looked straight at me and said, "Stay in the yard. No drinking the soup out in the road. We've lost too many dishes recently."

Without a word I walked to her, my back straight and my head high. "Take it, madam," I said. The look of astonishment on her face was one that I shall not soon forget. "At least you have not lost your dish." I turned and walked away without a backward glance.

October 25th. The lines on the page are made by the rain. The wind is blowing from the north tonight and at times a spray of water reaches it. If I move deeper into the stall water drips through the slats in the roof and that is worse. From my place here on the sacks I can see the lights from windows on the other side of the river. I can see smoke from the chimneys, from warm fires, from the burning wood. Some are warm, well-fed and content tonight.

I have been here since they all went home. To wait for sleep until

72

the pleasure-seekers leave is a terrible thing. I shall yet be a man of influence, a man of power, and when I reach that position I shall arrange things so that the comfortable and the condescending have reason to reconsider the value of their safety and their comfort.

They come here at night. I see them walking past, going along the avenue towards the beer garden, men and women together, walking in pairs. Sometimes they stop amongst the trees. But I know them. I have seen them on the Spittelberggasse and I know them. They cannot mislead me.

Pleasure seekers. They are nothing more than pleasure seekers. Their lives are spent avoiding hardship. They understand nothing of the nature of life. They do not understand the struggle of all things. To survive it is necessary to be the strongest and most ruthless. Germany cannot again be great by the seeking of pleasure.

The wind has changed and the water dripping through the roof slats is reaching me. If only the rain were not so cold.

They are hateful, weak and insipid. They are soft and cowardly. All they have are possessions. Character and genius are unknown to them. They have houses and warm beds, food on the table, and they have women. They should be made to stand alone, to endure, to take up arms. They should be made to fight.

Perhaps tomorrow old Frau Hesseman will give me something to eat.

November 16th. I did not want to do it. I had not forgotten the cold of the nights or the rain. But even I must eat. I saw myself in the window of a house and I could not believe the whiteness of my skin and how long my hair and moustache have grown and how uncombed they look. It is no wonder Frau Hesseman hurried inside and closed the door. I must have frightened her.

I did not want to do it, but the price I got for my overcoat will get me food for the next four days. If I am careful even six days might be possible.

November 23rd. Tonight I was in the labourers' quarters on Erdbergstrasse. The place where you sleep is a box with an old blanket inside. If it had a lid it would be a coffin. There are almost a hundred people every night, each in his box. Not far from me was a woman with three children. One of the children was sleeping with her and the other two in another box. They whimpered all night. One of them, a boy I think, lifted his head above the edge of the box and stared at me. It was an ugly little face, brown with dirt, the hair sticking together as if it was waxed.

I looked at the sleeping bodies around me. I should not have to share accommodation with people of this sort. To such, sleeping and eating are all that are important.

I was just falling asleep when the thought came to me that there might be bed bugs. At least on the bench in the Prater there were no bed bugs. Nor were there any in the stall. But they could live here. They could hide in the cracks of the boxes and come out when you are asleep.

Why, I reasoned, would the bed bugs wait until I sleep. The light was dim, too dim for me to see them. They might already have been crawling from their holes, creeping into my clothing, looking for my flesh, my blood. I leapt to my feet. I had eaten so little in recent months. There could be no unused blood in my body.

I rushed from the dormitory to find the front door already barred. In my haste to open the latches I woke the supervisor. He is a fat old man. He looked tired and angry, his thin grey hair standing up around his head. "What are you doing?" He asked me. "You can't go outside. Do you know how cold it is? You haven't even got a coat."

"I cannot stay here," I said, not stopping my work on the latch for a moment. "I cannot stay here and have my blood sucked dry."

He looked puzzled at my words. He is not a man of intelligence, not even mediocre intelligence. As I got the door open I heard him say, "To look at you I wouldn't thing you've got much blood." I plunged outside into the cold night air. I heard the old man shouting behind me. "You'll freeze, my boy. You'll freeze out there."

I found the stall open, but the night was cold. I should never have sold my overcoat.

November 29th. If I do not do something I shall die.

December 3rd. The cold, oh, the cold.

December 10th. I am in the asylum for the destitute. They have disinfected my clothing. The matron told me that there were dozens of bed bugs in them. She said that it is a wonder that I have

74

any blood left.

To think that my manhood and my genius were being drained by these parasites. This is where my problems lie, a deficiency of blood. They have nothing to do with the theories of that Herr Doctor Freud. Of this I am certain.

December 11th. Today I helped a young housewife scrub her floors. For this I was given a large piece of Bludwurst. I felt my blood strengthen as a result. My face is still very pale though.

December 12th. The matron has instructed me to cut my hair and trim my beard. I think that secretly she admires me.

December 19th. Nothing is private here. There are forty-eight beds in the dormitory. Most of the men dress and undress next to their beds. But I will not do it. I will not be put on display like an oddity. There is nothing wrong with me. Many great men have been as I am.

December 20th. I have a new friend. His name is Reinhold. He is definitely a person of higher intellectual standing than Gustl. Already he has taught me a great deal. "Survival," Reinhold says, "all is survival." He is a man of intelligence.

"Herr Hitler," he said to me. From the beginning he called me Herr Hitler. This was before I put him at his ease, telling him that Adolf was good enough. "Herr Hitler," he said, "I can tell that you are a man of breeding like myself."

"Reinhold," I asked him, "what brought a man like yourself down to this level?"

"The same reasons that brought you to this level. The fickleness of fate, the exigencies of a restless nature and the untrustworthiness of one's fellow men."

"Well spoken," I said, giving him a hearty blow on the shoulder. "I could not have said it better myself."

December 24th. Today we put to work the survival methods that Reinhold has taught me.

We started at the apartments on Schottenring, working our way from one building to the next. The method employed was for one of us to knock on the door of an apartment and when the wife answered

75

he would ask if she had seen his crippled brother. We had been visiting the cathedral and had been separated. We said that we lived over in the Meidling area and if the brother could not be found he would not be able to get home, struggling along on his crutches. Ten minutes later the other one would appear, limping, with a crutch that we had borrowed from another inmate at the asylum. For use of the crutch, we have to pay him five kreutzer from any money that we collect.

The first building that we tried Reinhold went first and I was the crippled brother. I am afraid it was not successful. The first wife that I went to said, "You have just missed your brother. Hurry and you might catch him." I tried to tell her that I was very tired and needed to rest, but she took me by the arm and rushed me to the front door of the building, going so fast that I forgot to limp. "Hurry, hurry," she said, "I'm sure you will find him." With those words she pushed me out onto the pavement and closed the door.

The second was an old woman of seventy or eighty. When I tried to tell her that I was hungry she said, "Blessed are they which do hunger, for they shall be filled."

I told her that I was very tired and she said, "Rejoice and be exceeding glad, for great is your reward in heaven."

I told her that there was a long way for me to walk home and she said, "I envy you your great courage, my son." Then she closed the door.

"You look sad enough, Adolf," Reinhold told me afterwards, "but you aren't charming enough. In this business you have to be both sad and charming. From now on you be the brother and I'll be the cripple."

It went better after that, excepting that Reinhold got all the food apart from one small piece of pie that he hid inside his coat. He shared the money with me. I received one krone and three kreuzer.

January 18th, 1910. Reinhold is very excited. I borrowed a pencil and paper and did a drawing of the asylum building. He says that if I can do such drawings in colour he will sell them and we can share the money. He says that all we need is a set of paints and some cardboard and we can be rich. At last I have met someone who appreciates my talents. If only the jackals of the Academy could have been replaced by men of taste and culture such as Reinhold.

February 15th, 1910. This is better. At last life is improving for me. Reinhold and I have moved to the hostel on Meldermannstrasse. I have my own room, big enough for a bed, a table and a clothes rail. There is also a window and if I stand before it I can see down into the street and watch the people coming by, dressed in their warm overcoats.

Having mentioned overcoats, I might add that I have a new one, long, black and not without a certain elegance. It was purchased from a pawn shop and is not more than five years old.

Food is available at reasonable prices and there are stoves for those who cannot afford the food. There are tiles in the washroom and the showers, beautiful clean white tiles. On the beds are white sheets that are changed once a week.

All of this from my painting. Reinhold and I are living in what is almost luxury, and it is from my painting. The gentlemen of the Academy would never be able to believe it. What further proof is needed of their incompetence?

February 18th. Today I tried something different. I have grown weary of painting the same cathedrals, museums and town squares to sell to visitors. Without intending it I found myself doing a study of the human figure.

Painting the human figure extracts from yourself a resource of the soul, not possessed by all. Strength flows from the mind to the finger tips and from there to the brush until stroke upon stroke flows sweetly to the canvas, the soul of the artist and the paint combining to make a thing of beauty, of inner joy.

As I studied the figure I had created on cardboard I was struck by the purity of line and the majesty of my conception. I looked at it admiringly for a while, then at once the condition began to ensue. I had not intended that. Perfection and purity had been my only aim. It grew, uncalled for and unwanted, a creature with a mind of its own, until, rigid as Bismarck's backbone, it pressed against the front of my trousers.

Reinhold had come into the room and I heard him speak behind me. "Now this is something to see," he said. His voice was filled with awe, like the voice of a sensitive youth who sees the work of Michelangelo for the first time, or first hears the music of Wagner. "I can sell those, my friend. I can sell those. Why did you never tell me that you could do something like this? I have been struggling to sell museums and cathedrals, and you can do this." He looked down suddenly to the front of my trousers. "Surely you cannot make a picture of this type without it affecting you," he said. "Let me see." Then he leant forward quickly and squeezed the point at which it pressed, angry and shameless against my trousers.

I leapt to my feet, at the same time turning to face him. "Go. Get out of here." I had not spoken. The voice that had spoken, the rough voice, breaking with anger, was not mine. I had heard it before, but where it had come from and to whom it belonged was not clear. It was also not something that I would spend time considering.

"Adolf . . ." he tried to talk to me.

"Go," the voice cried.

Reinhold's face was strange, his eyes fearful and his lips moving without speaking, but he left my room.

February 20th, 1910. Today Reinhold asked my forgiveness. He said that he was overwhelmed by the enthusiasm that gripped him when he saw the picture. He said that he would never do such a thing again and that I must not imagine his action as an expression of unwanted familiarity. He had not intended his action to be seen in that light. In fact he had not thought at all and was deeply ashamed and humiliated and begged me not to turn my face away from his.

Of course, I forgave him. I am a forgiving person.

The pictures, too, need to be sold.

March 7th. The new pictures are an amazing success. We sell at least one a day and the price is double what we charged for the pictures of buildings. I have a new cane, my shoes have been repaired and soon a second shirt will be possible. Reinhold and I are the aristocrats of the hostel.

March 13th. Today Reinhold looked at my new picture for a long time before saying anything. At last he spoke. "You know, Adolf, please excuse me for saying this. I hope you will. But you know, I have never seen a girl who is quite like this there." And he placed his finger on the spot that offended him. "I might be quite wrong, but I simply have never seen a girl quite like that."

How could I tell him that I have never seen a girl in that way at all?

He might have sneered at me. He might have laughed. But, in fact, I must have. I am not a man without experience Am I not the man who boldly seized the evil Martha from behind? Was it not I who fearlessly entered her apartment? "I am sorry that you don't like my painting, Reinhold," I said.

"It is not that I do not like it, Adolf. I like it. I love it. And I can sell it. Oh, without any trouble I can sell it. No problem there. It is simply that I have never seen a girl quite like that girl. In my experience, and excuse me for saying this, but in my experience it should not be so round. Perhaps a little flatter would be right, more sloping, if you see what I mean. Not so round like a balloon. But I'll be able to sell it. No need to worry about that."

April 1st, 1910. It might possibly be best to approach my destiny boldly. At least, so it seems to me. For this reason I have seen an astrologer. He asked my date of birth then he read the stars for me.

I knew it. I knew it all along. He looked at my stars carefully, taking no chance of a faulty reading. I was very clear on this point. There was to be no possibility of a faulty reading. I told him that I was willing to pay extra so that he would be especially careful.

I knew what the result would be. He looked straight at me when he spoke. It is easy to see that he is a man in tune with the universe. After a long pause he told me that I would lead a most unusual and significant life, that my name would be on everyone's lips. My life would be a blessing to all mankind.

He charged me four kronen. Rather a lot, but now I know the truth. Not that I ever doubted my future. This is where my career in art will lead me. My name will be on everyone's lips.

May 7th, 1910. Ah, Vienna in spring. It is good to be alive, knowing that my future is brilliant and secure. Reinhold and I continue to sell paintings as fast as I can produce them. He has only been arrested once for contravening the morality laws. He has an excellent nose for such situations and almost always he is able to avoid the police.

Ah, Vienna. How lovely it was when we set out this evening to promenade through the city where we are now a successful part of the artistic life.

It was impossible for me to know what sort of shock awaited me. How could fate have destined such a thing to be?

79

Yesterday Reinhold sold two paintings on the Prater, and I bought a second shirt. We dined on Bludwurst that I cooked myself. I feel that this is still necessary to strengthen the blood. The effect of the bed bugs has not entirely disappeared.

Our position in the hostel was further illuminated earlier in the week when we made use of the dining room. Herr Müller had been present and he had immediately gestured towards the empty seat next to his. "Please sit down, Herr Hitler," he had said. "I have been keeping a place for you." It is particularly satisfying to be treated in this way by the supervisor. During dinner I had discoursed at length on the need for a union of greater Germany. Everyone had been impressed. The few that had tried to leave, poor souls, had quickly been put in their place by Herr Müller.

Such was our position when the evening started, a state of joy and pleasure, a happy disposition on the future. We walked down to the river, strolling slowly in the warm evening. The air itself was like a drug to the senses, dense with the power of Germany.

On the bridge we stopped and looked down into the water, watching the reflections of the lights from the Prater, long shimmering, bobbing lines of light, pulsing with the life of the river. The Danube seemed to smell sweet as I leant over the railing to see it flow by, the resurgent life of spring absorbed into it.

As always our conversation was excellent, two scintillating young minds joined together in intellectual combat. What a pity that we have no one to note our words for the edification of those who come after.

On such a night, I should not have needed to face past horrors. But the joyous spring evening was about to be corrupted in a way that it was not possible for me to imagine.

Going home we passed the Opera. The performance had ended, a trivial performance of a trivial Italian opera, something of Verdi's. Such music should be banned in German cities where the glories of Wagner are available to all who have his spirit echoing within them.

The performance had ended and most of the audience had left. A few carriages were at the door, handsome open carriages, with coachmen in livery in attendance. The sight of such wealth sickened me. These people were the suckers of mankind's blood. They were the bed bugs of humanity. "Stop," I said to Reinhold. "Stop. I must see this decadence."

"Why, Adolf? Just a few rich snobs leaving the Opera. You've seen it before."

How could I expect him to understand the depths of their depravity? "Wait a while, Reinhold," I said. "Let me see them. I need to know these people."

Reinhold waited with me to watch the people of the carriages come out of the building. The women wore gowns that exposed their shoulders and hung in long folds to the ground. Jewellery of gold and bright shining stones adorned their necks and wrists. The men wore clothing that Reinhold and I could not have bought if we had sold paintings all year and not spent a kreutzer of the proceeds. They moved in a group towards the carriages, turning to each other to talk, to laugh and to gesticulate, aware of their finery and their wealth. At once our hostel, the honour of sitting next to Herr Müller, the joy of selling pictures for a few kronen and the tiny rooms, scarcely big enough for a bed: all of this changed in my mind. In a moment this group with carriages, diamonds and evening wear had made me poor again, aware of my patched and cracked shoes.

They reached the coaches, the coachmen standing to attention, the doors held open for the lords and ladies to enter, when one of the men, a young man, no older than myself, came towards a woman who was just a few paces away with her back towards me. The man's hair was so precisely trimmed and styled that each hair seemed to have received separate attention. His very skin seemed to have been powdered. It was white and unblemished, like the skin of a child. What hardship has he seen? I asked myself. What suffering has he ever endured for the Fatherland?

I heard his voice as he spoke to the girl, "Fräulein, won't you ride with me?" He spoke softly, but I was close enough to hear. "I have been watching you all evening and I would be honoured."

I heard her voice as she answered and I was stunned by what I heard. It was not what she said. Her words were, "Why, Herr Franck, you flatter me. I'd be delighted." Such words are as trivial as the entertainment in which they had just indulged. It was the sound of her voice that stunned me. It was a voice I knew. She turned and I could see the profile of her face, lit by the carriage lantern. She moved to the carriage and up the steps supported by the young lord and the coachman. As she turned to take her seat I noticed the back of her dress. It had a row of buttons, so close to each other that they were almost touching, stretching from her collar to her waist. I remembered such buttons. I remembered them and I remembered the weakening within me such buttons had once occasioned.

She had taken her seat and was looking down from the carriage as if she owned Vienna when her eyes met mine. I did not hear the sound of it, but I saw her lips form the shape of my name. "Adolf." Her eyes were wide with surprise. She was staring at me as the carriage moved away down the length of the street. It was Martha. The fashion of dresses that she chose had not changed, at least not as far as the buttons were concerned.

After a while I became aware that Reinhold had hold of my sleeve and was pulling it. "They've left, Adolf. Can't we go now?"

Editor's note: Volume four was not in the parcel Uncle Abdool Ebersohn left me. WSE.

VOLUME V

November 1917. We have had cat on the last five nights. This is a special treat. Wilhelm is an expert at catching them. He sets snares along the edge of the village, baiting them with some of the meat from the previous cat. It is astonishing how the cats have survived despite the shelling. They are fatter now than they were during peace. I think that it must be the bodies. There is always a trench wall being destroyed by a shell and an arm or leg protruding. Although the meat is not fresh, the cats find it very tasty. The rats also eat their fill, but we do not readily eat them. Only a severe shortage of cats would bring us to that level.

Most of the houses on this side of the village are in ruins, but the cats remain, fewer of them since Wilhelm got to work. When we have such good fortune it is always Wucherpfennig who does the cooking. He has an iron peg that he stole from the supply post. On this he spears the cat after removing its skin. Then it is roasted over a very slow fire. It is always Wilhelm, Wucherpfennig, Schmidt and I that share the feast. Sometimes we invite Sergeant Max Amman to join us. He is especially fond of the tail.

November 7, 1917. It is raining again. Even the village streets are little more than swamps. In some places the trenches are half-filled with water. Some of our barbed-wire barricades only just stick out above the mud. In one machine gun emplacement the men were squatting in water almost knee-deep yesterday. As a result of this we have seen less of the rats.

What a pleasure to know that this is not being endured for nothing. A little discomfort is a small price to pay for the Fatherland's eventual victory.

November 18th. Today I discussed with Lieutenant Wiedemann the question as to why I am still a corporal. I cannot believe his reply. He looked straight back at me and said, "Adolf, to tell the truth, you are without the qualities required in a leader."

I? I was scarcely able to believe my ears. "I?" I asked. "I, who have earned the Iron Cross, 2nd class? With respect, Lieutenant, you cannot be thinking of me."

"No one doubts your bravery and devotion to duty, Adolf," the Lieutenant said, "but why do the buckles not shine? And the leather? Why do the heels not click together smartly when an officer approaches? Where is the ram-rod back? Why is the chest not puffed out like that of a pigeon outside the Munich town hall? This is leadership, Adolf. Bear it in mind."

November 20th. Bombardment tonight. The trench wall is broken in a number of places in our area. It is no more than a metre deep at the place where Schmidt is normally on guard. First there were rockets from the French side, shooting up fast, but drifting slowly down, spreading their light over the trenches. And when the rockets stopped the guns started. One of the new men was crying and one was vomiting, but Schmidt, Wucherpfennig, Wilhelm and I were calm. We have lived through worse.

While the rockets were going up we sat in a line, watching them. One of them had a pink glow and as it dropped Wucherpfennig said, "Undergarments. They remind me of the colour of women's undergarments."

"How old were you when this started?" Schmidt asked. "Seventeen? What do you know about women's undergarments?"

"I know that is the colour I will want for my woman's undergarments one day when the war is over and I have a woman."

"Is that all you can think about?" I asked. "We are here on a great adventure for the Fatherland and is that all you can think about?"

"Adolf never thinks about women," Schmidt said. "He is pure."

"It is not a question of purity . . ." I tried to explain.

"He is pure as no-man's-land in a shit storm," Schmidt said.

The remark was without any meaning at all so I endured it in silence. I found Wilhelm patting me on the shoulder. "You have to think about these things, Adolf," he said. "The parts that inspire these thoughts are the most important parts in the body."

"The mind," I said, "the mind. . ."

"Don't shout, Adolf, the French will hear us." It was Lieutenant Wiedemann. He had come slouching down the trench in a very unmilitary fashion. "What is this argument about?"

"You settle it for us, Lieutenant. We were arguing about what is the most important part of the body." Wucherpfennig was speaking. He was grinning at me. I could see his great horse teeth shining in the light from the French rockets. "Perhaps you would be kind enough to inform us, Lieutenant."

"That's not difficult," the Lieutenant said. He looked nearly as stupid as Wucherpfennig. "You all answer brothel call, don't you?"

"Not Adolf," they all shouted.

"Not Adolf? And you want to be a sergeant, Adolf?"

I was determined to answer. I will not be made fun of by fools. "I . . . the girls . . . the girls . . ." I started to say.

"What about the girls, Adolf?" the Lieutenant asked.

"They're dirty," I said.

They all laughed, even Schmidt who is not usually as bad as the others. Wucherpfennig laughed so loud I am sure the French wondered what we were doing. The Lieutenant behaves in this way, but he has the audacity to say that I lack the qualities necessary for leadership. When at last he had managed to stop laughing he said, "Adolf, you cannot get warm at the fire without getting a little smoke in your eyes." At this the others laughed again like jackasses, but the Lieutenant held up his hand for silence. "In any case," he said, "you think they are dirty? What must they think of us with our lice?"

"They also have it, Lieutenant." Wucherpfennig was enjoying himself, the fool. "They have every imaginable variety of trench lice. It gets passed from one bush of hair to another."

"Adolf," the Lieutenant said, "next time you are on brothel call I want to see you there. Then we'll see about promotion."

December 3rd.   What if I go next time? What if I do go? Perhaps everything will be in order. Once during a bombardment I saw a new recruit shot through the stomach. In trying to assist him the medical officers removed his clothing. The condition had appeared and was present for ten minutes while he died.

Perhaps it will be in order. Perhaps the girls will be of a gentle and loving disposition, also helpful and not of a mocking type.

December 6th. Tobacco rations again. I lectured at length on the weakening effect on the body and mind of tobacco usage, but no one paid attention.

Mail was handed out at the same time. Most of the others received letters. Some received parcels of food from their families. I too would have received these tokens of love if my dear Mama had been alive.

December 8th. Last night we were in the front lines. The French bombardment was going over us into the village. I could see the houses burning. We will have a brothel call on the day after tomorrow. Wucherpfennig was worried that the French might have hit the brothel, but Schmidt said that, judging by the position of the flames, if they had hit anything it was the officers' brothel.

"What a pity," Wilhelm said. "I'll have to do an extra one for the lieutenant."

"Are you coming with us, Adolf?" Wucherpfennig wanted to know. He is a good comrade in battle, but he is a fool.

"Why should I not?" I answered boldly.

Perhaps the girls will be kind. Perhaps just one will be enough for what has to be done. On the other hand it could be that there will be important messages for me to carry and such a thing will be impossible.

December 11th. Duty above all. I too would have enjoyed visiting the brothel with the others, but duty would not permit it. Colonel von Tubeuf had an important message to relay to Divisional Headquarters and, as usual, the lines were down. "I'm sorry to ask this of you," my colonel said, "especially today."

"It is nothing, my Führer," I said. "Duty comes first."

"Spoken like a true soldier," my colonel said, "but I shall try to make it up to you."

"There is no necessity, my colonel," I said. Who is not officer material now?

December 16th. It is raining softly again. It has been raining for almost forty-eight hours. Since October nothing seems to have happened except the falling of rain. Even the French bombardments have been fewer. Perhaps they also do not like the rain.

Yesterday a French soldier died not more than ten paces from our trench. His comrades were on their way back when he fell. His boots were in excellent condition, unlike mine that were full of holes and letting in the water. The Frenchman's boots fit perfectly.

February 2nd, 1918. A general strike! We are here giving our life's blood for the Fatherland, and they are holding a general strike!

What is needed with such traitors is a firm hand, a firm hand and a firing squad. Let the strikers be sent to the front line. We will send them on the next assault.

There is talk of a Soviet in Cologne, and soldiers swearing allegiance to it. Such a thing cannot be. General von Hindenburg would not allow it.

March 27th. Another brothel call. Unfortunately my duties are now more demanding than at any time. Perhaps next time.

June 12th. What a day! Today I have ensured my future promotion. The mud in the trenches was worse than ever so I used an old trench in front of the lines on the way back from the wood sector. They call it the wood sector even though there is very little of the wood left. The French guns have cut it down like a scythe.

The trench is deep enough to give reasonable cover from the French lines. How was I to know that there had been a French assault earlier in the day and four French infantrymen were crouching ahead of me, too frightened to take either one step back or one forward? I came round a bend of the trench, running as fast as I was able, and the four of them were leaning against the side of the trench, smoking pipes. I immediately drew my pistol and shouted, "Prepare to fire, comrades," as if there was a platoon coming around the corner behind me.

The Frenchmen just stood and looked at me, none of them making a move towards their rifles. I turned my head and shouted back down the trench. "Spread out and surround them. Rifles at the ready." Then I pointed my pistol at them. "Don't move or I'll fire."

At length one of them spoke. His German was slow, but clear. "Herr soldier," he said, "we do not care if you are alone or one of many. The war is long. What is the food like that your prisoners eat?"

"Worse than the soldiers get," I said.

"At least no one will be shooting at us," the Frenchman said.

So I shepherded them back to our trenches and took them to Colonel von Tubeuf.

"Adolf, my boy," the Colonel said, "for this you will receive the Iron Cross 1st class, and also a special surprise."

"I was doing no more than my duty, my Führer," I said. I think he meant promotion.

August 4th, 1918. Today I received the Iron Cross 1st Class. What else is there that can be said? When you have received the Iron Cross 1st Class, you have fulfilled yourself in life. You are someone that others admire.

But what of the other surprise? Perhaps he has forgotten.

August 8th. Colonel von Tubeuf called on me personally today. He came to Lieutenant Wiedemann's office in the trench to find me. Wucherpfennig was there, also Wilhelm and Schmidt. He smiled at me. Colonel von Tubeuf is not a man who is free with his smiles. "Adolf, I promised you something special, did I not?"

I came to attention. My heels snapped together and I pushed out my chest until my back was arched like a cross-bow. I will show Lieutenant Wiedemann who is fit to be an officer. "As my Colonel pleases," I said smartly.

"Listen to this." Colonel von Tubeuf looked round at the others. "This is going to make your friends jealous." Even Wucherpfennig was not able to sneer. "I have made a special arangement that I have never made for any soldier before today . . ." What? I wondered. Could he be moving me directly to Lieutenant, without even stopping for the rank of Sergeant? I had never heard of such a thing. ". . . and why am I doing this? Because of Corporal Adolf Hitler's bravery and devotion to his comrades and the Fatherland. That is the reason." He smacked the palm of one hand down on the little folding field table, almost upsetting the Lieutenant's coffee and his chess men. "What do you say to that, Lieutenant," the Colonel asked.

"This is excellent, Colonel, but you have not yet told us what it is."

"Ah yes." The Colonel raised one finger to emphasize what he was about to say. "I have arranged for young Adolf here . . ." He paused to make sure that he had everyone's attention, ". . . to visit one of the young ladies in the officers' brothel. Not the men's brothel, the officers' . . ."

They were all swarming around me in a moment, congratulating me and slapping me on the back so hard that my backbone might easily have been dislocated. "Good old Adolf," Wucherpfennig said.

"I always knew he would be a success in the army," Schmidt said.

"Better than the Iron Cross any time," Lieutenant Wiedemann said.

And I am still a Corporal.

August 10th. The day after tomorrow at seven in the evening there is a briefing of all officers in our sector. At this time I am to report to the officers' brothel where Frau Engelhard will receive me. For my bravery all the girls are to be lined up and I am to have a choice. Once I have chosen I am forbidden to leave her room until eleven by order of Colonel von Tubeuf.

"What now, Adolf?" Wucherpfennig asked. "There's no getting out of it now."

"I am a German soldier and I have received an order," I said.

Schmidt put his hand on my shoulder. "Never mind, Adolf, it's not the same as attacking the enemy position."

"Do it for the Fatherland, Adolf," Wilhelm said.

"Also your comrades, Adolf," Wucherpfennig said. "Do it twice for me."

"And for art," Schmidt said. "Do if for art, sixty-four times for art."

"And do it once for yourself, Adolf," Wilhelm said. "Once should be enough for you."

Lieutenant Wiedemann had come in and was listening to the conversation with his usual stupid smile. He and Wucherpfennig are two of a kind. It is very difficult to show the necessary respect for an officer when you have such officers. "Just remember what is the most important part of the body, Adolf," he said.

"Explain it to him, Lieutenant." Wucherpfennig could never stay silent for long.

Lieutenant Wiedemann came over to me, placing a hand on my shoulder. He looked into my face, making a pretence of being stern and fatherly. And this is the sort of thing that has to be endured by a superior person like myself in the army of the Fatherland. "Adolf, my boy, have you heard of Doctor Freud?" There it was again, the hated name of that lying Jewish doctor. "Do you know what Doctor Freud says?" he persisted.

"Yes, I know," I said in military fashion. "And I do not believe a word."

"Don't shout at me, Corporal." The Lieutenant's imagination was functioning in an excessive manner. This was not unusual for him.

"What does Doctor Freud say?" Wucherpfennig wanted to know. He is a man of very limited knowledge.

"Doctor Freud says. . . " Lieutenant Wiedemann spread his arms wide. He loves to have an audience. "Doctor Freud says that all of mankind's troubles are in the balls. He says if you've got no problem there, then you've got no problem."

"I'll drink to that," Wucherpfennig said, taking a sip from his coffee mug.

"Lies," I said.

"Hah," Wiedemann said, "you think so, Adolf. Let me tell you that for you and me who have no problems in that area it might be hard to believe, but think of the fellow who can't manage it. Think of him. That's what I call suffering." A shell exploded nearby and Lieutenant Wiedemann sat down. "That's what I call suffering. The front line is nothing. But if you can't answer brothel call you're in deep trouble, deeper than the mud in no-man's-land." He turned to the others. "What do you say, my men?"

"It's a terrible thing not to be able to answer brothel call," Schmidt said.

"I'd say when that happens your troubles have got you by the balls," Wilhelm said.

"Heil the Kaiser," Wucherpfennig said.

August 11th. Everyone is waiting for tomorrow. They all seem to think that I am trying to avoid it. "Adolf, you lucky dog," Schmidt said. "No standing in the queue for you. You just walk into the officers' brothel like a man and take your pick. I'd give my Military Cross 1st Class for that."

Perhaps the French will hit the officers' brothel with a shell. There are still twenty-four hours, and the French gunners are very good. Perhaps if a cross was painted on the roof with white paint. But that is treason. What am I thinking of?

Wucherpfennig gives me advice every time I see him. "Warm up some water and get a good bath, Adolf," he says. "Take this chocolate I got from my parents. You'll need the strength," he says. "Walk slowly on your way there to save your energy," he says. "Have one mouthful of wine, just one, to get the blood moving."

Perhaps if I concentrate hard the one will be sufficient to do the thing. Perhaps the condition can be maintained by will alone. Why not? Schopenhauer says that strength of will must always triumph. The power of the will, that is what is needed. And who better to exercise such power than I? Therefore who better than I to do the necessary deed in the officers' brothel tomorrow night?

August 12th, 1918. All morning I had to endure the winks and nudges of the others. We spent the morning offloading supplies at the store on the east side of the village. At twelve o'clock Sergeant Amman ordered me to go and clean up.

"I do not need seven hours, my Sergeant," I said.

"You have received an order, Corporal Hitler," he said.

Wucherpfennig, Wilhelm and Schmidt all came to attention although there was no need for it and they had no order. "Up the Sixteenth Regiment," Wucherpfennig shouted.

Sergeant Amman turned to him as if to rebuke him, but he only smiled and said, "On your way, Adolf. This doesn't happen every day, you know." I saluted smartly and marched down the street. Behind me I could hear my three comrades cheering.

The house where we are billeted had lost the kitchen and one bedroom to a French shell. There was a fire place and we had been supplied with a steel bath. I made a fire and warmed a few pots of water and poured them into the bath. My uniform, sticky with mud and the sweat of the last two days and alive with lice, clung to my body as I removed it. This is not usual. Normally I wash daily and keep the lice and mud to a minimum, but for two days it has not been possible.

I washed and dressed in a clean tunic and trousers lent to me by Wucherpfennig. I only have one pair. By the time I had finished and my hair was combed and my moustache brushed (what a splendid moustache I now have) it was only two in the afternoon with five hours still to wait. To the west I heard a few French guns start up. How I longed to be back in the trenches, pressed against the mud walls as the shells come over, safe in the dug-out. Instead I was left helplessly waiting for five hours. The brothel is only five minutes' walk on the far side of the village. But I had to wait. I could hear the clacking of machine guns. Perhaps the French were about to attack

91

and I would be needed in the trenches. Every man would be needed to stem the French avalanche. It was my duty.

I marched to the front door and threw it open. Sergeant Amman was coming down the street. He saluted me. I could see a certain mockery in the gesture. "You look excellent, Corporal. Now stay out of trouble until seven."

"I heard machine gun fire," I said.

"Every day we hear machine gun fire, Corporal Hitler. I am sure that it is not important. In any event your comrades, Schmidt, Wucherpfennig and Wilhelm, together with half a million others should hold the line. For once they'll manage without you." He saluted again and went on in the direction of the stores' depot.

I went back inside and closed the door. The fire had burnt low in the grate and I watched the coals die.

Perhaps it would be successful. Perhaps, on its own, one would be enough. This is what Herr Doctor Silberman said years ago. For a Jew he seemed to be a man of fair intelligence.

Perhaps if I took hold of her violently and overpowered her. What if I overpowered her and there was nothing, no condition of any significance at all? In any event to think of overpowering a brothel girl was ridiculous. Resistance was not permitted.

There was another way. I had my service pistol. I took it from its holster and examined it carefully for the first time since I had been issued with it. Two months before I had used it to capture four French soldiers. Perhaps today it could do me another service. A single bullet and there would be only oblivion. The ordeal that I must face would have been avoided.

But what of Germany? Where will Germany find a ruler in the hard days to come when the war is over? What would Bismarck have done?

Bismarck would have faced the ordeal no matter how harrowing. He would have squared his shoulders and gone bravely to do the necessary. If sacrifice is needed for the Fatherland, then I must be ready to heed its call.

I ate the chocolate Wucherpfennig had given me. He said it would give me strength. I also swallowed one mouthful of Schmidt's wine as Wucherpfennig had said. To keep the blood moving, he had said. Was it important for the blood to move?

At length, at very great length, the hour of six arrived, then half past six, and finally ten to seven. I stood up, brushed down my tunic with my hands. I was about to stride out into the evening when I remembered the pleasant sensation the mouthful of wine had caused within me. I had truly felt the blood move. I went to Schmidt's bottle and took a second mouthful. The blood moved again, more strongly than the first time. My watch said that the time was eight minutes to seven. Five minutes was enough time to get to the officers' brothel. Even two minutes was enough if I walked fast. I took a third mouthful of wine and the pace of my blood quickened. I took a fourth. After the fifth the time was one minute to seven and I set out for my destination. My blood was racing, galloping like a cavalry charge.

I marched the length of the street, my shoulders straight, my chest out. I passed two officers and saluted them both in splendid Prussian style. They returned the salute tiredly. I heard one of them say, "It's amazing. There is a soldier who is still enjoying the war."

The officers' brothel is in a beautiful old house, overlooking the canal. They chose the best house for the officers' brothel and the second best one for Regiment Headquarters. Three houses down the road from it the men's brothel is housed in an ugly and dilapidated little building. The queue was out of the gate and twenty-five metres down the road. The idea of it was repulsive to a sensitive soul like mine. As I turned into the gate of the officers' brothel, I heard someone from the queue call out, "You're not allowed in there, Corporal." I neither turned my head nor paid any attention. "For such gross insubordination you might lose it completely," the voice called out again.

I strode up the steps and knocked purposefully on the door. A lady of middle-age opened it. "Frau Engelhard," I cried, "Corporal Hitler reporting for duty."

She looked at me for a moment. She had red lined eyes and skin that hung in wrinkled bags on her face. Turning her head, she called out, "Mimi, Corporal Hitler is here." To me she said, "I do the cleaning here. Come in."

I came through a narrow hall and into a big room with polished woodwork and a huge chandelier hanging from the ceiling. On all sides long couches with curving backrests were filled with cushions, girls and a few officers. The couches were upholstered with colourful material and the girls were dressed in evening dresses that showed off

93

their shoulders and more than their shoulders.

I kept my eyes straight in front, my head held high. My blood was flowing like a waterfall in the Alps. I could hear the rushing of it in my ears. Another middle-aged lady, but not so middle-aged as the first one and also wearing the same kind of dress as the girls, came smiling up to me. "Corporal Hitler reporting for duty, Frau Engelhard," I said. My feet clicked together, my chest was pushed out and I saluted smartly. We will see who is of the right material to be an officer and who is not, I thought.

"At ease, Corporal," she said. "By the look of you, you seem ready to take all of us by storm." She was smiling, but it was the smile of business. "Would you like a drink first?" While I was seriously considering this question she continued, "Or would you like to choose a girl right away? We don't normally have such young men here and even then we sometimes have a fair amount of impatience to deal with." She gave me only a moment to think about this. "Either way you might just as well remove your helmet."

My blood was a torrent, a throbbing pulsing jet, being driven by a high pressure pump of which I could feel the pounding in my temples. "The girl," I said.

"There they are. Make your choice."

I removed my helmet to look round at them, but I got no further. One of the girls cried, "No, he's mine." My eyes found hers. I had recognized the voice. Again I had recognized it. Now I was faced with her and the recognition was complete. Her long curling black hair was falling over her shoulders and down to her bosom. Seeing me enter, the officers rose to applaud. Clearly my bravery had become the talk of the regiment. Martha. Would I never be free of her?

But my blood was a flood and its pressure was irresistible. I leapt forward, took her by one arm and, my eye falling on a nearby door, dragged her in that direction.

She was resisting me. "Not that way, Adolf," she said. "The kitchens are in there. Let me lead the way."

I could hear the other girls laughing. "At least he's not a general that you have to help up the stairs," I heard one say.

Martha had her arm around mine and was directing me across the room to a staircase on the other side. I had my helmet under my free arm and I was holding my head erect and my shoulders back in true military fashion. My blood was a waterfall inside my head, a torrent roaring so loud that I could hardly hear Frau Engelhard say, "You'd better cool this one down, Martha, or you might never recover."

"Jealousy will not help," Martha cried. "He's mine." Then she pressed her mouth against my ear. "Secretly all the girls would like to work in the men's brothel. It's just the long hours and the hard work that stops them from applying."

Suddenly we were in a bedroom. She had closed the door and was leaning against it as if afraid that someone might come in or that I might try to escape. She was doing things with her shoulders, a movement like a caterpiller makes as it progresses along a branch, and her dress was slipping down. I was at attention, my arms stiffly at my sides. The condition was a proud reality that could not be denied. "My God, Adolf," I heard her say. "Why did you put your helmet back on?"

I would have answered, but military dignity made it impossible. Also my throat had swollen closed. I was swollen everywhere.

The dress had gone. It was a red floral pile on the floor. My eyes were still straight in front of me, looking over the top of her head, but down in the bottoms of my eyes, obliquely, vaguely, I could see white flesh, flesh in the shape of mounds and hollows, undulations, plains and peaks; and it was coming towards me. "Your helmet, Adolf." Her voice was a whisper above the sound of my blood. "Take off your helmet."

I was immobilized, rigid and inflamed. My arms were pressed so tightly against my sides that my elbows hurt. My neck was so stiff it could have been used as a bridge across an Alpine river. She was working at my tunic and my trousers. Suddenly my legs felt cold as if a blast of air had struck them. There was also an itching, spreading down the bottom of my stomach and between my legs, as the trench lice scurried away from the light for cover. Martha was climbing up me like a monkey. Her arms were wrapped around my shoulders and her legs around my waist. "Adolf," I heard her gasp, "you are quite extraordinary." Then she said, "Aah," long and drawn-out like a sigh or a deep breath, taken slowly. "I don't mean it as a compliment," she said. "Aah, that's good." The pressure of her arms around my neck became stronger, like a creature with tentacles. "I was good at sports at school, which is just as well. I cannot believe in a person like you. Perhaps you don't really exist. I made you up, I think. Aah, you fool."

Some military aspect was needed, a sense of discipline was lacking. "Forward, my Courtesan," I said, my speech clipped, neat and precise.

"Jawohl, my Corporal, aah," she said, "sofort, my Corporal."

She continued in a similar manner, saying a great many things of a similar sort, none of which are worth repeating. The rushing of my blood had stopped. Now there was quiet. All I could hear were the sounds that Martha was making, the nonsensical jumble of her words, her breathing (she seemed to be making a great effort) and the aahs.

Everything inside me, my whole self, was being drawn to a point. At once in agony I remembered the sinful deed that had taken place at Uncle Anton's farm. "Aah," Martha was saying. "Adolf, you fool," she said. I remembered in a flash the feeling of exhaustion when my whole being, the very potency of my soul had erupted from me through the confines of one narrow passage. "Aah," Martha said. "I feel like a monkey up a pole." It was going to happen. I could feel the surge, the urgent upward pressure. "Aah. For God's sake, Adolf, that helmet is ridiculous. Aah." It was moving and could not be avoided.

I closed my eyes at the horror of it. What if the one single one exploded with the effort of trying to do the work of two? What if I was left with only an empty shell, a hollow vessel of no significance at all? "Aah."

The eruption came like that of a volcano, a thousand years of molten lava bursting forth in one mighty bolt. "Aah."

I sat down on the edge of the bed and took off my helmet. There is no dignity in being naked from the tunic downwards. The shining points of my boots were protruding from the rumpled heap that my trousers formed on the floor.

I leapt to my feet and pulled up my trousers. A trench louse moved, scurrying from near the bottom of my stomach to a place just behind my one single one, that is to say, if the one was still there. I was compelled to scratch.

"Even the officers have them," Martha said.

But there was a weakness upon me. I sat down again on the bed, slowly, very slowly, the feather mattress sinking beneath my weight.

"We have to make up the bed after every assault. At least that is not necessary with you." Martha's voice was bubbling along like a stream.

"Assault?" I asked.

"We're in the army now. We use military terms."

She was still naked, except for her shoes that seemed to be covered by a gleaming red satin, her stockings that were black but not so black that you could not see the white of her skin shining through them, and her garters, broad and with little bright red frills. I turned away so as not to see her. In turning the weakness came over me like a wave. My strength, every vestige of my potency, had been drawn from me. I felt myself sinking further back onto the bed. "Adolf?" I heard her say. "Adolf? Adolf, wake up." Her voice was reaching me from far away. "Adolf, you fool, open your eyes." I could barely hear her. I was sure she had killed me. "Adolf, damn you." It was no good. A dark wave was flowing over me and she was on the far side of it. To die this way, in the officers' brothel, was beyond imagining. The thought came that at least it had been in the service of the Fatherland. Martha seemed to move away and I heard her voice reaching me from further than ever. "Frau Engelhard, Frau Engelhard, come, come, please come. I think he's dead."

August 15th. "That is what happens when you do not answer brothel call regularly," Wucherpfennig said. "When you do answer it, it is a severe shock to the system. The constitution cannot handle it. It is the same as giving a starving man too much to eat. It could kill him. Adolf needs to be broken in gradually."

"Explain to us," Schmidt said, "how someone can be broken in gradually."

"One centimetre at a time," Wucherpfennig said.

August 20th. I am completely recovered and on frontline duty again. There is no hardship of war that I have not braved, no obstacle that I have not conquered.

September 6th. The writing of notes such as these needs to be approached in an orderly fashion. It is possible to fill the pages with trivia, but of what value will they then be to the generations that come after. Where will they find inspiration?

It is because of considerations such as these that I write only of the most significant events of my life. The generations to follow will be my beneficiaries.

VOLUME VI

July 20th, 1919. I am a man. I am thirty years old. I have lived through the greatest of wars. I have discovered genius within myself. I have developed a powerful basso profundo voice. I am quite tall and of a fairly imposing physique. I have trimmed my moustache to give me a more sophisticated and intellectual aspect. I have also changed my style of hair, combing it smoothly and elegantly over my forehead, my carefully trimmed fringe reaching to the edge of my left eyebrow. I am a man, physically and intellectually mature, ready to serve my country in whatever capacity she needs me. Naturally I expect it to be a leadership position, upper leadership, not middle or lower. The upper of the upper.

September 12th, 1919. Today I attended a meeting of the Workers' Party on the orders of Major Hierl. The meeting was held in a little beer hall called the Sterneckerbräu. Nine people attended. One old man was deaf and his friend translated the speech into sign language for him. I slept.

My report will be handed in tomorrow. I will say that there is nothing to fear from these people. They are quiet and peaceful by nature and not even a leader of the most potent sort could rouse them to revolution or war.

September 13th, 1919. Last night I did not sleep at all. Perhaps the reason was that I had slept in that stupid meeting. A Workers' Party with only nine workers, imagine such a thing. The only phrase I heard was one of them saying,"We need a party for the people." The fool. Who needs a party for the people? I need people for a party.

Because of my inability to sleep I placed breadcrumbs on the floor for the mice. This I do as a demonstration of my generosity and compassion. It is also the reason that I make reference to it here. It is only fitting that succeeding generations should know of my compassionate nature. I placed three crusts of bread next to each other on the floor. This is a great deal of food to mice who are very small creatures and for that reason do not have large appetites.

After watching them for a while I began to wonder whether there might be any parallels between the behaviour of mice and that of men. With this purpose in mind I tried very cleverly to catch one of the mice. I accomplished this by balancing an upturned bowl above the crusts of bread. Holding up one side of the bowl was a fork and attached to it was a boot lace. As soon as a mouse got close to the crumbs all I would have to do was pull the boot lace and the bowl would come down, imprisoning the creature.

But as soon as I had my trap constructed the mice stayed away from the breadcrumbs. This was a surprise to me. I had not expected cowardice in mice. From my experiment the use of logic indicates that men too are cowards unless they have strong purposeful leadership. What the mice needed was a Bismarck, then they would have marched in and secured the breadcrumbs for their feast.

As soon as I came to this realization I saw that I had been hasty in judging the Workers' Party. Their problem does not lie in their small numbers, it lies in the fact that they have no leader.

I have learned from my experiment with the mice and I have solved the problem that is holding back the Workers' Party. Tomorrow I shall offer myself as leader.

September 19th. They refused me. I explained carefully to them that they needed me, but they refused. I sat through all of their discussions and arguments, their beer drinking and their falling asleep, and after all that, they still refused me. When I made the suggestion, in the most pleasant and reasonable of tones, their present leader, a little fellow by the name of Drexler just looked up and said, "God in heaven." You would have thought that mine was a surprising or unusual request.

I must admit that after the meeting he came to me and apologized, saying that I must understand that they already have a national leader, a fellow by the name of Harrer. "National leader?" I asked. "How many branches are there?"

"Just this one," he said.

"And how many other members?"

"You've seen them all," Drexler said.

September 21st, 1919. I must remember the mice. The Workers' Party is, as yet, without a leader. They should not be judged too harshly. When I am leader they will have no excuse.

October 1st. Today I was called into the Captain's office. He started speaking without looking at me. "Corporal Hitler, you are being given a new room upstairs. You will pack your belongings." He was clearly troubled at having to tell me this.

"But why, Herr Captain?" I asked. "I am happy in my quarters."

"Nevertheless, I have decided that you are moving to new quarters upstairs."

"But, Herr Captain," I said, "I do not believe that we have empty quarters upstairs."

The Captain looked out of the window. He had not looked in my direction since I had come into his office. It was not soldierly conduct. He cleared his throat. It sounded like gravel pouring down a shoot. "The old broom cupboard, we have cleaned it out . . ."

"The broom cupboard . . ."

"It is of a fair size. Also there is a window, not a bad window . . . I looked through the window. If I stood on the tips of my toes I could see onto the roof of the store room, not a bad view . . ."

I brought my elbows in tight against my sides, squared my shoulders and raised my chin so high that I could no longer see the Captain. "I believe that I am entitled to an explanation, Herr Captain," I said.

"There is really no need . . ." The Captain began. His voice was uncertain. It is this sort of weakness that caused the German army to be stabbed in the back and brought the infamy of Versailles upon us. "All right then, Corporal," he said. "There have been complaints."

"Complaints, Herr Captain?"

"That is correct." I could imagine him looking out of the window in order to avoid looking at me. Of course I could not see him.

"What sort of complaints, Herr Captain?"

He took a long time composing his answer which, when it came, was of such feeble simplicity that the long period was difficult to understand. "Something about body habits," he said.

"Body habits, Herr Captain?"

"That is correct. Corporal Hitler, your body habits are your own business. I do not wish to pry into them. For this reason you are now going to have your own room where you will be able to exercise them in private. You are dismissed Corporal."

Body habits! Is it for this that we fought? It is to this level that the Fatherland has fallen.

October 4th. My office, as I call it, has become a sanctuary. When I enter and close the door no one may follow without my permission. There is room enough for my bed and my locker and in the afternoon there is a patch of sunlight from the window. It starts at the foot of the bed, then climbs the wall to finish near the ceiling.

If I stand on the bed to see out of the window it is as I was told by the Captain. I can see the roof of the store room, and also the grey wall of the administration building. Administration. An army of clerks. No wonder we have Versailles.

I lie down on the bed and I am shut off from the outside. At such times the strength of the mind dominates all else. I am given a chance to exercise the pure logic that has been demonstrated in these pages. Also the voices of the mind speak to me. Since Vienna they have spoken more and more often, directing me in the path of leadership and the pursuit of glory.

Today while I lay on my bed I heard one of the voices speaking. It was the female voice. She said that I should take her, that if I had to use force she would understand. But first, she said, I should woo her with the power of my voice and the wisdom of my words.

After the voice had stopped I stayed in the same position for a long time, holding fast to the moment. It was a time of great wonder. Germany does not speak directly to many of her sons.

October 12th. This Harrer with his limp, his dirty shirt collars, his long meaningless discussions and his unpleasant winds: is this a national leader. What is needed for the meeting is an advertisement in the newspaper, a carefully worded invitation. "Germans, awake to the insidious lies, frauds, corruptions, deceits and treachery of the Bolsheviks and the Jews." Something striking that people will remember is needed.

But no, Harrer says. We do not have the money. We must look to the budget. We must look to the membership, all seven of them. We must first raise money with a collection. Each of the seven members must put a few kronen into the hat. In this way with the passage of

101

time an advertisement will not be impossible. In such a way we are going to save Germany.

October 13th. Too many soldiers, Harrer says. Where do the soldiers come from? he wants to know. From Hitler, he says. Where is the worker? he asks. Swamped by soldiers, he says. Soldiers from Hitler are swamping the worker, he says.

All seven workers.

October 14th. Tonight at the meeting I spoke of destiny, of nationalism, of patriotism, of history and of Aryan glory. I ended on a fine note. With these words I ended: "There must be an advertisement in the newspaper."

October 15th. Tomorrow night is the meeting in the Hofbräuhaus and we have placed an advertisement. Drexler supported me. Harrer is angry. The national chairman does not like new faces in the audience. Seven is his lucky number.

Harrer is the main speaker. I am to speak before him, but fortunately I do not have to introduce him. That sad task falls to Drexler.

October 17th. Last night it was impossible for me to work on my writing. My triumph was still too close upon me. I was too much in awe of the forces at work within me.

I was to speak for ten minutes, not eleven minutes, not even nine minutes. When the time came for me to speak Harrer took out his pocket watch and, with a great clicking open of the cover, placed it on the table where I could see it.

Before the meeting he had stopped me outside the Hofbräuhaus. "Remember," he said. "If no one comes there will be no collection to pay for the newspaper advertisement, and if there is no money for the newspaper, the German Workers' Party will be bankrupt, destroyed by your excessive ambition. Think of that, Herr Hitler. We have a solid little membership, but this is not good enough. You and Drexler are power hungry. And the German Workers' Party will be sacrificed."

Instead it was a triumph. Forty-five people attended, five of the old guard and forty new people. Harrer sat next to me on the platform, his arms folded and his eyes dark with anger. At one stage before I was due to speak he leant towards me and whispered, "We might still not collect enough to pay for the advertisement."

I had prepared every line, every word of my speech. In my broom closet I had practised every gesture. Whenever I used the word Germany I stretched my arms wide on either side to denote its greatness. When I spoke of Bolshevism my finger pointed down towards the earth, showing how we were going to grind them into the dust. When I spoke of the German people my voice grew soft with tenderness. And when I spoke of the sacrifices of German mothers I almost wept. All this I had tempered to a point of perfection. There was drama. There was oratory. There was romance. And there was vision. All this I instilled into one ten-minute speech in the privacy, the solitude, of my broom closet.

It was with these hours of preparation as the foundation of my speech that I stepped forward. My opening words were as I had prepared them. "Dear Germans," I said. Then my eyes fell upon Harrer's watch, lying there on the table, ticking at me with the measured clicks of time being chopped away, each tick a fall of the axe.

"Dear Germans," I said. The abominable humiliating watch was staring at me, challenging me to go beyond ten minutes. I looked at the audience, forty-five men of all ages, young and old, military and civilians. Forty-five. It was a meeting of substance.

"Dear Germans," I said again softly. I had forgotten my speech. Harrer still had his arms folded. He was looking at me out of the corner of his eyes. I could imagine the sneer. Drexler was leaning forward in his chair. His face was puzzled, as if he did not understand what was happening. All the preparation in my broom closet, the memorizing of every word, the planning of every gesture, every intonation: it was all gone. "Dear Germans . . ." There was nothing else.

Then it happened. The voice was there and I was listening, instead of speaking. It had a harshness that surprised me. I had heard it before, a few times but only a few. Now it was filling the hall. My hands were gesturing, not the gestures I had practised. These were shorter and more precise, little stabbing movements, and short sweeping strokes, like a scythe cutting away grass. I felt perspiration flowing down my forehead and cheeks, plastering my lock of hair to my left eyebrow. My head lifted, the voice flowing out and filling the hall. The sound was coarse and rough, but it possessed a rhythm, like the rhythm of the sea, or of the mind. Soon the rhythm of the voice was the rhythm of the crowd, and the rhythm of the crowd was the rhythm of Germany. I was above the crowd, swooping like an eagle, a black steel eagle, an Aryan eagle flying over the heads of the listeners, lifted high and towering over them. And the power within me, and going from me to every soul in the crowd, was the power of the voice.

As suddenly as it had started, so suddenly it ended. The eagle swooped to earth and again I was on the boards of the little raised podium. I heard Harrer behind me. His voice was hoarse with agitation. "Two hours, two hours," he was saying. "He was supposed to speak for ten minutes. There is no time for me. Two hours."

But the audience was standing and applauding, shouting and clapping their hands. Some even threw their caps into the air.

We collected enough money for ten newspaper advertisements.

January 25th, 1920. It is especially pleasing for me to lie down on my bed and think about the time I spent defending the Fatherland in the great war. It is pleasing to remember that even at that stage my qualities of leadership were being recognized. I remember how my Lieutenant ... his name was Wiedemann ... I remember how he wanted to promote me to the rank of sergeant, but I said, "That is all very well, Lieutenant, but the Fatherland is short of frontline messengers. Who will replace me, if I accept promotion?"

At this the Lieutenant immediately saw the difficulty of our position. "Are you willing to make such a sacrifice?" he asked at length.

"I am willing to make even greater sacrifices for the Fatherland," I said.

I have also been thinking about this Doctor Freud. I have decided that perhaps he is right. Perhaps if all problems of the soul come from the same area, then if the area is halved, the problems also are halved. Perhaps this is the root of my genius. Perhaps the great men of history have all been blessed with an absence of this nature. For that reason they would have had fewer distractions. All their energies would have been directed towards the task in hand. I have no doubt that Julius Caesar, Alexander the Great, Charlemagne, Napoleon Bonaparte and Bismarck all had a similar physique in this respect.

This is logical. And I am a master of logic.

January 30th, 1920. This Freud is a fool.

February 7th. I am a man of more than average height. I have taken note of this when standing face to face with others. During the last week I have stood face to face with twenty-three men. I have been taller than twelve of them, of the same height as seven of them and only shorter than four of them. This proves beyond any doubt that I am a man of substantial height. Fair height.

As for women, I am taller than all women I meet.

February 8th. Not only are the voice and the gestures important when addressing a gathering, also the stride is of consequence. When approaching the platform a measured stride of military nature is needed, the head raised in commanding fashion, the eyes a cold blue, the intensity of the eagle combined with the vision of the mystic.

But the stride, the military posture, this is what the audience can see. This is leadership they can accept.

My hair is unfortunate. I am naturally blonde, but time has darkened it. A light dye might be in order. I shall consider this.

February 10th, 1920. What do they expect? Should we allow them to attend our meetings and shout their slogans?

While Harrer's workers are cowering, my troops of the storm take control. Five years of war have made them as strong as lions, as tough as front line stew and as hard as the power of my resolve.

And should we allow them to run their own meetings without interference? Should treason be permitted in the name of freedom? Who gives the Social Democrat the right to side with Germany's enemies? My troops of the storm will have to be encouraged and extended. There is much for them in the years to come. Germany must be defended.

February 17th. Every political movement needs slogans. For this reason I have been working on a few stirring sayings that are easy for the mass to remember. They all have a powerful triumphant sound to them: *To victory with our leader. Führer, we thank you. The leader is always right.*

Strong words for a strong movement. But first Harrer must go. Such sayings will not fit him at all. How can you chant "The leader is always right," when Harrer is the leader.

February 22nd. Among the new members is Doctor Wilhelm Schubatt. He is a man of immense learning and unrivalled understanding of natural forces. He has invented the cosmic pendulum. By the use of this device it is possible to detect the presence of a Jew within five kilometres. He has covered the whole of the Fatherland, testing the air, and everywhere without any exception he has obtained a reading on the face of his instrument, a clear indication of the extent to which the Fatherland has been infiltrated.

March 7th. More and more people of quality join the party and Harrer is terrified. He is frightened of our success. He would have been happier with the seven members the party had in the beginning.

National Chairman, pah!

One of the new members is Captain Ernst Röhm. A homosexual, Harrer says. How can we have a party member who is a homosexual? he asks. But I know from personal experience about these doings with women, and it is not surprising that someone like Captain Röhm prefers boys. In any event these evil children must be put to some use. What I need is a man who is not afraid to crack a few skulls, a man who understands that Germany is sanctified by blood. For such a need a man like Captain Röhm is required. He understands the use of necessary violence.

Also we have thinkers now. A young philosopher by the name of Alfred Rosenberg has decided that his destiny is with us. We have poets and artists, men of the soul, as well as soldiers, men of the arm, also Harrer's workers, men of the stomach.

April 4th, 1920. I have left the military life. My new home is at Theirschstrasse 41. I have a fine room, nearly as large as my broom closet and not very much colder. If I am fully dressed and I am wearing two pairs of socks and my overcoat, the temperature in the room is quite bearable. All in all it is an excellent accommodation for a serious-minded person.

For nearly six years the military has been my home. It has supplied my food, fed my inspiration and provided an audience. It has been my shelter and my life. Now destiny calls me from it.

106

August 13th. Tonight the Hofbräuhaus nearly burst with the enthusiasm of the party supporters. There was scarcely room left for even one of the mice I had used in my experiment to determine the nature of leadership. Every table was crowded, every chair taken. Supporters, Germans anxious for clear decisive leadership, filled the aisles and blocked the doorways.

It was not necessary for me to prepare or consider in any way. Without thought and without introspection the voice murmured and climbed, exhorted and roared, and the crowd responded to its mystery.

I listened to the words. "We are not proletarians. We are Germans." There was a wisdom and an elegance of phrase on which no one could have improved. "We are not anti-capitalist. We are anti-semite."

At the end they stood and applauded, shouting their agreement. As for me, I sat down at the end of it, soaked with perspiration, a happy vessel for the use of the greater powers within.

August 27th, 1920. We continue to attract men of an outstanding calibre. Rudolf Hess, an air hero of the war, is the newest of these. After attending a party meeting he came to me and said, "Germany needs a leader of strength and firmness, one who does not suffer from an excess of human sensitivity, from misplaced gentleness. Germany needs a leader who will be willing to trample on his oldest comrades and smash his sweetest beloved. You, Adolf Hitler, are such a man."

He is a man of extraordinary insight. What a pity about his buck teeth. Without them he would have made a fine cabinet minister. "You have the eyes of the mystic," he said, in parting, "and Germany can only be led by mystery."

August 28th. At night I lie in bed with the window open. If the night is quiet I can hear the sound of the presses of the *Völkischer Beobachter* thud-thudding softly away, a sound to fill the heart of any patriot with tenderness. In the early hours of the morning when ordinary souls, happy people who are not burdened with the destiny of nations, when such innocents are asleep, I lie awake in my Spartan cell, denying the needs of the flesh, my will directed to the higher needs of mind and soul: at such times the soft thudding of the presses is a great comfort to me, filling the night with a rhythm in tune with the heart of the nation. Throughout the night, all night long, the presses are at work, bringing the deep thoughts of Alfred Rosenberg to the people, warning them against the *Protocols of the Elders of Zion.* What a lullaby for the tired heart.

September, 1920. They want a party flag. What is wrong with the German flag? I ask. But no, they must have a party flag. And what an emblem, a stupid little cross with crooked legs, called a swastika. I will have no part of it.

September 10th, 1920. At last I am a statesman. Yesterday General Ludendorff sent a message that he wished to see the man destined to lead Germany out of darkness into light.

And today a driver arrived to bring me to the General. I was taken to the front door of his house and the driver, wearing a neat military-style uniform, leapt out to open the door and lead me into the house. I was wearing my new green suit, purchased for three marks in the second-hand clothing store down the road from my room. I looked very elegant and dignified as I entered the front door of the General's house. The owner of the shop had told me that the fit was very good for a second-hand suit. Also a size that did not fit too tightly was good for health, allowing greater air circulation. For this I was grateful. The threat of germs is always present and one cannot be too careful.

I was only kept waiting ten or fifteen minutes in the hall before a servant arrived to show me into the General's study. He was sitting at his desk. The great oak surface was completely empty, a clear indication of the order, the military discipline that he exercises in all things. "Ah, Corporal Hitler," he said.

What a pleasure to be addressed once again by the rank I bore with honour in the service of the Fatherland. My heels clicked together as if by magic and my right hand flew up proudly in a salute. "At your service, my General," I cried.

"Sit down, Corporal," the General said. His hand pointed toward a chair, almost as well cushioned and impressive as his own. "So this is the man to whom the gods are going to entrust my country?"

"As my General was ready when Germany needed him, so will I be."

"Of course you will. Sixteenth regiment, weren't you? The men of the sixteenth never once let me down." He banged his fist on the desk. "When others faltered the men of the sixteenth held the line, heroes all."

"There was one by the name of Wucherpfennig who had unfortunate opinions, my General. Otherwise we were . . ."

"Wucherpfennig!" The General's face grew angry. "Never heard of him. We should have put him in front of a firing squad while we had the chance. Bolshevik, was he?" He shook his head in disgust. "But that is not the reason I summoned you."

I tried to come to attention but it was impossible to get my heels together while sitting in the General's armchair. "I am at your service, my General."

"Of course, of course." He coughed, raising his closed fist to cover his mouth. His eyes had a look of intense resolution. I could imagine him, standing on a hillside overlooking the trenches, his feet spread wide and his hands clasped behind his back, the wind perhaps pulling or rather tugging, even swirling around him. "In the path of greatness there are many pitfalls," he said.

"Yes, my General," I agreed.

"There are hidden dangers that would drag us down and make of us less than we should be."

"Yes, my General," I said again. My mind passed to all of the many pitfalls on the path of greatness. Could the General be referring to the treachery of comrades, the fickleness of the mass, the ignorance of those who do not recognize in me the qualities that are there for all to see? Could he be talking about women, the dark passion that sucks the strength from a man, leaving him an empty shell?

"Women . . ." I started to say.

"Of course, women, have your fill of them, my boy. But remember that there are other things. Consider the mass. The mass is ignorant. The mass is bourgeois. The mass needs to be led the way a man leads a dog or a wife."

"Altogether so, my General."

"Where would the mass be without such as you and I? Wearing skins. They would be wearing skins of animals and dancing around fires, like Turks. Germany would be decadent, no better than the Italians or the Spaniards. The mass needs leadership."

"They are nothing without us, my General." His views are deep and perceptive. Perhaps he is a little kind to the mass. His criticism is of a gentle nature.

"They are limited in intellect and we must shape them." The General was looking past me as if to a distant battlefield. "We must bend our proud spirits to the needs of the mass. This is the first duty of leadership."

Ah, sacrifice. The General was speaking of sacrifice. And who knows sacrifice better than I? Those cold nights on the Prater. The indignities of the asylum. Frau Zakreys's bed bugs. No one performs sacrifice with greater enthusiasm than I.

"The mass demands of its leaders a proud bearing."

"Yes, my General." My shoulders had squared as he spoke the words.

"The mass needs the bearing of leadership in those it calls Führer. It is not enough to have the soul of a leader, the eye of a leader or the heart of a leader. One must have the appearance of a leader."

I thought of my hair, carefully greased across my forehead and my moustache, no more than a centimetre wide, a neat little wedge of bristle. This was surely the appearance of a leader.

"You agree?" General Ludendorff asked.

"Of course, my General."

"Your tailor?" the General asked, "Who is your tailor?"

September 27th. This swastika, it irritates me less now. Also I noticed that seven party members saluted it, without thinking, the first time they saw it.

October 7th. Meetings and more meetings. Germany is rising to the future. I appear suddenly, marching resolutely to the platform, and wait until the audience quietens. Then I wait again to achieve the correct sense of expectancy in the mass.

I begin to speak slowly, giving them time to consider my words, absorb their wisdom.

Then suddenly, just when I have them leaning forward in their seats, their faces frowning with concentration: at that moment it happens. Always and without fail the voice comes, roaring from the depths of the soul, to hold them fast and dedicate them to Germany, and to me. I know the voice now. At first it was a mystery, but now I know it.

November. Food riots! For what do they want food? Why do they complain about warmth? They should be brought, every one, to see my room. They should be made to look at sacrifice.

December 7th. Protest, disorder, riots. They say they are hungry. Let them dare to complain when I am in power. Let them shout about their empty stomachs then. We shall see about empty stomachs. A few lessons will have to be learnt.

December 10th. This disorder is an opportunity. These dissatisfied dogs must be made still more dissatisfied.

January 17th, 1921. The other nationalist parties want to join us in a protest meeting. I have told them it must be soon. Something might change. The national bankruptcy might ease. The Foreign War Council might cancel the national debt. Food might become freely available. Fuel might appear on the market. Any number of disasters might be in store. Dissatisfaction might disappear. The mass is not to be trusted in any way. If matters improve their discontent will disappear like party workers when there is work to be done.

February 20th. The fools are still undecided. They are afraid of the Bolsheviks. They say the Bolsheviks will break up the meeting. They say there will be violence. They say blood might be spilt.

And they shrink from this? In the meantime the weather is getting warmer. There might soon be more food. Conditions are improving. How will I build a military dictatorship with happy Germans?

February 23rd, 1921. I can wait no longer. We go on without them. Would they have me speak to an audience with full stomachs?

February 26th. Seven thousand people. Seven thousand joining together with one impulse to sing *Deutschland, Deutschland.* Seven thousand people with empty pockets and stomachs. Seven thousand, listening to every syllable, every intonation. Seven thousand followers of Adolf Hitler. Where is Harrer's membership of seven now?

March 7th, 1921. I have a new friend. He is a party member and his name is Emil Maurice. Also a young man from Berlin by the name of

Joseph Goebbels. This one has a rather dark complexion, by no means the perfect Nordic type. He has already told me on more than one occasion that he envies my clear blue eyes. Also he walks with a limp, like Harrer. Perhaps we can find something for him to do, opening letters in the party office, or giving out handbills.

Emil is a fine fellow though, light brown hair, eyes nearly as blue as my own, and a quick mind. When I explained to him that nonsense such as democratic procedures would have to be removed from the party principles and that the *Führerprinzip* would have to replace it, once I am Führer, he understood perfectly. "Then you will be the boss?" he said.

"Exactly," I said.

"Then we will not have to worry about Drexler and Harrer and all those other old women?"

"What I say will be law, absolute law."

"Is this the way it is going to be for the party?"

"For the party now, and for the nation later."

We were in my room and the cold there was as it always is in spring, just bearable. He leapt to his feet, rubbing his arms with his hands. "I need a drink, and a woman," he said.

I should never have accompanied him. Someone of my intelligence and sensitivity should not partake in the more vulgar aspects of human behaviour. I only followed him down into the road because of my deep interest in all aspects of the life of Germany. The Führer must be a man of wide knowledge. In order to govern Germans it is essential to know them. My following him down into the street, and to the café across the road from the park, had nothing to do with the small amount of excitement I experienced at his words or the slight and only partial appearance of the condition. I have learnt too well the lessons of this sort of thing and I remember too clearly that night three years ago.

Martha, the thought came to me. What if Emil led me to Martha? What if it was my destiny to suffer further in this way?

At the thought of Martha the condition worsened, became a thing of granite, of diamond, of Krupp steel. It possessed an unyielding hardness, such as that of German resolve, my own.

Emil led the way down Theirschstrasse with me following a few steps behind, the stiffness in my loins impeding my stride so that I walked like a man unable to bend his knees. "Hurry, Adolf," he kept saying. "I want to fix us both up with something soft and willing." Every time he spoke he would turn to me and wink. "Know what I mean?" he would ask.

I was astonished to find that Emil did not want to enter the first café. He stood in the doorway and his nose twitched like the nose of a rabbit. "Not here," he said. "Here we are wasting our time." We walk to another café where again Emil tested the air with his nose. A small group of girls, wearing overcoats and with hair cut short around their ears, were sitting near the door, but Emil only glanced in their direction. "No," he said, his nose working delicately back and forth. "No, not this one."

On the way to the next café I began to doubt whether it was wise of me to have come. I am a man to whom seven thousand people come to listen. I am a man possessed of a great purpose and a great patriotic passion. Should such as I be doing this? I asked myself. If a woman is required an order should be issued. There should not be a walking of the streets with one such as Emil.

"Perhaps this is not the night," I said.

"Every night is the night," he said.

At the fourth café Emil went through the same procedure, but this time his blue eyes seemed to grow bright. "This is the one," he said.

"The time is getting late," I said.

"Always duty, Adolf? Our future Führer needs some pleasure too."

"How do you know this is the right place?" I asked. It was an old and dirty café, noisy, crowded and too hot inside. The tables were close together, but Emil led the way, squeezing between the patrons, following his nose. I do not think that he heard my question.

The girls were plain country girls, broad hipped with round faces and wide skirts. There were two of them and they were drinking beer from large glass mugs. "Good evening, ladies," Emil shouted above the noise. "May we introduce ourselves?"

Emil introduced me as the distinguished leader of the German Workers' Party and himself as my adjutant. It is not yet true of course, but Emil is a forward-looking person. I could see that it helped his confidence with the girls to call himself my adjutant. The girls got off their chairs and curtsied. They both called me Herr Hitler, not Adolf. They asked what important people like us were doing in a cheap café. I was about to say that I did not know either

113

when Emil said that even the great need relaxation. He said that in fact the great need more relaxation than anyone else and for that reason was it possible that we could buy them two more beers?

The girls accepted the beers and they were soon calling Emil by his christian name. "Perhaps you should call me Adolf as well," I suggested.

"Oh no, Herr Hitler. We could not think of such a thing, Herr Führer." They were good German girls who had learnt respect for their superiors, a quality that might have to be fostered by decree in years to come.

One of the girls was short and fair while the other was a little taller and darker. They told us that they were employed as baker's assistants. They were fine girls, good girls of excellent farming stock, such as have made Germany great. Their eyes were as blue as mine. There was nothing wrong with them at all. But I prefer a leaner type. It has to do with having the eye of the artist. Also fat ankles are a source of difficulty: Martha has ankles that to see just a fraction of them protruding from an evening gown would have been enough to have started a stampede in the Sixteenth Regiment.

Emil talked almost continually, pausing only long enough to order more beer, while the girls seemed to find his sayings amusing and laughed often while I, I maintained a dignified presence, in keeping with my rank. It was not long before we left the café, to go to the room in which the girls lived. I do not know how Emil arranged it. I was not paying attention to the things he said. As always my mind was filled with matters of greater importance. But soon we were walking through the cold streets, Emil's chatter still going on like a machine, the controlling apparatus of which is damaged and just keeps running on and on without purpose or function. And what was to happen when we reached their room? I asked myself. I could already imagine the narrow cubicle, containing two beds and a cupboard, I could imagine Emil seated on one of the beds, his arm around the shoulders of one of the girls, and myself with the other girl on the other bed. And what then? Would Emil try to switch off the lights? And when we were in darkness what would the girl expect of me? And could such a thing really be expected with the lights out and Emil and the other girl on the other bed, and what would she be expecting of him? And dignity, where is dignity at such a time?

We reached the building, only four streets away from Theirschstrasse, an even older building than the one where I have my room. The paving in the courtyard was cracked and broken, and there seemed to be unswept dirt in the corners. We reached the stairs and the girls were still giggling and Emil was still talking, his foolish remarks being the cause of much amusement. I could see the dark staircase, twisting to the right as it rose, narrow and steep, with just a little light coming from above.

"Girls, this has been a charming evening." It came unexpectedly, without intent or planning, but I felt the power just as I had at the Hofbräuhaus, only more briefly.

"But, Adolf . . ." Emil's eyes were filled with panic.
"Aren't you coming up?" the taller of the two girls started to say.
". . . to the room?" the shorter one finished.
"As you know, Emil . . ." and there was wisdom as well as power in the voice, ". . . as you know, we have important duties in the morning. We cannot afford a late night."

"But an hour . . ." the taller girl said.
"Even half an hour . . ." the other suggested.
"We would love to, but tonight it is impossible. Come, Emil." I took him by the arm. I do not think he truly believed what was happening. Poor Emil, such are the sacrifices that come from associating with the great.

We were out in the road again, having left the girls at the foot of the stairs, before he regained control of his mouth. "Adolf," he said. "Adolf, I have no important duties tomorrow. You go on to the duties and let me return to the girls."

"Which is more important," I asked, "the Fatherland or a moment of pleasure?"

"I will have to think about that, Adolf," he said. But I knew that he was joking and held tightly to his arm, leading him in the direction of Theirschstrasse.

April 3rd, 1921. Committees. All Drexler, Harrer and the others can think of are committees. They have arranged an arts committee, a workers' committee, a military committee, one for municipal affairs, one for propaganda, one for German traditions, one for the place of German mythology in the struggle, for urbanization, social welfare, industry and so on. Others are being planned for inter-party co-operation, for the study of Bolshevism, for foreign nationalist groups, capitalism, patriotic radicalism, also music as a force to be used in politics, party polemics, sport, and corruption in the Reichstag.

Committees. The party will founder under an avalanche of committees.

April 7th, 1921. I live in two worlds. One is the sublime world of the public meeting when the voice takes over everything and the people are mine, easily wooed and as easily won.

The other world is the world of the party committees, Harrer's committees. All last night I walked the streets of Munich. I could not sleep and I could think of nothing but Harrer usurping my position, limping from one committee meeting to the next, calling himself National Chairman of the German Workers' Party. National Chairman!

April 21st. I die for lack of sleep, but that sublime state will not come. First the future must be resolved.

April 28th. I need an inspiration, some way to destroy Harrer. Some sweet and beautiful plan to annihilate the imposter.

May 7th. I spoke to Emil today. Immediately he said, "What a pity that we cannot have Captain Röhm and his men just use their canes on old Harrer and his friends. That would be simplest."

Sweet Emil. He is so naive.

May 13th. Tonight I shall certainly sleep well. Tomorrow I make contact with Captain Ernst Röhm. He and I are men of character and action. We understand each other.

June 1st. Captain Röhm is a person with whom I can deal easily. I feel comfortable in his company. He is a man of pride and military bearing and manner. Also he admires me deeply. He has heard me speak. And he is shorter than I am.

I met him in the Hofbräuhaus. To meet at party offices where Harrer has an ear listening at every wall was out of the question. I thought that perhaps we should meet out of doors, but Captain Röhm said no. "The Hofbräuhaus," he said, "the scene of great victories. Let us meet there," he said.

He was waiting for me as arranged at a table in the corner. Outside a platoon of his men stood guard to watch against Harrer's unexpected arrival, while inside we were surrounded by another platoon to give us privacy. He leapt to his feet as I came in. "Heil Führer," he cried. At that his men all came to attention, echoing his cry, "Heil Führer." Their arms all flashed out in a salute. I was wearing my blue suit, together with a neat black tie, but my hat is nearly five years old so I slipped it quickly behind me with my left hand while I returned the salute.

"Captain Röhm," I said softly, "those other people will hear of this. Are we not a little conspicuous?"

"My Führer, we are utterly conspicuous." At this I tried to laugh, but the sound barely left my throat. I could imagine Drexler and Harrer and how furious they would be to hear of this, and the conniving that would result. I sat down at the table and the Captain sat down opposite me. "This is a time to be conspicuous, my Führer. This morning rumours of our meeting are reaching them and they are sending their own men over here to see the truth of the rumours. And what will they see? They will see you and me talking and they will see us surrounded by the steel of the Sixteenth Regiment. And their small hearts will faint within them. I guarantee it."

Of course, I thought, of course. Here was an excellent man, a man of understanding. He carried bullet wounds, from the war, on his face. It was a square face like the front of a tank or a battering ram. "These committees," I said, "these committees are the problem."

The captain slapped his open palm down on the table. "The *Führerprinzip,* that is what the army wants, the *Führerprinzip.*

"Captain, we understand each other," I said.

"Ernst, my Führer. If my Führer can find it in himself to call me Ernst I will be indebted."

Of course I was willing to do him this kindness. "Certainly, my Ernst. But how to proceed in this delicate situation?"

"This is a military problem. The political necessity is clear. These committees must be removed. The rest is a matter for military action." He struck the table with one huge fist, making both beer mugs and teeth rattle with the strength of the blow. My Führer should tender his resignation from the party unless he is made leader. Give them seven days to decide and insist upon the central committee

117

meeting at party headquarters to hand over their decision personally."

This was insane. I knew they would not accept me. I would be giving them the chance they wanted. I should have known better than to talk to a military man about political matters. Emil also should have known better.

"Then, my Führer... " Röhm's thick neck was bulging over his tight shirt collar. "Then I will arrive at the meeting five minutes before time and surround it with three platoons. When my Führer arrives I will march in behind him with my staff sergeant and two corporals. I will carry my cane in my hand."

Could it be this simple? "This will work?" I asked.

"We are dealing with clerks and dreamers, my Führer. It will work. I guarantee it. These are not men of action, such as you and I."

June 10th. It is well for Ernst and Emil to say, do this thing, but if it does not work?

June 15th. How can I sleep? Sleep is impossible. If I do this thing and it fails I will be out of the party. My destiny will have been aborted.

June 18th. Committee meetings. I wrestle with such problems and they want me to attend committee meetings.

June 22nd. Ernst visited me today with Emil. Now is the time, they say. For them it is easy. They do not bear the burden of leadership.

July 1st, 1921. Last night I dreamt of Martha. She was with me in the bed, caressing me. The condition had grown to proportions of courage and dignity. Then suddenly she had a knife in her hand and she was screaming, "Give me the one. I want him. I will cut him into slivers and feed him to Harrer."

When I awoke the entire bed was wet with perspiration.

July 9th. Captain Röhm was here again. "Perhaps I was wrong about you," he said. "Perhaps Hess might be a good leader."

Hess? With his buck teeth?

July 11th. I did it. They have a week to decide.

118

July 17th. Tomorrow I meet with the central committee. I have been patient long enough. Harrer will crumble before the strength of my will. Röhm says so. And Röhm knows. This is quite certain.

I am convinced of it.

July 18th. Today I met with the spiritual invalids of the central committee. Harrer was there and Drexler was there and four of their cronies, six of the seven original members of the party. When I came in they were all smiling and shaking hands with each other, even slapping each other on the back. Harrer was limping from one to the other, calling them comrade and thanking them for coming. But as soon as they saw me (I stopped just inside the door) there was silence. Harrer was insolent enough to say, "Today we get rid of our biggest problem."

"Today we purify our party of unworthy elements," Drexler said.

As for me, I said nothing. I stood alone, one man against six, with only Emil behind me. Ernst Röhm and his platoon were in the beerhall down the road, while I stood alone against the central committee.

He had said that he would be present with his men when I arrived. Instead I was left to meet my destiny alone.

"So good of Herr Hitler to join us," Harrer said, bowing to me. "His presence enables us to deal with a pressing matter. Shall we sit down, gentlemen, if Herr Hitler is ready?" He waved an arm in the direction of the table and limped to the seat at its head. I sat down a the opposite end. This was the seat that Drexler normally occupied as deputy leader of the party. The little man turned red and his Adam's apple bobbed once up, then down again as he swallowed his own saliva. "Never mind, Anton... " Harrer was again letting his voice be heard. " ... never mind. Sit somewhere else. Today all is put in order." The others sat down. Poor Drexler's face was still red and his Adam's apple still bobbing. "Now, Herren party leaders, let us give attention to the agenda. Comrade Drexler, would you be so kind as to tell us how many items there are on today's agenda."

"One," Drexler said. His face was pink now.

"One? If there is only one, our business should not occupy us for long. And the nature of this item?" Harrer winked at one of the other committee members. The fool was finding great enjoyment in this matter.

119

"Would Comrade Drexler be so good as to tell us what is the single item of the agenda?"

"Certainly, comrade," Drexler said. "The item... "

Harrer held up a hand. "Before you tell us, comrade, perhaps Comrade Bielenbaum will tell us if the champagne is chilled for the celebration that we are going to hold after the meeting."

"The champagne is chilled, comrade."

"Good. All are invited, even Herr Hitler, should he choose to come. It is possible, of course, that he might not choose to come." Harrer looked very pleased with the meeting, also pleased with his champagne, and even pleased with himself, a situation that is not easy to understand.

From down in the street I heard Ernst Röhm's voice, it was raised loud in command. "Company, present arms," he cried.

"A parade passing in the street," Harrer said. "I heard of no parade."

"Nor did I hear of a parade," Comrade Bielenbaum said. "I like parades."

"Let us attend to business quickly," Harrer was smiling at all, excepting me, of course, "then we can attend the parade. Comrade Drexler, if you please."

Drexler's formerly pink face had returned to its usual colour of old and motheaten paper. "The item on today's agenda is the ultimatum given to this committee by one of its members, namely Herr Hitler. The member in question has given the committee until today to appoint him party leader under the so-called *Führerprinzip* or he will resign his membership of the party."

Down in the street Ernst Röhm was shouting again. Some of the words were lost through the closed windows. " ... form up ... single file ... follow... "

"The parade is getting closer," Harrer said. "But first our own business. Is the meeting in agreement that we should vote on this matter." The heads of the fools all nodded back and forth like rocking chairs. "Of course this is the democratic method and the German Workers' Party is a democratic party. It is true that Herr Hitler does not subscribe to democratic methods..." He winked at Bielenbaum again. " ... perhaps he has an objection to this method of making decisions... "

His face still had its half-witted smile, but he was unable to look directly at me. The sound of footsteps, loud military footsteps, was coming from the stair. I raised my chin and answered in a voice firm with military precision. "No objection," I said.

"Then let us discover the will of the majority by means of a vote. All in favour..." The footsteps on the stair were of thunderous proportons. "The parade..." Harrer started to say.

If he finished what he was going to say no one heard him. The door was thrown open so hard that it crashed against the wall and Captain Ernst Röhm and perhaps a dozen of his men marched in. In one hand he was carrying his parade ground cane, as he had promised. Bielenbaum leapt to his feet. The other committee members were wiser and thought it better to stay in their seats. Ernst's cane landed against the back of Bielenbaum's head, knocking him back into his chair. "Don't get up for me, Herr committee member," Ernst roared. In a moment he and his men had formed a ring round the table. He personally took up a position directly behind Harrer.

Harrer's eyes looked like those of a sheep in the moment before the wolf strikes. I cleared my throat in order to bring the others' attention to myself. "A vote," I said in soft and civilized tones. "A vote was about to be taken."

Harrer looked at me for a few seconds as if he did not understand what I was saying, then he turned round to look at Ernst. Finally his eyes flickered to Drexler and Bielenbaum. "All in favour of acceding to Herr Hitler's demand, raise the right hand," he said.

"Heil Hitler," Ernst shouted and his right arm shot out in a salute, with his men following. They stood still, backs straight and shoulders squared, their right arms stretched out before them. With his other hand Ernst tapped the edge of the table with his cane.

Harrer's hand came up first, then Drexler's and Bielenbaum's, and finally all the members of the committee. "Unanimous," Ernst said as his arm snapped back to its place at his side.

"Thank you, Herr committee members," I said. I am a person who is well-known for magnanimity in victory. "Thank you, very much. From now on we will abolish the decadence of democracy. As the new leader of the party I declare that the party will be run on the *Führerprinzip* and I am the Führer. This committee is therefore disbanded and its members will now take their places as ordinary party members. Herren ex-committee members, you may go now, unless you wish to stay to share the champagne."

Drexler, Harrer and their friends crept furtively from the room and down the stairs, trying to make no noise. From the window I watched them go down the path left for them by Ernst's troops. Poor Harrer, he was limping even more than usual. Not one of the committee members dared lift his head high enough to look upon the immobile faces of the men. This is an excellent method of settling arguments. It shall find uses in the future.

Someone coughed behind me. I turned to face Ernst. "Ah, my Captain," I said. My voice was stern but friendly.

"Heil Führer," Ernst Röhm shouted. It has a pleasant sound to it.

VOLUME VII

August 3rd, 1921. As Drexler creeps away, so Drexler creeps back, he agreed with me all along, he says. He was never really in doubt, he says. It was Harrer all along, not him. It was Harrer, that intellectual midget.

But I am a generous-hearted person. I am reconciled to Drexler. There will be room in the party for him in some suitable position, adviser to the Munich Gauleiter in time to come, perhaps, something of that sort. As long as he does not deviate from the *Führerprinzip.* As for Harrer I might allow him to retain his party membership.

August 5th, 1921. Emil has found an excellent astrologer, Frau Blomhorn. Today he took me to her and for the modest sum of two marks this happy woman consulted the heavens on my behalf.

Before she started speaking her eyes half closed and her voice became more distant in the manner of mystics. I myself am a person of the same sort. "You are Aries, the ram," she said. "None shall stand in your way. Power shall be yours," she said. "Women shall also be yours."

This sublime person spoke for half an hour, explaining how I was fortunate to be born at the moment when the power of Uranus and Jupiter coincided to exercise their influence over the earth. In this way even the heavens conspired to assist me. She said that the paths of fortune written eternally in the sky cannot be denied.

Also I have become a vegetarian. The killing of animals as food is a cruel and unnecessary business.

August 6th, 1921. Faithful service to the party shall not go unrewarded. Emil's reliability and resolute support of the party has been acknowledged: he has been given the position of my driver. He is very pleased.

August 7th. The physical aspect of the leader's existence cannot be ignored. Even the strength of my will does not seem to be sufficient. It would be better if I was like Röhm.

That is a solution. Perhaps I will discuss the matter with him.

August 8th. I must arrange to see Röhm soon. This is the sort of advice that a faithful party functionary will willingly give to his Führer. Can the method of that sort satisfy? Is it more easily accomplished than in the other case, that of a woman for instance? At what age did he commence with matters of this sort? And the subordinates, the partners, are they easily obtainable?

August 11th. I have made an appointment for Röhm to see me tomorrow. It will be an opportunity to ask him a number of important questions.

The vegetarianism has given me a feeling of inner cleanliness, almost spirituality. For the first time I realize that I am a spiritual person of mystical inclinations.

August 12, 1921. Today I received Captain Röhm at the party offices and under what different conditions did we not meet this time! Instead of sharing a table in a beer hall, I was seated at my new desk and Röhm was allowed to wait in the ante-room for a minute or two before Emil went out to bring him in. After he had marched in Emil discreetly backed out of the door, closing it behind him. Such are the new manners in the party offices. "Heil Hitler," Captain Röhm cried, his right arm shooting out to just above shoulder height in a fierce military salute, the flesh of his neck bulging over his collar as his chin was drawn in.

"My dear Captain," I began.

"My Führer has forgotten my christian name?"

"No." He is a fine man, my Captain Ernst Röhm, a man of dignity and humility in dealing with his Führer. "No, my Ernst. How can I forget one who serves as you do?"

"My Führer is too kind to a simple, immature and ungodly man like myself."

"Simplicity, immaturity and ungodliness, my Captain? These are characteristics that can be put to use."

He sat down, but, even seated, his posture was that of the soldier, his head held erect on his short thick neck. "It is because I am a simple and immature man that I am a man of action, my Führer, a man who likes to crack a few skulls on occasion."

"Germany needs such," I told my Ernst, "for the difficult days ahead."

"And I am told that I am an evil man because of certain desires that are a part of me."

There it was, certain desires. He could keep nothing hidden from me. "It is about this that I wish to speak to you, my Captain," I said.

"I am at my Führer's service."

"This is a delicate matter," I said. "It is a matter for the ears only of you and me and no one else.

"I have felt the need as well," he said. The broad fleshy hands with the thick square fingers rested on the edge of my desk, moving restlessly on the oak surface.

"It is a matter that you will understand, I am sure. No one need coach you in this."

"I thought my Führer required this." A little column of perspiration had formed at the bottom of the centre parting in his bristly blonde hair. "I myself have felt it to be irresistible."

"Then you are not surprised?"

"No, my Führer, I have even thought of a name for it."

"A name?" I looked carefully at his face, but the expression showed only respectful interest. "What do you mean by a name?"

"A name," he said, "that would be descriptive and create a sense of pride in the boys."

My mind struggled with the thought. What name could he possible imagine suitable? Hitler's hellions? The Führer's fellows? Adolf's angels?

"Stürmabteilung."

"Stürmabteilung? Storm troop? Is this a joke, Captain Röhm?"

"A joke?" Captain Röhm had leapt to his feet. "On no account, my Führer. I am surprised that my Führer thinks of this as a joke. I will call them the Storm Troop because they will always be at the centre of the storm, keeping order at our meetings and at the Bolshevik meetings... there they will keep order of a different sort."

Storm troop? I wondered. How could such boys be a storm troop? *"Stürmabteilung?"*

"I see the idea begins to find favour with my Führer." Röhm was leaning forward, looking down at me, his chin pressed towards me as

125

far as his short neck would allow.

"They will solve my problem?"

"I personally guarantee it. I stake my military reputation upon it."

"Ah. A storm troop?"

"Exactly so. Then I have my Führer's permission to go ahead with the idea?"

"Yes, yes. Why not?"

"Heil Hitler," Röhm shouted.

August 18th. I begin to wonder if Captain Röhm and I understood each other completely yesterday. I have seen some of his selections for the first storm troop and they do not seem at all suitable, big strong young men. I do not like the look of them —from a certain point of view.

August 20th. Perhaps I should speak to Röhm again. This husky mob looks more as if they have been recruited to beat up people.

August 24th. Today I saw Röhm. "These young men." I said.

"My Führer," he shouted at me.

"You are satisfied with your selection?"

"These men will strike and strike hard," he said.

"Strike hard?"

"Heil Hitler."

September 15th 1921. Last night the Bolsheviks tried to break up our
it is that he is planning.

Hess is doing a little public speaking of his own, nothing of any consequence. It is not easy for him, addressing an audience while concealing his buck teeth.

September 15th, 1921. Last night the Bolsheviks tried to break up our meeting at the Löwenbräukeller. Röhm and his storm troop were present though. Afterwards most of the Bolsheviks needed medical attention. This troop of Röhm, they might after all come in useful.

They are no use at all for the other matter.

January 7th, 1922. Now at last I have a worthy lieutenant, a man among men, a gentleman, a man of the aristocracy, commander of the Richthofen squadron, a man with a background. This is a man I can deal with. So often I find myself surrounded by party riffraff, tramps and beggars, only partly educated, people of no breeding.

Ah, the name of my new convert? Hermann Göring. What an excellent man! What a German! A man of action like myself, a man who received the highest of military decorations, just as I did, a man who married into the nobility, just as I might easily have done. Of course I put Germany first. That is the difference.

Nevertheless he is an acceptable and useful member of the party. The first thing he said on meeting me was "Damn the Treaty of Versailles. I spit on it." That's my man, I thought at once.

Also he has perfect Aryan features, a fair skin and eyes as blue as my own. This Hermann is going to be useful to me. I can feel it.

February, 1922. This memoir, rather these notes for a future memoir, will not be complete unless I explain the relationship between the mass and the Führer. It is only the true leader that understands this relationship and it is fitting that it should be revealed by one such as I. There may not be another.

The mass is a woman, not intelligent, not given to rational reflection, not imbued with strong powers of reasoning, and not loyal, but sensitive, moody, immoderate, fickle, wayward, easily hurt and seeking stimulation. In meeting after meeting, in each gathering the mass has to be wooed afresh and brought to a moment of submission to the leader's wishes, the moment when surrender is more pleasurable than resistance and when the leader, having established his dominance, presses home his advantage with ruthless passion.

In each speech, of necessity, the wooing begins slowly. I have to employ the vanity of the mass, explaining not in what measure Germany needs me, but how I need them. Just as no woman ever feels altogether fulfilled and has to seek fulfilment in the arms of a lover, so the mass is never fulfilled. The mass is empty. I draw them to me and in me they find fulfillment.

I woo them, ease my way past the barriers within, until they are mine for the taking, helpless, submissive and seduced . . . but the orgasm, the orgasm is not mine. I become as helpless as the mass. I am a victim of the forces within me. When the mass lies helpless, seeking only the final thrust, I have lost them. They slip away from me. In a moment the voice is there, roaring and climbing, tearing to the heart of the German soul, reaching the climax without me. And I,

I return to the room in Thierschstrasse, empty and weak, a masturbator at the greatest orgy in history.

February 14th, 1922. Alois! How dare he come knocking on my door? "Ah, dear Adolf, my brother," he says, "how good to see you. We were always so close," he says. "Now that you have become a great man," he says, "I know that you will not forget your family."

"You," I cried. "I have been hearing of your doings, living in England, living among the enemies of Germany."

"Not England, Adolf." He made a poor pretence at dignity, trying to puff up his anaemic little chest and look like a German. "I lived in Ireland."

"Enemies of Germany all," I cried, my voice vibrant with outrage.

He took a step backwards, trying to get closer to the door. "You are not being fair to me, Adolf," he whined. "The Irish hate the English."

"On which side did they fight in the war?" The tone of my voice was insistent and demanding. I could see how it cowed him. "Where were you in the war?"

"This is not fair, Adolf."

What did he expect from me? A hero's welcome? Stupid sentimentality? "And there was an Irish wife. Where is the Irish wife?"

"She was a bad woman. I should never have left Germany. It was a mistake. I should have married a good German woman." Alois has always been a fool. Now he was a greater fool than ever before. Imagine such as he looking to such as I for sympathy. "Oh, why did I ever leave Germany? How could I have been so foolish?"

I pointed an accusing finger at him. "The greatest war in all history and you are lying abed with an Irish wife. Think of that. While the men of the Fatherland are in the trenches, dying, you are planting seeds in the womb of an Irish wife. Think, Alois. Think of that."

"I am a great fool, Adolf." At last he was coming close to the truth. "I am a great fool, but I know that you will find it in your heart to forgive your brother his foolishness. I know you will be able to understand."

"Why have you come here, Alois?" I asked him.

"To see you, Adolf. Should I not come to see you?" he whined.

"Why, Alois? Why did you come? Answer."

"First, to visit you. That was the first reason."

128

"What was the second?"

Alois was standing at the door by this time. He seemed to be crouching slightly, ready for flight. "A beer hall, Adolf, a café. I could be a happy man if I could have my own café, just a small one. It's all I need in life. I could be satisfied with my lot, Adolf. And now you are a great man, I know..."

"You come to me for money?" I felt a great anger within me, but my voice was calm, my control impregnable.

"Please don't scream at me, Adolf. Two thousand marks. What are two thousand marks to a great man such as you have become? I will be a happy man, Adolf. I will be an asset..."

"Emil," I shouted. "Emil, throw this fellow out into the street."

April 20th, 1922. My birthday. The inner circle gathered at the party office for a small celebration. Josef Goebbels made a speech, saying that this day is the most significant in all of German history. It is possible that my early judgement of this fellow was not altogether accurate. No, it was accurate. In fact I have always favoured him, now that I think about the matter. He is a good man, if a little sallow of complexion for a leadership position.

Röhm was there with his leading S.A. officers, also Eckhart, Hess, Göring, Hanfstaengl and even Drexler. He is a weak and ungrateful man, this Drexler. He should realize that there are limits to my magnanimity. He does not appreciate his good fortune. When I seized power in the party I could have ejected him altogether. I could have reduced him to nothing. But no. I chose to keep him. I allowed him to remain a member of the party executive.

And what thanks did I get? He sidled up to me during the celebration and whispered. "That rhinocerous-hide whip," he said, "walking around, cracking it against your jack-boots, it looks a little cheap."

Cheap? He uses the word cheap to describe the behaviour of his Führer. In any event I noticed the effect it had on the ladies when I struck the coiled whip against my boots. It was clear that they found it a very impressive spectacle.

Putzi Hanfstaengl brought his beautiful wife Hélène with him. What an aristocratic lady! What beauty and breeding in perfect union. But let no man say that Adolf Hitler does not know how to behave in the presence of a fine lady of breeding. "Führer, I would like you to meet my wife," Hanfstaengl said.

"How do you do?" The lady said, at the same time reaching out her hand to me. Her skin was white, glowing, translucent, silken and so smooth in the grasp of my fingers that I was afraid of bruising it. Her hair was dark and falling in curls around her shoulders and her eyes were deeper than the heart of the Aryan soul.

I held her hand gently, bending over it, with my heels neatly together and my hat in my free hand. "My lady," I murmured.

"It is an honour to meet you," she said.

"My lady," I said so softly that only she could hear.

"Putzi thinks so highly of you. He is impressed by everything you say." Her smile was like a bright star.

"My lady," I said.

"We all feel that destiny has chosen you."

"My lady."

Let no one say that Adolf Hitler does not know how to behave in the presence of a lady.

June 1922. The great men of history were all men of steel and blood. Julius Caesar, Alexander the Great, Genghis Khan, Napoleon Bonaparte: they were not stupid sentimentalists. They did not allow a few worthless inferior lives to come between themselves and their destinies. Even Jesus Christ said. "I have not come to bring peace, but the sword." It is a tragedy to me that such a man of iron should have been the founder of something as weak and effeminate as Christianity. But then he was not a success. All he did was talk while he should have been raising a *Sturmabteilung* such as I have. But perhaps it was not his fault. After all he only had Jews to call on. Of course one can see clearly in all the paintings of the great masters that Jesus himself was an Aryan. And as God was his father this indicates beyond all doubt that God is an Aryan. This conclusion is the product of rational thinking, an area in which I am particularly adept. The use of logic is one of the many factors that separate the great from the mediocre.

June 23rd. The voice spoke to me again last night. I had been asleep in my room and I woke suddenly without special reason to a quiet such as I have never experienced. From the sleeping city there was no sound at all, no roar of motor car engines, no clicking of horses hooves, no human voice or closing door, no sound of any description.

The significance of the moment was immediately apparent to me. I lay still, not looking to the right or to the left, waiting for the moment that I knew would come. When it came the voice was distant, calling to me across the great vastness of history. "Adolf Hitler," it said, and I recognized it from the meetings. "Adolf Hitler, you are called to sacrifice for your country. You are called to give everything."

"Everything?" I asked. I was not unwilling, but it was necessary to seek clarification.

"Everything. Everything has to be given for Germany, down to your only piece of manhood."

"Heil," I said.

"The time is coming," the voice went on. "Your hour is at hand. The year 1922 marks the turning of destiny's tide. It is you for whom all Germans are waiting." When the voice stopped the silence continued for a while, then the night sounds of Munich returned. I heard footsteps in the road, the rattle of the milk wagon and the crying of a child. I knew the moment was over.

July 7th. Emil brought a woman tonight. "Führer," he said. "You are working too hard. A little relaxation is needed." He left the woman inside the door of my room and was gone. Another country girl with thick ankles and mighty thighs, recruited from one of Munich's endless beer halls.

"Heil Führer," she said, bending and starting to unbutton her frock.

"Attention," the voice roared. She straightened up like a steel spring being released. Her great legs coming together and her huge breasts bouncing.

"Dismissed," I said.

"Dismissed, Führer?"

"Dismissed."

July 14th. I visited the Hanfstaengls on Sunday at the express invitation of Hélène. It was she that wanted me to come, not Putzi. She wore a gown that did not cover her shoulders and the pure whiteness of her flesh, flowed like a glacier descending a precipice to the entrance of a cave.

"Adolf," she said. "I'm so pleased to see you again." Her hand reached out to mine, but as I tried to take it she withdrew it suddenly with a quick little laugh.

"My lady," I said. She should really address me as Führer, but it does not seem to be important. I can see in her eyes the passion she feels.

"Adolf, you are such a famous man," she said. "I really want to listen to you today."

"My lady."

"And you must say more than usual. You really must. I want to quote you to my friends so that they can see that you really are a friend. They would never believe that all you ever say to me is, my lady."

"My lady ... " I started to say. It was only the start of something far more complex and profound though, but Hélène interrupted me.

"There you go again," she said.

I took her by the arm, drawing her close. The scent of her was overpowering, like *Deutschland* being sung by the Sixteenth Regiment or the sailors' chorus from the *Flying Dutchman*. In my mind I was forming wonderful chains of words.

"My lady ... "

"Adolf, Adolf," she said. "There's no hope for you."

Drexler was also invited. For what reason it is difficult to imagine. He had the audacity to approach me while we were alone and say, "I do not think that the piggish eating of many cakes improves the image."

Piggish eating? He risks his life to suggest such a thing. It is well known that my eating habits are of a moderate and conservative nature. In any case, there were many cakes. What was the sense in letting them go to waste.

July 16th, 1922. Last night I lay awake thinking about Hélène. I tried to think only thoughts that were worthy of one such as she, but other thoughts, ideas alien to my mind and her nature, intruded continually. Her spiritual presence was before me, but so was the silken touch of her skin, the glory of her hair and the volume of her bosom. I do not easily admit to such a thing, but unworthy thoughts prevailed.

It is a thing of shame. I lay on my back and my hands became parts of Hélène, taking the place of those parts, raising urges that should only have been raised by her gentle touch, that had only in the past been raised by the touch of the infamous Martha.

As I lay there, my imaginings transforming my hands into Hélène, the memory of Martha and the night in the officers' brothel in 1918 returned to me, blotting Hélène from my mind. I had risen to the point of explosion, to the depth of the one great degradation of my life, the moment when Martha overwhelmed me. I remembered the weakness that had followed. I remembered the shame and the dishonour.

I leapt from my bed, drew on my clothes and marched out into the night. Never, never, never may such a thing be repeated. Never.

Fortunately I found Emil in bed. "Rise," I said, "immediately."

"You want a girl?" Emil asked as he stumbled out of bed.

"I want you to drive, just drive."

"You don't want a girl?"

"No. Just drive."

Emil drove and the sound and movement from the car soothed me as it always does. Soon sleep was engulfing me and not once did I think about Hélène. Or Martha either for that matter.

July 20th. I have instructed Emil to drive more slowly in future. What will happen to Germany if an accident befalls me?

July 21st. The voice is more insistent that ever. My hour is not far off. Also I have seen Frau Blomhorn. The visit cost two marks, a large amount, but she is a person of high standing in her profession. She agrees that my time is soon.

July 23rd. Hess is busy at public meetings again. He has learnt the technique of hiding his buck teeth through much practice. I congratulated him on this, but he showed no interest in pursuing the subject.

August 1922. I have seen Hélène again. It was after a party meeting at the Café Neumaier. She arrived at the end of the meeting and I could see by the look in her eyes that she is infatuated with me. In the crush of people we only came close for a moment. "Still mute, Adolf?" she asked.

October 11th. Yesterday Mussolini seized power. An unnecessary presumption. The land of Verdi and Caruso cannot possibly assume leadership of world fascism. From such decadence it is unthinkable.

November 3rd. All the great men of history have been vegetarians. This is a well known fact. The reason is clear. It is far more difficult to apply poison to vegetarian food than to meat. The strong taste of meat completely overpowers the taste of the poison and one is dead in minutes. But the soft taste of vegetables enables the tongue to distinguish the presence of poison immediately. For this reason vegetarianism is essential in the life of the great.

February 3rd, 1923. Oratory is important, but so is the atmosphere that must be created. A great address delivered in an atmosphere of coldness and scepticism is worthless.

The artifacts of patriotism are required. The mass needs a feast for the eye as well as for the ear. Great eloquence is lost without marching troops, row upon row of uniformed patriots standing shoulder to shoulder in their country's cause. And music: there must be music, the sounds of military brass and drum, such music as causes men to come to attention without thinking, music that beats to the rhythm of the blood in a man's veins.

Also flags: the red, white and black of the swastika waving overhead, in time with the music and the blood and the marching, all drawing the spirit upward. And over everything the banners, crested by the eagle of Germany, above the heads of those in the crowds, drawing forth the last thrust of courage, until all are impelled to their feet and the German salute, arm held stiffly pointing forward, becomes a sea of salutation; ten thousand, twenty thousand, a hundred thousand arms raised to the glory of Germany and the Führer.

Such must be the atmosphere when the speaker rises. Under such circumstances the voice comes of its own, needing no coaxing, rising freely from the depths of its citadel.

February 27th. Last night we met with Ludendorff. Goebbels was there. Eckhart was there. Also Hanfstaengl, Göring, Julius Streicher and of course Ernst Röhm. Emil too is now a member of the trusted inner circle. He was there with Rosenberg and Scheubner-Richter. But not Drexler, never Drexler. I have had enough of discretion being the better part of valour. This is the time for fanaticism and action. We will leave Drexler to sharpen pencils in the party offices while we go on to seize power in Germany.

Julius Streicher promises to be a man of many uses. He is of the same persuasion as Röhm, as regards boys. There might be a certain wisdom in this. It bears examination in spite of the *Stürmabteilung* episode.

The General only kept us waiting for ten minutes this time. I noted it on the pocket-watch Emil gave me on my birthday last year. When we came in he rose from his desk to meet me. The expression of joy on his face was wonderful to see. "Ah, Corporal Hitler," he said.

"My General," I said.

A number of chairs had been arranged around his desk and he waved a hand towards them. "Sit down, men," he said. But he showed special respect to me, holding my hand a little longer than the others and continuing to shake it. By the time he released it and I turned to sit down all the seats had been taken. For a moment no one spoke, each looking angrily at the other. Julius Streicher was the first to say something. His eyes glinted fiercely and he pointed to Röhm. "Ernst, stand up for the Führer," he said.

"You are the junior," Röhm shouted in reply.

"What about Hanfstaengl? He's a civilian," Göring suggested.

"I am official liaison with the overseas press," Putzi Hanfstaengl said.

"Try Eckhart. He is of little importance."

"Me? Of little importance?" Eckhart was more than usually indignant. "What about Rosenberg?"

"Editor of the *Völkischer Beobachter*, that's who I am." He leapt to his feet, pointing a finger at Eckhart.

Rosenberg had taken a step towards Eckhart when Streicher pulled his chair away from behind him. "A chair for the Führer," he said.

I sat down and Rosenberg slouched off to stand against the wall at the back of the study. The General looked slowly from one of us to the other. His admiration was plain to see. It was clear that never before had he seen such fire and enthusiasm in a body of men. He struck a little bell on his desk and a maid entered. "A chair for the editor," he said. Then he turned to look at me, his cheeks moving up and down as he thought. The General's cheeks always move when he thinks. "Well, Corporal, are we of one mind?"

"One mind and one soul, my General," I said. "Also one spirit, one blood. . ."

"Yes, Corporal, I follow the idea." He looked slowly from one to the other, pausing for a moment while his eyes searched those of each man. Any traitor among us would have been flushed out immediately. When he spoke it was slowly and deliberately. "The vons must go. Since when is Bavaria ruled by a triumvirate? Who allows such a thing? The time is past for von Kahr, von Lossow and von Seisser. Do you know what this means?" He looked straight at me. "Tell them what this means, Corporal."

"A *Putsch*, my General."

"A *Putsch*, that's what it means. First Bavaria, then all of Germany. Munich today, Berlin tomorrow. . ."

"Paris and London the day after," I suggested.

"Moscow and Washington," the General roared. "But first Bavaria. The vons must go. We need men fitted for rough work. He leant towards us over the desk, his cheeks moving like an unruly sea. "We need men with the balls for such a task. Do you agree, my Corporal."

I look straight back into the General's eye, unflinching. "I agree, my General."

"Men with the balls for such a business, that is what we need." He fixed his eyes on me again. "What do you say, my Corporal? Do you have the balls for such a task?"

My eye was held by his like a magnet. "I have the ball, my General."

"The ball? The ball?" The General's face turned towards the sky, he rocked back in his chair and laughter roared from his throat. "Humour in the midst of adversity. That's the spirit." His voice was like a cavalry charge, the galloping of many hoofs. "I am beginning to like you, Corporal Hitler." He turned to the other men who were also laughing. "Did you hear that? He has the ball. Only one of Corporal Hitler's is enough for this matter. What happens when he brings both into play?" The laughter erupted from the depths of his stomach.

Julius Streicher had his arms wrapped round his sides. "One is enough for the three vons," he moaned. "One is enough."

March 5th, 1923. Drexler has got to hear of the *Putsch*. "We are democrats," he says. "How can we preach revolution?"

Democrats? There is no room for the weak stomach of the democrat in an order based on the *Führerprinzip*. For what purpose should there be voting, the turgid irrational wishes of the mass? Mob rule?

We shall have to watch this Drexler. Goebbels has put him in his place though. "Let those rule who are born to rule," he said. A good man, this little Joseph. A pity about his complexion, though, and his brown eyes. I am afraid that with those features and his club foot he will never rise above the rank of *Gauleiter* of a small town, perhaps Linz, after the *Anschluss.*

March 8th. I hear from reliable sources that the Bolsheviks are planning a *Putsch* of their own. These dirty brutes, they have no respect for human life. Give them power and we shall all be murdered. Unless we seize power first. Then we shall see who gets murdered.

March 21st. What holds us back? Drexler is still complaining about unnecessary violence and even Ludendorff says we must wait for a more propitious time. What does the word propitious mean?

It is only I who have the will.

April 20th. Today I saw the Magnificent Hélène again. Putzi invited me to their home to celebrate my birthday. The children were present, each with a gift for me. How sweet they are, how gentle and good-natured, typical of all true Germans.

Hèléne herself had knitted me a pair of warm woollen socks with her own hands to wear with my new *lederhosen.* This is what it is to be a member of a family. Oh the warmth and tenderness. It reminds me of my own mother, what a lovely soul. She would do everything for me. No sacrifice was too great for her brilliant son. Such is motherhood.

Putzi himself gave me a history of the Franco-Prussian wars in three volumes, bound in leather with my name engraved on each one. He is a true patriot. Such as he would think nothing of allowing his Führer certain liberties with his wife if such a thing would profit the Fatherland.

Hélène wore a bronze coloured gown that buttoned tightly around her throat and wrists. The sleeves formed small puffs at either shoulder, accentuating the smoothness of her flesh and the sturdiness of her bosom. Unfortunately I had no opportunity to speak to her. I did speak to Putzi and the children though.

The children have been taught to call me Uncle Dolferl, the little charmers.

May 1st, 1923. So we were forced to yield our arms to the state troops. This is a small thing, a minor reverse, not even a reverse, an incident, no more than that.

Where were the Bolsheviks? We held our parade to meet with them, not the state troops. It was the anniversary of Munich's liberation from Bolshevik rule, but the Bolsheviks stayed at home. That we were forced to hand over our arms to the state troops, this is a matter of no concern, a tactical device on my part.

As for those who have lost faith as a result: to them I say we cannot afford the inept and the weak-willed. This is not an impediment, not to Adolf Hitler.

May 2nd. Now there are two possibilities, to *Putsch* or not to *Putsch*. I am considering this matter.

There are also two possibilities concerning Hélène, to have dominance of her or not. Such a thing was after all possible in the officers' brothel of the sixteenth regiment in 1918. It can be possible again. I am considering this matter also.

August 6th. Frau Blomhorn insists that my time is almost here. She says it is before the door, or at least reasonably close to the door. If not that, it is coming closer, mounting the front steps, perhaps. Her fee has risen to ten marks, an amount easily encompassed by the party funds.

August 10th. It is necessary to make a decision soon in the matter of Hélène. It is not fair to keep her in suspense to this degree.

August 14th. Is not Munich the centre of the world's culture? Why else would Frau Cosima Wagner, widow of our greatest national genius continue to live here? Also her beautiful daughter-in-law Winifred. What a pleasure it was to meet them in their home where the master himself lived and worked. I was tongue-tied with joy. When Winifred came to speak to me I managed only to take her hand in mine and whisper softly, "My lady," I could see how moved

138

she was. Perhaps she also deserved consideration, not only Hélène Hansfstaengl.

But the *Putsch*, this comes before all else. It must receive my full attention.

August 19th. Fate is on my side. Once again destiny has taken a hand in the affairs of men. It singles out its favourite sons for refinement.

Money has lost all value. One mug of beer costs a million marks. A sack of potatoes costs twenty million marks. The bourgeois middle class have rooms full of worthless banknotes that have no value for anyone and will yet be the destruction of them all. People can afford nothing but potatoes, and the potato stocks are running short. The weak of will jump from the roofs of buildings they once owned.

Everything must be paid for in millions of marks and every day more millions are needed. The purchasing of goods becomes more and more impossible. Only bartering and stealing remain. Ordinary Germans have been dragged to their knees by the treachery of Versailles and Weimar.

What joy! What a time in which to live! What an opportunity! What a victory lies ahead! The traitors of Weimar can be seen for what they are.

Also this matter of money no longer having any value is of another use. It has made it very easy to repay the debt on the *Völkischer Beobachter*. The price of running a newspaper at that time is the price of a case of schnapps now.

One thing remains constant in price. Membership of the party is free. This sublime fellowship is still available to the ordinary German. Heil Hitler!

September 3rd, 1923. Drexler, the fool, he says the time is not right for such a thing as a *Putsch*. Also Eckhart and even Putzi. They say this is a time for caution. All should not be thrown away on a toss of the dice.

Fortunately there are also those of sterner will and more ready to abide by the words of their Führer. I think of Emil and young Goebbels, Ernst Röhm, Hess, Streicher and Göring, even the General, if I could only establish the opportunity to convince him. But he is in favour. Everyone is in favour. I hear no voices of dissent, only the clamour of patriots. We go forward united, with no voice raised against us. This is National Socialism. This is leadership.

The end is in sight for the three vons. But I am a man of compassion, and they are men of education. I will allow them to officiate in the prison library after the *Putsch*.

September 18th. I will not again address a public meeting. I have gone as far as I am able to go and to go further is torment beyond endurance. I speak but a few words, a short carefully planned introduction, then the voice seizes control both of me and of the meeting. The hall is filled by the cheering of the mass, the shouting of Heil and the stamping of feet, and I am exhausted, my voice hoarse and my face running with sweat, but the voice has spoken without my concurrence, or even my permission. I cannot do it again. It is impossible.

September 20th. Perhaps there is no alternative. At least the voice is the voice of Germany.

September 21st. Is the voice that speaks within me the same as the one that speaks from me? Who can tell me this? Perhaps if I listen very carefully it will be possible to tell.

November 7th. A nationalist rally? von Kahr has the audacity to call his meeting a nationalist rally. And they have the greater audacity to invite me to sit with them on the same platform.

This evening I held a meeting with Scheubner-Richter and the others. And not one of them had seen the opportunity, only myself. There was much talk about how von Kahr had outmanoeuvred us now and how we might never recover, much ill-considered talk until I silenced them with a word. "Gentlemen," I said, "they are playing into our hands. This is our chance."

"But the propaganda," Goebbels said. "With respect, Führer, propaganda is a hobby of mine. The propaganda they will make at tomorrow's meeting might destroy us."

"Ah, the propaganda," I said wisely.

"Do not underestimate the force of propaganda, my Führer," the sallow Goebbels said.

"They cannot make propaganda if they have no meeting," I said. "They also cannot make propaganda if they are under arrest." At this I saw Ernst Röhm rub his hands together, spitting on them first. "All three of them are to attend the same public meetings. They will be chickens for the plucking and the flesh will be ours."

Rosenberg turned white and his eyes grew larger. "My Führer," he said, "perhaps this is a time for caution." Clearly it was a mistake to make him editor of the party newspaper.

I did not have to answer him though. Ernst did it for me. "You remember what General Ludendorff said? This is a time for men with balls."

Rosenberg had been sitting forward. Now he sank back into his chair. "Perhaps this is a time for caution, I said. I did not say definitely. I said perhaps."

"Perhaps you have an empty bag where the other things should be," Röhm said.

So in an atmosphere of enthusiasm preparations were made. We looked at our list of socialists and communists. Röhm said that he knew of a young blonde communist from Bayreuth with a fair skin and dimples on both his cheeks. He said that he would like to take this one into his personal custody.

Göring said that he doubted there would be enough prison cells for all of them, but this young Joseph of the swarthy complexion was quick to react.

"The English," he said, "they had an excellent idea in the war with the Boers. Concentration camps. I'm sure we can do something of the sort, a good place for communists, misguided democrats and other Bolsheviks."

A fine mind this young Joseph Goebbels has. He should be useful in future.

November 8th, 1923, 3am. Today is the greatest day of my life, and for this reason I am going to keep my notebook with me every moment. It is impossible to think that any part of such a day might be lost, forgotten amongst the trivia of everyday life, not that there is any trivial part of the life of one such as I.

I cannot sleep. There is an evil ferment in my stomach. I can feel the reaction as conflicting chemical substances war upon each other. Perhaps I have been poisoned. A Jew or a communist might easily occupy the quarters above mine and allow poison to drip down the walls, infiltrating the air of my room. This is something to consider.

November 8th, 1923, 4am. There is still no sleep. I have been sitting quietly in the chair at my desk, waiting for the night to pass. I have kept my eyes on the far wall of the room, holding to that old cracking surface with all the power of my senses.

All at once the wall was far from me. It had not moved and I had not moved. I could clearly see that it was in precisely the same place, and yet there was now a great distance separating me from it. There was distance and the mist of distance, the vagueness of outline and the softness of form. Then I noticed that the desk also was far from me and even the chair on which I was sitting was now at a great distance.

Nothing was close, nothing was touching. I was in the midst of an immense isolation. Then the voice came. Its tone was strong and echoing like a cry in a cave. It filled my soul and all of my being. It was speaking with the power of the soul, not with the words of the mind. I could distinguish no single word, but the message flowed into me like an alpine cataract. "Today," it said. "Today, today."

November 8th 1923, 9am. It is cold. The wind is blowing and it is cold. How can one conduct a *Putsch* in such weather? No one will want to take part. This is not fair. The forces of destiny are dead. Or at least asleep. My brown suit is a fine replacement for the blue one that served me so well and that General Ludendorff admired. It fits well and I shall wear it today. The small tear along the seam, between the legs, will not be noticeable.

11am. I met Emil at the Café Edelweiss. He says that he has heard that the State government has six thousand men. This is a great many, perhaps too many.

Noon. They probably have others as well, secret batallions. Perhaps they have eight or nine thousand.

1pm. I have met with Göring. He says they have at least ten thousand, but that courage always wins in the end and we should not let ten thousand troops bother us. What he had to say was very inspiring. He is mad.

Also the ferment in my stomach is worse than ever. if this continues I shall become intoxicated by the juices from my own intestines.

2pm. Göring says that we can easily call it off at this stage. He says that we are outnumbered by four to one, maybe five to one. This is the voice of discretion. Captain Hermann Göring cannot be counted as a coward. Not he, the last leader of the Richthofen squadron.

Getting out of the red party Mercedes, the tear lengthened. It can still be easily controlled by the use of simple devices such as the taking of small steps when walking (the military stride can still be regal even if shortened) and getting in and out of cars with the feet close together.

4.30pm. Ten minutes ago I left Ernst Röhm at the Café Heck. These cafés are going to be the end of the National Socialist movement. If only we could crack as many Bolshevik skulls as we drink litres of beer we would take over Bavaria by nightfall.

Röhm arrived at the café, red in the face, sweating and breathing hard. "My Führer," he said, "the party will have to decide upon one café for meetings. This is the twenty-seventh one I have visited. I have been looking for the party leadership since nine o'clock."

"Security, my dear Röhm," Esser said.

"Precautions, Röhm," Göring said.

"What about communications?" Röhm said. "Has the great National Socialist army heard of communications?"

"This man is criticizing the Führer," Rosenberg said. His white face was even whiter than normal and his eyes their usual anaemic grey.

Röhm had sat down, causing the wooden chair to creak. He leapt again to his feet knocking it backwards. "Heil Hitler," he roared, his heels clicking together like castanets. "Not Ernst Röhm," he shouted. "Ernst Röhm does not criticize his leader."

"If he shouts any louder," Hanfstaengl said, "he will hang his leader before nightfall."

Röhm's chest was rising and falling quickly with the anger in his soul. "You," he shouted, pointing at Hanfstaengl, "and you," pointing at Rosenberg "You two. . ." The pointing finger shot back and forth from one to the other.

"My Ernst," I said.

"My Führer," he said.

"Why were you looking for me?"

Röhm sat down again. His thick neck was bulging over his collar

143

and his little pig eyes were staring into mine. I have not yet forgiven him altogether for that *Stürmabteilung* matter. "My Führer," he said "I heard something, some small insignificant thing, that cannot possibly be true. I know that it cannot be true because I know that there is not a cowardly hair on my Führer's head, not in his moustache either, or either . . .

"We follow you, my Ernst," I said.

"This was a thing so unlikely. . ." His cheeks were still red and dampened by perspiration. "My Führer, they said that tonight's *Putsch* is cancelled. Such a thing cannot be."

"This is not for you to say," Rosenberg's icicle voice was insipid as always.

"My Führer. . ." Röhm's chest puffed up and for a moment his pig eyes almost became round. ". . .such a thing cannot be."

"Why not, my Ernst?"

"Firstly. . ." He pointed towards the ceiling with one finger. ". . .we cannot contact all the storm troops in time. They have instructions to attend the meeting tonight to support the Führer's action."

"Do they know what the action is to be?" I asked.

"Of course not."

"Then there is no problem."

"The problem comes with secondly. Secondly," he said, "I have taken a prisoner."

"A prisoner?" All at the table asked the question together.

"One small prisoner, my Führer."

"Who?" I asked.

"A man of little significance."

"His name."

"Minister President von Knilling."

"von Knilling? Where are you keeping him?"

The little pig eyes went from one face to the other, but kept coming back to mine. "Anyone would have done it, my Führer. Why should I be blamed?"

"Where are you keeping him, Ernst?"

"Well, we do not have control of a prison yet, also not an army camp or even a police station. . . and I was passing the gasthaus where my Führer lives. . ."

"Where I live?" This time it was the voice. Röhm was at the end of a long red passage. I could see nothing else.

"I was passing there." Now his eyes were imitating the rhythm of castanets, with the quickness of their blinking. "I was passing there and I thought, not having a jail or police station or an army camp, I thought, why not keep him in my Führer's room. My Führer is not using it today . . ."

"My room?" It was the voice again. I had decided to be silent and aloof and I, personally, had not spoken a word. "My room?" The voice was like a thunderstorm, a long rolling reverberation.

Röhm spoke very quickly, so quickly that it was difficult distinguishing one word from the next. "He is bound and gagged, chained under my Führer's bed. He cannot move, so well is he chained."

5.30pm. That fool Röhm. Von Knilling tied up under my bed. Now there is nothing for it but flight. I have a place booked on the seven-thirty train to Vienna. There is no alternative. Our four thousand against fifteen thousand state troops.

As I sit here at my table in the Café Heck I am aware that if I miss that train I might never write another word. I cannot even return to my room to pack. Von Knilling under the bed. I will have Röhm court-martialled. The revolution will have to begin in Austria instead. I will have him court-martialled as soon as the revolution . . . as soon as I . . . soon. I will have him court-martialled.

Göring has come in. He says that all over Munich members of the SA are coming home from work and changing into their uniforms. He says that bravery will make up for numbers. He is a worse fool than Röhm even. Also he asks what I am writing. "Notes for my speech tonight after the *Putsch*," I say. His eyes glow.

6pm. There is a continual coming and going through the doors of the café. It is being left open continually. No sooner do I despatch a messenger to close it than someone else leaves it open again. Normally I would not mind, but a draught is caused, a cold and low wind, and the tear along the seam between the legs has widened. Only by sitting with my legs clamped tightly closed is a necessary degree of protection afforded, also warmth. A chill in this region cannot be contemplated.

6.30pm. I have to slip away from the others soon to get the train. It is

145

well that I possessed the great presence of mind two weeks ago to reserve the ticket. Emil has it in his pocket, also one for himself, second class. It is never wise to be too confident.

I have my rhinocerous hide whip here.

6.45pm. A few cracks of the rhinocerous hide whip certainly bring excitement to a gathering. I swung it above my head and cracked it a few times to get attention. Immediately the atmosphere in the Café Heck changed. I could see the admiration in the eyes of all.

The lady of the café came in. "Not the chandelier, Herr Hitler," she cried. "Try to miss the chandelier."

7.05pm. The whip is a wonderful thing. In the hands of a true leader it is authority and purpose. What a pity I shall not get the opportunity to use it tonight.

7.10pm. "Behold these proud Germans," I said, my hand sweeping broadly over the young men in the Café. All eyes turned to look and immediately I dropped my hand to examine the breadth of the tear.

Four fingers fit into it with no trouble.

7.20pm. I shall stride carefully to the podium, swinging my whip above my head to raise the level of attention to a suitable height. Tonight they will see a true figure of command.

Emil whispers in my ear, "We must go, Führer, before it is too late."

"To the beer hall," I cry and the whole café breaks into applause and singing. My rhinocerous hide whip cracks against the chandelier and a lamp smashes.

"Another one, another one," the lady of the café cries. She is a small broad person with bosoms like the udders of a cow, a productive Bavarian cow.

Emil has hold of my arm. He hangs onto me like a limpet. "Not the beer hall," he whispers, "the train."

What train does he mean? There is no train to the beer hall.

November 9th, 1923, 5.30am. Things have gone well. I am Minister President of Bavaria now, or perhaps Ludendorff is. He sits opposite me, drinking wine for breakfast while the *Putsch* percolates like

146

coffee coming to the boil. Even his cheeks are damp.

If I sit with extreme care, not moving the position of my buttocks on the chair, the tear in my trousers does not widen. I have marched with it, strode the length of the Bürgerbräukeller, with smallish steps, even stood with legs apart while addressing the mob, not far apart, a small amount, two or three centimetres perhaps.

Also a small tear exists in my nether trousers, nothing to make mention of, a tear of minute dimensions, the result of my frugal manner of living, but situated in a place of delicacy, great delicacy. The thought occurs that secrets could be revealed by such a split and such a tear, secrets of a nature that should always remain secret. Standing with legs apart could lead to terrible revelations, or at least one terrible revelation.

This Ludendorff, I shall no longer address him as General. Whenever I do he calls me Corporal. How can the party Führer be addressed as Corporal? He sits there, his elbows resting on the table, his cheeks working as he takes in the wine, and his red eyes looking at me. He has his mind on the position of Minister President, I can see it.

Last night at the beer hall there was no resistance, not from the vons or from the crowd. It was destiny, destiny upon destiny, fate upon fate.

It was destiny that decided that Göring should wear his Luftwaffe uniform. When the police tried to block our way into the hall he shouted, "About turn. Quick march." One look at his uniform and hat was the last we saw of the police. Von Kahr was standing on the platform, calling out in a weak voice for them to come back. But he was not wearing the uniform of a Luftwaffe Captain.

I strode to the podium with steps of modest length, but purposeful design. I could feel the tear in the nether trousers, scratching. There was a moment of fear. Even Napoleon felt fear, even Bismarck, even Charlemagne, Julius Caesar. The podium was a foot above floor level. If I stood on the edge there was no telling what perspective the audience might have, what angle from which matters might be viewed. Perhaps if I stood with my feet close together, or my legs crossed. The podium drew closer. I could hear the thrilling shouts of Heil from all sides. Von Kahr was no longer speaking. He was looking at me and his pale short-sighted eyes were filled with fear. Or perhaps it was puzzlement. I do not think that he could see me yet.

Something needed to be done. A distraction was necessary, a small diversion, some small matter of interest to lift the centre of attention to a more elevated point, one above waist level for instance.

Without thinking, I drew my pistol from its holster, held it above my head, pointing skyward, and pulled the trigger. Every eye in the hall turned in that direction. At least attention was now in the right area. I had just reached the edge of von Kahr's range of vision. I saw his eyes go wide, then narrow into two little points.

Behind me Göring shouted, "The revolution is upon us. The hall is surrounded." They were the words I was supposed to shout. I turned to see him, but he was behind the others.   "That was for me," I said to Hess.

"I know, my Führer. Let us bear it in mind, regarding Göring," he said. "Such a one is not to be trusted, especially in the matter of deputy leadership."

By the time I reached the podium poor old von Kahr was already seated. This was clearly the most sensible thing for him to do. I went up the steps carefully, one at a time, still waving my pistol in order to keep attention in the right area. Suddenly I realized that I was saved. There was a table with a broad apron on the podium. Von Kahr had been standing in front of it. I went round to stand behind it, right amongst the vons.

There was a scattering among them to make room for me. In a loud voice, filled with patriotic pride, I shouted, "The revolution has begun. The hall is surrounded."

Ludendorff sits there like a statue, only his cheeks moving as he swallows down the wine. Ten minutes ago he spoke for the first time. "You did not follow my advice, Corporal." I looked straight into his eyes, straight into the eyes of a General of the army, a hero of the Great War. Of course, I am also a hero of the Great War. "You did not change your tailor." He was looking at my trousers. I have changed my trousers for a pair provided by a member of the *Stürmabteilung*. Except that he has longer legs and the turn-ups have been folded over to shorten them, they fit fairly well. In such a crowd it is not possible to see the flapping of the trouser legs or the fold at the waist. In any event the belt pulls in the fold at the waist so that it is barely visible.

"There are matters of greater importance," I said. It is not for nothing that I have come to be party Führer.

148

"To be sure," he said, going back to his wine.

A matter occurred to me, a matter of some importance. Von Kahr, von Seisser and von Lossow, what had happened to them? "The vons?" I asked. "Where are they now?"

"I have released them," Ludendorff said. He leant back in the chair as if to see me more clearly. "On my own authority," he added.

"Released them? The enemies of the revolution?" I could not grasp the possibility of such a thing.

"Seisser gave me his word as a German officer that they would cause no more trouble." His cheeks puffed up with these words and his skin turned a shade of pink in the area around his eyes. His officer friends, standing in groups around the room, all turned to face us. "No German officer has ever broken his word and no German officer ever will." His friends look at me as if I am a person of no understanding. I take a good look at the faces of each one to remember them against the day when I am Reich Chancellor and Ludendorff is decomposing beneath the earth. Then we shall see something.

The General was still glaring at me. It seemed a good time to show the breadth of my learning. This would ease the tension. Also a more intellectual note would not be amiss. "I am against industry," I said. "Industry promotes both communism and capitalism." Ludendorff said nothing. His cheeks twitched once. "It promotes capitalism in the capitalists and communism in the communists," I explained.

"Who will do the work?"

"My dear General, you have overlooked the genius of the German peasant," I said.

"Is the German peasant in his backyard going to manufacture eighty-eight millimetre field guns for us?" He is a man of limited intellect and no understanding, this General. Something will have to be done about him after the revolution. On the other hand, this thing of the eighty-eight millimetre cannon is a problem. The peasantry must be made to know that no excuses are acceptable.

November 9th, 7am. A message has just come in over the radio, saying that von Kahr, von Seisser and von Lossow repudiate the *Putsch.* "I will never again trust the word of a German officer," Ludendorff says. "Not one of them has ever kept his word and not one ever will." His friends from among the officers just stare at me again, as if I still do not understand.

7.30am. The *Putsch* is a success. Munich is in a state of rapture. We have rounded up two thousand enemies of the Führer. Enemies of the people, Hess calls them.

As long as the people are careful to have the same enemies as the Führer I have no objection. Röhm has occupied von Lossow's headquarters. This will place the young blond lieutenant in his custody, a state of affairs that will be satisfying to him. Max has occupied two banks and one hospital. We are also in charge of three beer halls, twenty-one cafés and the police station. The cadets of the infantry school, with three brass bands and a horse-drawn carriage, have also joined. Also the printer who prints the state money, together with last week's production.

At the Bürgerbräukeller Streicher made a speech of such obscenity that Esser had to drag him off the table he was using for a podium. Afterwards he made amends by arresting five hundred and twenty-seven known communists, all of whom were living in a Jewish old-age home, as if so thin a disguise would fool us.

Noon, November, 1923. Röhm is besieged at military headquarters. This is the treachery of the vons. How could Ludendorff have been such a fool? He has clarity in only one matter. It is truly impossible to trust the word of an officer.

"Röhm must be rescued," Ludendorff roared at the others. He dare not address me in this fashion. "Röhm must be rescued. We march on headquarters."

I could not believe my ears. The old fool was clearly having an attack of some kind. This was a time for negotiations. But all around me there were cries of "Jawohl," and "Heil," and "Germany!"

"The heavens will fall, the earth will move and the oceans divide before one member of the Bavarian Reichswehr fires one bullet on a troop commanded by me," Ludendorff roared.

All of our people were on their feet and shouting. They have gone crazy. What could I do but get slowly to my feet, moving with deliberation and majesty, and raise one hand in a solemn salute. Immediately they were all saluting, even Ludendorff.

What can I do? We march.

8pm. Dead, all dead. Ludendorff dead, Emil dead, Göring dead, Esser dead: all fallen valiantly in battle, giving their lives for the cause of Germany. I, I alone of the leadership, have survived. Destiny has seen fit to spare only me.

I am lying down on a couch in the home of Hélène Hanfstaengl. Schultze brought me here. He is not a doctor, a man of very inferior talents. He says that I have only dislocated a shoulder as a result of falling to the ground when the firing started. "This is impossible," I said. "How could I have fallen to the ground if I had not been hit. It is clear that I was struck by a bullet."

"But, Führer," he said, "the skin is not broken."

With a word I silenced him. "There can be many explanations for that," I said.

"Of course, my Führer," he said. At least he has the grace to yield before superior wisdom.

But Hélène is the biggest surprise. What a fool I was to think that beauty and racial purity necessarily coincide in the same person. This is completely untrue. Despite her blue eyes there must be a trace of some inferior blood in her ancestry. This is the only explanation for her behaviour.

She has been sitting opposite me, pointing a finger at me ever since I arrived here. "You men," she says, "you are little boys, little boys playing Red Indians. Not one of you has ever grown up. Both sides should be issued with rubber bullets before you start. It would make more sense. Also it would be more in keeping with the intelligence employed on both sides."

"Please, woman," I said, "I am in pain. I have been wounded in the cause of the Fatherland. My shoulder feels as if it is torn from its hinges, and there is a gaseous reaction in my stomach."

"I am glad you are suffering," she said. "You are the worst of them. As for having a problem in the guts, I am not surprised. I would have been surprised if it had not been so." I tried to speak, but her lips were moving too fast, also too fast for her brain to keep pace. "And where is my Putzi? And where are the others? Most of them are madmen anyway, but if my Putzi is not back by tomorrow morning I am handing you over to the authorities. No Putzi, no Adolf."

"You blame me?" She was perpetrating a terrible injustice.

"Of course I blame you. Who is the so-called Führer?"

"So-called?"

"This is what they call you, I think. Is it not?" Her voice was corrupted by a nasty sneering tone.

151

"Well, yes. . ."

"You are the so-called Führer. And I hold you personally responsible for my Putzi. And what about Carin Göring's hubby, such a nice little fellow? He would not hurt a mouse. And where is he now? I don't suppose that his Führer knows."

And so on and on. It is impossible to say which caused greater pain, my shoulder, the turbulence of my stomach or Hélène's accusations. No, it is not impossible to say. Hélène's pointing finger and pointed tongue were by far the worst. To think that I once considered honouring her with the potency of my manhood.

All this might have been forgiven, if it had not been for the laughter. I had grown weary of her scolding and had risen to leave the room. Getting up had caused me great pain. I stood before her, hunched over in agony when her eye fell on my trousers. The complete lack of moderation in the scene that followed is too painful to relate. Eventually with tears running down her face and her finger now pointing in derision at my trousers she gasped, "Adolf, where did you get those. Are they standard issue for Führers?"

10.30pm. It was all the fault of Ludendorff and that madman Göring, also Röhm and Streicher. It was a time for negotiation. Anyone could have seen it. The vons would have come to terms.

But Ludendorff was the worst, marching next to me at the head of the column, puffing and wheezing, snorting and snuffling, his cheeks twitching more than ever, pretending that he was not scared, the ridiculous old fool. Officer corps, pah! As he said himself, they are not to be trusted, none of them.

Esser was close behind me. "Order the band to play," I said, as we started out. The cadets could march and the SA could march, and the students and working men could try.

"There is no band, my Führer," Esser said.

"There were three last night."

"They went for breakfast and have not returned, excepting the oboe player of the cadet band. Also it is very cold weather for conducting a *Putsch*."

"Band or no band, forward march," Ludendorff roared, and se off down the road. "Let the oboe command the time."

"The oboe, Herr General?" Esser asked. "Is this a musical com edy?" But his voice was lost in the cursing as the entire colum lurched once, heaved mightily as men bumped into each other and stepped on each other's feet, then set off after the General, shoving me along with it. This is not the way a *Putsch* should be conducted. Who, after all, is the Führer?

I hurried to catch up to Ludendorff. "What about the cold, Herr General?" I said. "This is very cold weather in which to conduct a *Putsch*. Such a thing might be more popular in the summer."

"Corporal," he said, without turning his head to look at me, "a man can die for Germany as easily in winter as in summer."

I knew he had gone mad. I had known it all along. He and Göring were subject to the same malady. It had the effect of exaggerating the natural German tendencies of bravery and of turning the brain to stone. I glanced back down the column. The bodyguard and the SA looked like soldiers, but they were a small group. The cadets looked like cadets, but the others were workers, old soldiers, students and even café owners, they looked like nothing I have ever seen, certainly not an army. And above the cursing, shuffling and jostling of the column the oboe kept time, sounding like the rhythmic flatulence of an elephant.

The length of the borrowed trousers was also a problem. If the turn-ups were folded over only once they rode on my shoes and dragged along on the road. An extra fold exposed my stockinged ankles. I started with just one fold, but walking was difficult, also the trousers hooked on any uneven place in the road. I stopped to introduce a second fold and a young party member by the name of Heinrich Himmler bumped into me. "Excuse me, my Führer," he said, "I did not see my Führer stop."

"Quite all right, my Heinrich," I said.

Seeing what I was doing, he said, "Exchange trousers with me, my Führer. I will gladly accept such extreme humiliation in the cause of the Fatherland." A sweet and gentle soul, this Heinrich. He is one who can be used in future, in a non-violent position, I think.

We had arranged to exchange trousers at the first opportunity when Ludendorff led us into the Weinstrasse, another mistake. I could have told him, but no, no one asks the Führer. And there they were, state troops, blocking the road, hundreds of them, thousands, armed to the teeth.

Before I could persuade the ridiculous old fool to withdraw they started firing. I felt the pain of the missile that struck me and I fell to the ground, wounded in the chaos of battle. Emil fell on top of me and through his legs I could see Ludendorff still marching, straight into the firing. I could imagine his grunting and growling, and his cheeks puffing and trembling. He had no business walking to certain death that way. He only did it to show up his Führer.

November 10th, 1923. The state police arrested me this morning at the Hanfstaengl villa. "Even prison trousers will fit better than those, Herr Hitler," the sergeant said. How pleasant is the solitude of my cell after spending last night listening to Hélène Hanfstaengl. Her scolding is gone and I can hear the inner voice speaking. Only one word is clear: "Victory, victory."

Just before the lights were switched out the head warder visited my cell. "Yesterday was a black day for Germany," I said. "Great Germans died, great patriots."

"Like who?" The warder asked.

"Like General Ludendorff," I said, "and Captain Hermann Göring, also good honest Germans like Emil Maurice and Putzi Hansfstaengl."

He stroked his beard. "Not dead," he said.

"What?"

"Not dead at all. We've got them all here."

VOLUME VIII

December 7th, 1923. They lied to me. Göring and Putzi Hanfstaengl escaped. They are in hiding. But then it is not given to them to be leaders, as it is to me. It is not they who must be crucified for their country as I must be. Like Jesus I am sacrificed in the cause of my destiny. We have both been plotted against by Jews and both been destroyed, he by the Pharisees and I by the dissolute Doctor Freud.

December 8th. I am alone. There is no one here at all. My solitude is complete, excepting only Hess, Ludendorff, Emil, Kriebel, Weber and a few others. It is in the midst of such solitude that great souls are tested. It is a time of refinement such as lesser beings can never understand.

Also the food is of poor quality and the warders are slow to carry out my commands. One of them even had the audacity to suggest that the Social Democrats are reasonable people.

December 9th. Hypocrites! That is what the democracies are. They are forever preaching human rights, but what about our rights? Their newspapers call our *Putsch* a minor beer-hall revolt, a cowboys and Indians adventure, a schoolboy prank with guns and, more infuriating and disgusting than anything else, they are calling me Ludendorff's noisy Corporal.

If they had any interest in human rights their leaders would close down the newspapers that write such lies.

December 25th, 1923. Christmas day and I am suffering terrible agonies. My body is being eaten away by a dreaded venereal disease. I can feel its tentacles insinuating themselves throughout my body. It is that Martha. She is an evil woman. I contracted the disease from her in 1918 and it has been lying dormant within me ever since, waiting for a moment of weakness in which to strike. And it has found the moment. Now while I am wounded and suffering in prison, my strength drained from the frail structure of my body: now at this moment it has chosen to mount its assault.

The prison doctor has examined me and found nothing. This is further proof of the ignorance of professional people, especially when they are faced with genius. He is a very weak fellow. He as much as admitted to me that his wife has a Jewish uncle.

January 1st, 1924. We have an excellent man here by the name of Patrick Gutenberg. He is an accomplished fortune-teller. His case is very similar to mine. He too is a victim of a miscarriage of justice. He was found guilty of stealing a horse and carriage, a man such as he. The idea is ridiculous. As he rightly points out, a man such as he would steal a motor vehicle, not a horse-drawn carriage.

Justice will not prevail until a National Socialist meaning has been given to it.

This Gutenberg's fortune-telling is of the highest order. Immediately he looked into the palm of my hand he could see that I was no ordinary person. He said that I am to be Germany's saviour. He also said that a vegetarian diet will dispose of the venereal disease that is destroying me. He has kindly agreed to dispose of the meat in my prison diet himself.

January 7th. My life is at an end. The criminals who are going to conduct the trial are pretending that my act was treason. And the penalty for treason is death.

My entire existence has been a series of unfortunate mistakes. If my mother had lived I would have been a great composer, another Wagner. But perhaps Germany is not ready for another Wagner. Perhaps we have reached a level of decadence from which there is no return. If it was not so the entire populace would have joined the *Putsch* and success would have been ours.

I sit at the window, looking out at the trees, and I find that if I do not move for a long time the voice speaks. It comes out of the darkness, very softly at first, but growing in strength. I cannot separate one word from the next or one sentence from another. The meaning is not always clear, but the strength is without question.

Yesterday I sat there from breakfast time. In a small breeze I watched the naked branches of the trees moving with the rhythm of marching feet. And the voice came. It came and remained throughout the time I was there. It was stronger, louder and deeper than it had ever been.

A warder interrupted the passage of my vision when he took me by the arm. "No need to cry, Herr Hitler," he said. "Look, even your collar is wet." He led me back to my bed in darkness. Only a little light came from the passage.

I do not know what happened to the day.

January 13th, 1924. Drexler! How dare he come here and pretend to be giving me courage, a coward like him who did not have enough ball to join in the *Putsch*? I should have killed him. The voice should have destroyed him. He said, "All is not lost," and, "Do not despair," and, "Germany will rise again," and, "Look to a bright and resurgent future." He is fortunate indeed to have left here alive.

January 14th, 1924. All these visitors, Frau Bechstein with her sentimental stories, Hélène Hanfstaengl without even an apology, Knirsch with all his talk of the National Socialist revolution in Czechoslovakia, even Harrer.

After Harrer had left I summoned the head warder. "No more visitors," I said, "unless they are first cleared with me. Understood?"

"Yes, my Führer," he said. He did not salute. I do not find it necessary.

February 3rd. The trial is to take place later this month. The end draws near.

February 7th, 1924. Today something happened that I have not experienced for a long time. I will not go so far as to say that it was a significant event. Possibly it was a sign of weakness. As yet there is no clarity on this matter. The voice is yet to speak.

The incident of which I write was an appearance of the condition. It was a great problem to conceal and it remained for an overly long period, causing extreme strain in the one singular area that should never be mentioned. No leader should discuss such a shortcoming or deficiency even if such a thing has no bearing on his life and is barely a deficiency at all. Or no deficiency even.

Angela visited me. She looks nothing like Mama. Her face is round, like a pudding, not elegantly carved like Mama's was. She is also without Mama's large and beautiful eyes. Hers are not little pig eyes such as old Alois had and the brat, Paula, possesses. But they have not the beauty of Mama's.

With Angela was little Angela. Geli is what they call her.

It was at the moment I saw her that the condition occurred. It was present in abundance and of a hardness befitting a Führer. Since they left I have been considering this and it is clear that this should be so. The true leader cannot after all be inferior to others in a matter of this nature.

I had not seen Geli since she was a very small girl. Now she is fifteen and soft at the angles and corners and roundnesses of a woman, soft of mouth and eye, and touch and curl of hair, soft everywhere, soft as silk or butterfly wings. I had barely greeted Angela when she came into the cell and my eye fell upon her. The condition was an inevitability. The eyes, the large round dampness of eye and the contours of face, as perfect as Lohengrin's narration. There was a quality that made it almost the face of Mama.

"Hasn't my Geli grown to be a big girl, Adolfus?" Angela asked. The condition was a steel point struggling against the front of my trousers. Angela was looking at my face. I wriggled to free the tormenting organ but it was wedged fast. It took a quick movement of the hand, a brief and flashing stroke, to dislodge it, so fast that it was barely visible. Angela had turned to look at Geli. She turned back to me. "Isn't she a big girl, Adolfus? My how you look at her. Never mind, Geli, it's just that Uncle Dolf likes you."

"I can see it," Geli said. Her face was red and her eyelids flickering like a candle in the wind, looking quickly at me and as quickly away. Sometimes her glance was aimed at my face and sometimes at the area just below my belt. "It's a hard love," she said.

"Geli," Angela said, "how can you say that? Uncle Dolf has a soft heart." Geli looked quickly at me again, her eyes aiming for the lower target. "A soft heart, but a hard love," she said.

"Geli, how can you say this? To hear you a person would think that you do not believe Uncle Dolf loves you."

"I do, Mama. I can see it."

"Of course. Look at his soft blue eyes."

"Yes, I can see it there too."

"Adolphus. . ." Angela must have been looking at me again, but I was looking at Geli. How could I help it? Such perfection is beyond

158

the reach of mortals. Mama must have looked just as she does at the same age. A lock of hair was curled across her forehead. I reached out to move it back. She watched my hand come towards her, without pulling away. She is fearless, a child of the German soil. She breathed deeply once as my finger brushed her forehead, causing her bosom to rise and fall. "Adolphus . . ." Angela was speaking, addressing her remarks to me, but I heard nothing more. Geli's eyes were round and moist, gleaming brightly, and the condition was aching with the hardness of it. ". . . such glory to the family," I heard Angela say. "We are all so proud. This is not the end. Everyone knows that. Everyone is saying it." Geli's eyes met mine, then rolled downwards to the point on which they had fixed before. The condition was a wild thing, harbouring an independent life, burrowing angrily against the flannel of my trousers, trying to escape.

". . . such an honour for my little Adolphus to be the party leader," Angela was saying, "but you look only at Geli. You see, Geli, Uncle Dolf is just as surprised at what a big girl you are as everyone else. And remember what an important man he is, and consider yourself lucky that he has a soft spot for you."

The red of Geli's face deepened. "A soft spot, Mama," she said. "That's nice, Mama."

February 8th. Emil and I were walking in the garden today when he asked what it was that I wrote every night. I explained to him the nature of leadership and that the most intimate thoughts and actions of the man of destiny should not be hidden from generations to come. I explained that others should understand that triumph of the will that is the fruit of greatness. "Do you understand, Emil?"

"Of course, my Führer. It's a wonderful idea," he said. "And by the way, I was wondering who is the pretty woman who visited my Führer yesterday. But I suppose it is only the Führer who gets such tasty morsels brought to his cell."

"My niece," I said. "A charming and innocent child."

"Of course, my Führer," Emil said. "That is just the way I saw her, a charming and innocent child."

February 26th. It is Angela who is at fault. She had no right bringing this young Geli into my cell. It was to be expected that something of this nature would take place. For years my thoughts have been of a refined and intellectual nature, unsullied by anything dark and of a sort to weaken the resolve. For years every gram of my energy has been directed towards the course of perfection, without diversion, distraction or corruption. I have been the pure sword of fate.

But now, in my cell at night, the worst of horrors overtakes me. The condition rouses itself like a creature possessed, keeping me awake through the long hours, throbbing and writhing, until finally I fall asleep only to waken in the cold lifeless early hours of the day, the condition gone, but the signs of its passing clinging to the sheets like a stigma of past sins, the lone centre of my manhood shivering in a tight knot, all strength drained from my body.

A smaller matter: the trial started today.

March 7th. My strength is almost gone. One more such night and Germany will need other options for the future. Geli, the name itself means torment.

The trial proceeds without a thought for justice. Today I was interrupted by the prosecutor after an address of less than two hours. This is typical of the treatment I am receiving. Yesterday I was interrupted after three and a half hours and I had not yet reached the point I was making. It is very comfortable for these honourable gentlemen to make all the rules.

March 9th. Only my will keeps me alive. Today in the small hand-mirror in my cell I examined the focal point of manly problems, the curse of all leaders. It has retracted, withdrawing itself until it is just a tiny protruberance. It is clear that the strain of the last month has been almost enough to destroy it.

The trial proceeds. The voice took over as soon as I rose to speak. Poor little Judge Neithardt almost dirtied his trousers.

March 15th. I did not ask for it. It was not as a result of any request of mine. The head warder should have known better than to do such a thing. He had no business bringing in a man of that sort. I summoned him immediately afterwards to tell him clearly that I take the strongest exception to such an action.

"I am Doctor Schwarz," this person said.

"Schwarz?" I was not surprised at such a name, from such an

individual. "This is no name for a German," I said.

"I apologize for my name, Herr Hitler," he said. "Your friends here have summoned me. They feel you might need someone to talk to."

"My friends? Is this Hess?"

"You have many friends here, Herr Hitler."

"Many friends? I have no friends. I am a man suffering agonies and trying to forget the injustice of the past and the treachery. . ." A thought came to me. "Emil! Is it Emil?"

"No, Herr Hitler," he said, "it was not Emil." He bent his head forward so that I could see his eyes above the rims of his spectacles. This was clearly done to impress me. Such is the bourgeois nature of these so-called psychiatrists, that they imagine such a gesture will impress me. "You have been losing weight, Herr Hitler. Also you look pale, as if you are sleeping badly, and apart from this, at night two distinct voices have been heard, coming from your cell. I thought that you might have something that you wanted to discuss with me."

Discuss with him? I, Adolf Hitler, discuss anything with a fellow by the name of Schwarz? And it is for nothing that he speaks to me about losing weight and looking pale, as if these matters are important in even a small way to such as he. I know only too well which part of the body it is that interests him. It is no use him asking question about two voices coming out of my cell when what he is curious about are two of something else altogether, and if he finds only one then there will be more questions as if such a person is a freak or worse. There will be nodding and ah-ha and this was to be expected and well, well, and what have we here or what do we not have here?

I folded my arms and looked sternly back at Doctor Schwarz. I said nothing at all, thereby thwarting all his insidious plans.

March 20th. This morning the head warder came to see me. His manner was polite and respectful as befitted a person of his rank when addressing a person of my rank. "With respect, Herr Hitler," he said.

"Speak," I said.

"With respect," he repeated. His eyes were blinking quickly. 'With respect the daily showering is a prison regulation. It is also good for the health. There is also a problem with the court guards. They say the close proximity becomes problematical. So they say. I

161

am sure the daily shower will not be found to be distasteful in any way." His hands were clasped in front of him as if to shield a certain delicate area. This is all part of the sense of inferiority suffered by those who have both. It is clear that they realize that one of the two is superfluous. They have my pity. It is only so keen an observer as myself who would notice these clues. "It is a small thing, Herr Hitler. I am sure that it can be done as a favour from one man to another. After all, regulations are regulations and where will I be if word reaches my superiors that regulations are being ignored? It will be a sad day for me. I'm sure you realize that."

There was a certain unseemly audacity in the man's request, but his manner was humble. "This is a matter for dignity," I said.

"Dignity?" He is a good soul, this jailer, but lacking in true intelligence.

"Certainly," I said. "It is a matter of dignity for the Führer of a political group."

"Ah, dignity." The troubled expression left his face. "Herr Hitler wishes to shower alone?"

"Clearly," I said. "In a cubicle with a latch on the inside of the door."

April 1st, 1924. Five years. They have the insolence to pretend that they are able to lock me up for five years. Let them take note that my time in prison will be far briefer than that.

April 17th. Rosenberg was here to see me today. He brought a charming fruit cake in the shape of the swastika. It had little roses of icing along the edges with a row of little marzipan babies along each leg of the swastika. What a noble emblem. I have always loved the swastika. In large lettering on one side the icing said, "Happy birthday, dear Führer." My birthday is in three days' time.

"Eat it in good health," Rosenberg said.

"Thank you, good Alfred," I said. "If only I could do something for you."

"Not for me, my Führer, but for the party."

I looked carefully at him. Unlike myself there is no laughter or human kindness in this Alfred. He is not a warm and happy person. The face is white, almost without colour and the voice like the voice of an icicle, if such a thing were possible. "What is it you want for the party, my Alfred?" I said.

"The work of the party must go on, my Führer," he said.

"Of course, my Alfred."

"We cannot afford to lose five years." His eyes were blinking and his mouth was twitching. He looked like a corpse, one of reasonable age, that had recently been disinterred.

"Five years, my Alfred. How is it possible to lose five years?" My eyes were fixed upon him with a great intensity. I could see him cower before their force.

"Five years, my Führer, was that not the sentence?"

I resolved to remain silent, to show my disregard for such an idea. I turned my head towards the window. But, without warning, the voice spoke. "Sentence," it said. "What sentence? Five years?" It asked. "Who sentences me to five years? Who?"

"Forgive me, my Führer," Rosenberg said. He was even whiter than usual. "The court did it, my Führer."

The voice withdrew and I answered him. "The court is a fool," I said.

"Nevertheless, my Führer, the party. . ."

"Alfred, it is not necessary to say, my Führer, with every sentence."

"Yes, my Führer."

"Every third or fourth sentence will be enough for propriety's sake," I said.

"Yes, my . . ." The speech froze in his flaccid throat, or perhaps it was his feeble mind in which it froze, or perhaps just stagnated.

"What about the party?"

"The party leadership, my Führer. It is vacant. . . in a manner of speaking. . ."

"Vacant?" The voice was a shaft of ice.

"My Führer, they all want it. Esser wants it. Eckhart wants it. Strasser and Streicher want it. General Ludendorff says he should always have had it. He said, pardon me, my Führer. . . he said, it was no job for a Corporal. Röhm says it is right that a military man should have it, but Ludendorff is too old and he should be the one. Hanfstaengl says a man of the world is needed, one who can talk on equal footing to heads of state, one such as he. Little Joseph Goebbels, can you believe it, says that he is the best orator and an orator is what is needed. Even Göring, my Führer, he is reported to be forming a government in exile. As for Hess, it is just as well that he is locked up with my Führer so that he can do no harm. . ."

"And you, my little Alfred. . ." His shoulders looked to be even rounder than usual and his eyes turned down at the corners, like the eyes of a heartbroken Dachshund. "You. . . what do you want?" He was gazing at me with those sad eyes and I could read his thoughts as if they were the banner outside the party headquarters. "What do you want, my little Alfred, pertaining to the party leadership?"

"Nothing for myself, my Führer, nothing at all. I want not anything for myself. Such a thing never crossed my mind. Personal ambition is not for me, as my Führer very well knows . . ." He was rubbing his thin white hands together, partly out of fear and partly from the thought of being the next leader of the National Socialist German Workers Party. Suddenly the words poured out of him, like beer being poured into a mug. "The work of the party must continue, my Führer. The party must be placed in the hands of one who will not ignore the sacred trust. . . Only one who is a true devotee of his Führer, who can be trusted, who will never, never . . ."

"My little Alfred," I interrupted him, my voice as soft as the sound of the deadliest snake as it slides over the bare sand of the wilderness.

"Yes, my Führer. Before answering I would beg my Führer to forgive me raising such a matter. It is only because. . ."

"Granted. Forgiveness is granted."

"Thank you, my Führer."

"Dormant," I said.

"Dormant, my Führer?"

"I want the party to be dormant until I am free."

"Dormant? But, my Führer, five years. . ."

"Dormant, my little Alfred. And it is not going to be five years. Altogether dormant. Do you understand?"

"Yes, my Führer."

"Good, my little Alfred."

April 18th. Do they really think that I am going to allow them to play at being leader while I am here? Do they imagine that they are going to make speeches and plan strategies and organize another *Putsch* and wave banners while I am locked up in Landsberg prison? A temporary Führer? And what if the temporary Führer decides that he would like to be the permanent Führer?

There will be nothing of the sort. They will wait until I return. I have given permission for them to celebrate my birthday. It is no more than fair to make an exception in this case. After all their joy is quite natural.

But the party will sleep until the Führer returns. It is I for whom all are waiting.

April 19th. My little Hesserl put the matter very well today. "Goebbels, Streicher and the others must get their minds in order," he said. "The Führer is right and he will always be right. They must learn to want the Führer."

April 21st. Just when I was getting over it. Just when the torment is subsiding it begins again. And on my birthday. Mama used to say that everything that happens to you on your birthday happens again on every day for the rest of the year. It cannot be so. Mama was a dear gentle creature, a person of exquisite softness and warmth, but from her I inherited purity of soul, not the immensity of my intellect. My intelligence is a spiritual entity that needs no factor of heredity.

To endure what I have endured yesterday another three hundred and sixty-four times is impossible. Even the steel of the Führer's soul cannot be tempered in this way. Such a flame will consume everything.

They came again, Angela and Geli. No one said anything to me. There was no, "may we come", or "will you see us", or "by your permission". They simply came. The first knowledge I had of their visit, the first murmur that reached me, came when the head warder entered my cell. He stood at a respectful distance, his hands folded protectively in front of him as before. "My dear Herr Hitler," he said, "I wish you to know that all of us here in Landsberg wish you a most happy and pleasant birthday."

I nodded graciously. "The staff's good wishes are acknowledged."

"Thank you, Herr Hitler. There is another matter." His folded hands were wrestling against each other. Perhaps one side of the old jailer was struggling to gain ascendancy over the other. In the humble there are many conflicts. The will is without the purpose that is to be discerned in the great.

"What is the nature of this other matter?"

"Visitors, Herr Hitler, there are two visitors." It was said very quickly.

"Two visitors? Who are these two visitors?"

"Herr Hitler might remember the lady with the beautiful daughter who came to visit in March or was it February. Herr Hitler might remember the daughter. She is a girl with long brown hair that hangs down to the shoulders and soft eyes like a little mountain cow, also beautiful straight legs and in the region of the chest . . ."

"I do remember her. It would seem that I am not the only one."

"Quite so, Herr Hitler." He had stopped just inside the door. Now he moved a little closer to it, a move clearly intended to facilitate sudden flight. "Shall I allow the ladies to come up?"

I raised a finger, beacon-like, to emphasize the point, but before I could speak the voice burst forth: "I gave no such command. I said no such thing. There was no such instruction."

The jailer's heels clicked together like Spanish castanets. "Yes, my Führer," he said. "I will send them away immediately." Before I could answer he was gone. I heard his feet clattering down the passage.

The cell door was open as it always is at this time of day. I went as far as the door and looked in the direction he had taken, but he was already gone and I could hear his feet on the stairs. No one had given him permission to run away like that. Another warder was standing close by. "What is the name of that fellow?" I asked.

He came smartly to attention. "The head warder, my Führer?" He was a brave intelligent young fellow. He would have looked good in the uniform of a storm trooper.

"Yes, the head warder."

"Schmundt, my Führer. Herr Schmundt."

I went back into my cell. Schmundt. This Schmundt had run off without consultation. He had dared to anticipate my wishes.

Geli had come and my will had stood firm. No more torment. No more indecision. No more fruit of my manhood dirtying the sheets. My will had remained pure, a perfect instrument of destiny.

I went back to the door of the cell and listened. Had he told her yet? Was she already leaving the building? Those eyes flashing at strangers in the street, and the straight legs, walking with sharp little steps that cause her buttocks to bounce like two rubber balls, the flat stomach that might press stomach to stomach, and the long hair, the small soft hands and narrow ankles, even old Schmundt could not

166

help but notice. . . and as for the region of the chest . . . if it had been music only Wagner could have composed it.

That fool Schmundt, no one told him to send them away. No one gave any such instruction. But the will, ah the will. Here was resolution. Schmundt, the idiot.

The eyes, of the eyes, of eyes, of eyes. Only in one of Uncle Anton's heifers have I seen such eyes. Such eyes are beyond price. Also the sweet heart-shaped face, a softness just like Mama possessed. Schmundt! I might yet kill him. The roundness of the upper arm and the buttocks more like two small cushions than rubber balls.

Suddenly the condition was upon me, ensnaring itself in the folds in my clothing, a thing of intense discomfort. She had probably left already, was walking down the road away from the prison, her buttocks moving from side to side with each step, the region of her chest bouncing a little. The condition ached with the intensity of its being. I ran to the door of the cell and cried out into the courtyard. "Schmundt!"

In a moment he had appeared below me, he and a few of his underlings. "Herr Hitler, what is it?" His hands were wrestling with each other again.

"Have they gone?"

"Forgive, Führer, but they will not go. They do not believe . . . I tried to explain. I will put the matter more clearly . . ." He started back toward his office.

"Schmundt!" The voice was a shaft of iron, nailing him to the spot. The condition, meanwhile, had become wedged in the iron railings as I pressed against them. I tried to wipe it free with a swift stroke of one hand.

"Heil Hitler," Schmundt shouted from the courtyard.

"Let them in," I said. The condition was still wedged fast.

"Immediately," the jailer cried. "Pille, you fool," he shouted to one of his men. "Let the women in."

"Wait." I stopped them again. "Just the girl."

"Pille, you worthless fool," the head warder shouted, "just the girl."

Holding onto the railing, I pushed myself away from it, plucking the condition free. Then I returned to my cell to prepare myself. How to position it was a problem. The trousers I was wearing were too small and my underwear was being washed. There are many such problems of organization in prison. I tried pushing it downwards but this was impossible. To achieve that would have necessitated a complete fracture. Twisting it to face either side caused a bump of obvious dimensions. Straight upwards was the best possibility, but even that gave me the appearance of someone with a broomstick in the front of his trousers. I was still struggling to get the condition into a suitable position when I heard footsteps outside the cell door. I sat down quickly on the bed and covered the problematical area with the cushion from my bunk.

Schmundt came in first, with Geli close behind. She was warmly robed with scarves and other woollen garments. The jailer gestured towards her and tried to smile.

"Here you are, Herr Hitler, just as you . . ."

"That's enough, Herr Schmundt. You may go."

"Of course, of course . . ." He backed towards the door, smiling and nodding, his head bobbing up and down like a ball on a string. As he left he closed the door behind him.

Geli remained, just inside the door. Her face was as gentle as a summer breeze, a very light breeze, just a stirring, no more than a kiss, a wafting of air. Her eyes were large, brown and round. I could see no more of her. All else was submerged in her woollen mufflings. I wanted to rise to meet her, but the condition was still an irresistible presence in the heart of the cushion. To have risen would have been to embrace catastrophe. "Geli," I said, "your beauty . . ."

"What about Mama?" she said. There was not the love in her voice that one would expect from a young girl for her dear Uncle Dolferl.

"Mama?" I asked. I used a sharper tone to my voice. It works very well in dealing with party members. "What have I to do with Mama?"

She pointed a finger at me, a beautiful, soft, subtly padded, gentle finger, but harbouring a nail that was sharply chiselled like a dagger. "Mama," she said. "Mama is downstairs and she is not allowed in. Why not?"

The question and the manner of its asking were a surprise to me. "Prison regulations," I said.

"No, Uncle Dolf. Herr Schmundt said it was your express wish that I should come alone. He said that Mama had to stay downstairs and now Mama is in his office and she is crying and it is not right." The brightness in her eyes flared as if there was fire within them.

168

Could she be no more than sixteen?

Beneath her wrappings I knew that there was a body of such sublime proportions that it could only belong to a woman of the German soil. Despite her angry manner the condition thrust into the cushion like a lance of Bismarck's cavalry. But it was imperative that I deal with her spirit of rebellion. "Remember who you are speaking to, young lady," I said. My chin was raised in a gesture of pride and grandeur.

Suddenly her manner changed. She cocked her head lightly to one side and looked at me out of the corners of her eyes. "What are you hiding under the cushion?" she asked.

"Cushion? What is this about a cushion?"

The one on your lap, Uncle Dolf. If you look down you will surely see it." I looked straight at her with a granite fixity of eye. "Look down, Uncle Dolf," she said. "You can't miss it."

"I look where I please. No one prescribes to such as I . . ."

But she interrupted me in the rudest most ill-mannered way, a way that did not show the breeding that I had expected to find in her. She darted forward and grabbed the pillow away. "Ah hah," she said. "Is it always like that?" Before I could answer she had slipped through the door and I heard her laughter echoing down the corridor as she fled. It was a thin tinkling sound, like a sleigh bell, but it could have been made by all the devils of hell, it was so charged with torment.

I lay down on my bunk with my face to the wall, covering myself with a blanket so that the cushion would not be needed again. But the condition remained. I tried consciously to think about other matters, the matters of the mind and the spirit, of the greatness of Germany and the role of the leader, also the qualities needed in statemanship and the purity of the Aryan race. But the condition was unaltered. I could hear Geli's laughter. I could see her brown eyes, also her straight legs and the region of her chest, the heaving of it: invitations to hell, every one of them. It was steel, adamant, diamond, an organ of such hardness and brittleness that a sudden shock might have shattered it beyond all hope of repair. Schmundt! It was all Schmundt's fault. When the time comes the little jailer will pay dearly. He will suffer for the Führer's humiliation.

Seized by an inspiration, I leapt from the bed to the door, holding the cushion close. The young warder was in the corridor again. "Schmundt," I cried. "Tell Schmundt I want them both to come to my cell, mother and daughter."

"Heil Hitler," he said. "Is there something wrong with the cushion?"

"Forget the cushion. Get the women."

He ran for the stairs and I returned to the cell. But the women did not come. They had already left. It seems that Schmundt, the fool, sent into the town to find them and have them return, but they had gone. I am not going to forgive this easily. Kriebel tried to come in and talk to me, so did Weber, but I instructed them to leave.

The condition had become a thing of pain. How long could it last without easing even a little? And what of the poor single organ, struggling alone, shivering with the effort of maintaining such a state? Could it rupture? Could one, one lone heroic organism, in a moment become nothing at all? Might the strain leave it limp and exhausted beyond all hope of recovery?

At one point there seemed to be an easing, a slight weakening, an infinitesimal softening, but unbidden Geli returned to my thoughts, looking at me slyly out of the corners of her eyes, and immediately the microscopic softness was gone and the hardness was again total. A memory returned. I had heard that a swift blow, carefully placed, causes immediate relaxation. It is like striking a man over the skull with a club. A swift blow and the offending object is rendered without consciousness, in a manner of speaking.

To inflict injury upon yourself in the call of duty, this is the ultimate proof of true courage. To strike the blow that lands upon one's own flesh, to suffer the pain caused by your own arm: here is true heroism.

I withdrew the cushion and looked upon the offending bulge. Naturally for the sake of dignity I did not remove the clothing. I raised my clenched fist above the bulge. Then brought it down in one quick precise stroke. There was a moment of flexing like the coiling of a steel spring, then it leapt again into the same inflexible state, quivering like a dagger thrown into the trunk of a tree, possibly more rigid than it had been before. I tried again. And again. Then from a different angle, and aimed to land lower down, but not so low as to cause possible damage to the singular source of my manhood. Nothing helped. It held firm.

I had given up the struggle and was lying on my bunk, my mind and soul immersed in the terrible despair that is at times the curse of the great when Schmundt entered through the open door. To say that he entered does not accurately describe his action. He stopped in the open doorway, pressing his back against one side of the door frame. "Herr Hitler . . ." he said. The fellow thinks that he can go back to calling me Herr Hitler any time that he chooses. "Another visitor . . ." he said. His left cheek was twitching like the tail of a cow trying to rid itself of a fly. "She assured me . . ." But he got no further. Martha wafted past him, surrounded by furs and feathers. Even in this weather her neckline revealed the upper areas of her bosom. Her black hair swung around her shoulders in long turbulent locks. Any chance the condition might have had of disappearing was irrevocably lost. "I explained to her . . ." Schmundt tried to say.

"That's enough, Herr Schmundt," Martha said. Her voice was friendly, almost intimate. She is an evil woman. "Go along," she said. "One must look to the future. No sense in angering Herr Hitler at this stage."

Schmundt went out and closed the door. Martha stood in the centre of the cell, looking at me. She had the same little smile around her eyes and the same twist of wickedness along her mouth. "You did not expect to see me again. Did you, Adolf?" Her flesh was white, snow white, milk white, better yet it was Aryan white. Her legs swelled slowly from the ankles to soft and fleshy calves, beyond which there were knees, thighs even, and hips. The mind could extend no further. Even the imagination of genius has limits. "You are staring at me very strangely, Adolf. Is something wrong? I know you didn't expect to see me, but I do turn up every few years, you know. What are you doing with that little cushion." I clung more tightly to the cushion than before, my eyes exploring this woman who has in the past exercised such evil power over one such as I.

Her eyes were narrow, hiding some part of her spirit, or some part of her intentions, but letting the poor victim, myself, know that she was hiding something. Her eyelids closed a little further and her eyelashes swept downwards like the tail of a peacock I saw at the zoo in the Prater. She took a deep breath and her bosom rose like a wave swelling before it breaks.

I threw the cushion aside and leapt to my feet. Martha's eyes widened as they found the spot that I had been hiding, but before she could speak I was upon her. I heard her voice in my ear. "You can't be serious, Adolf. This can't be real. Oh, oh, oh. Adolf, you're not

171

going to let me down again, are you? You can't do this then let me down again, you hear . . . Oh, Adolf, I don't believe it. Have you been sick. Oh! Adolf, you devil. You've changed. All right, just don't let me . . . oh . . . just don't . . . let me down. Oh, the floor is cold. We could have at least used the blanket. Now careful, don't lose it. See you don't. Hold on. Oh, oh . . . no preparation, just straight . . . ah, I don't . . . mind . . . some might, but . . . me . . . ah . . . Adolf, you devil . . . ah . . ."

A trap. Of course it was a trap. My manhood, my unconquerable masculinity has been taken away from me. In a moment it was gone, sucked into the lugubrious depths within Martha. All strength, all will, all genius had been drained away in one mighty quaking extrusion. I felt the weakness assaulting me, wave upon wave, a black cloud enclosing me, cutting away consciousness . . . Through the fog that was covering my soul I heard Martha's voice. "Adolf, you fool, must you always be like this?"

When my senses returned I was lying on my back on the floor and Martha was kneeling next to me. For the first time I saw ordinary human pity, such as one finds in all people, present in her face. "Adolf," she said, "are you all right. You poor brave little fellow. I never realized. I tried to return your trousers to their normal position. Oh, Adolf, the Hochstetter is quite a respectable organ, but only one peanut. My poor Adolf . . ."

May 23rd. The National Socialist Freedom Movement! How can Ludendorff do this to me? First they have a new name, soon it might be a new party. The party must be dormant, I said to Rosenberg, but no, they are compelled to win thirty-two seats in the National Assembly. And who won them the seats? Adolf Hitler won the seats with wonderful oratory during his trial. And who takes the credit? Ludendorff takes the credit while I suffer in prison. Treachery, treachery.

June 6th, 1924. It is of no consequence that I sometimes miss a day or two. This is the record of the most illuminated moments, perhaps a basis for future history, a catalogue of great thoughts, an inspiration to unborn generations. It is beyond imagining that I might write anything as trivial as a diary.

July 1st. Today I asked Gutenberg if he is sure that the venerea disease will not return. He assured me that as long as I eat only vegetables there is no danger at all. Every day he takes the meat from my plate, also his own, and wraps it in his handkerchief to dispose of it. A fine man, a truly fine man.

August 6th. I walked in the garden with Emil today. "That Geli," he said, "will she come back again?"
  "How am I to know such a thing?"
  "I only wondered if you might know, my Führer. She is such a sweet and innocent child."
  "Clearly," I said.

August 15th. The whole thing is Hess's idea. I personally want nothing to do with it. A book about my life and thoughts is something that others should do. It should be the work of many interested parties. It would be more fitting for me to stand aside and let others compose such a volume. Let history speak above the deafening thunder of my silence.

September 3rd. Perhaps a small role overseeing Hess's work on this book will be in order. After all Hess can surely not know my thoughts better than I do.

September 6th. My struggle, he calls it. He has no business calling it his struggle. What about my struggle? Who is it who is doing the struggling anyway?

September 7th. Hess says he has no objections to the book being about my struggle instead of his. I explained that his struggle was really of very minute proportions when compared to mine. He agreed of course. I have taken the pages he has done for careful checking.

September 14th. My little Hesserl, he is such a sweet soul. The book evokes my spirit in an entirely accurate way, far-sighted and clear-thinking, especially as regards the nuisance value of minority groups, communists and the inherent virtues of true Germanic stock.

September 18th. My little Hesserl is doing good work.

September 21st. Perhaps a few authentic thoughts are necessary. A few notes from which Hess can work might be in order. I will write down a few and pass them on. My little Hesserl will be so pleased.

September 30th. This book is all very well. Hess is doing his best, but the style ... the style. ... If I was writing it myself how different it would be. What elegance of prose, what memorable turns of phrase, what music would flow from the page. What a pity that Hess is not a better writer.

October 3rd. He is doing his best. There is no question about that. One cannot blame a man for trying. It is not his fault that he does not have my clarity of mind, or my way with words. He is certainly working hard at his task.

October 4th. Hard work is all very well. The greatness of the German people was built upon hard work. But the genius is lacking. What kind of struggle am I to suppose is going to come out of this? A tired second-hand sort of struggle, that is the kind of struggle. . .

October 7th. I have decided to take over some of Hess's duties, regarding the book. I will do the actual writing, also the thinking. I am not cutting him out though. This was my little Hesserl's idea. I am not a man for taking the credit that is due to others. There is still plenty for him to do, a little proof-reading, a little typing, that sort of thing. Oh no, I am a fair and just person.

October 9th. The book is looking better already. Such form, such unity of thought. If only I could see now what later generations will think of it . . .

Editor's note: At this point the bottom of the manuscript page had been torn away and the last few pages of Volume 8 lost. Volume 9 is also missing.

W.S.I

VOLUME X

May 3rd, 1928. The craftsman hones and polishes the sword until the steel gleams, keen and unblemished. The artist studies his work until every line and every tint is perfect. The writer prunes and trims his work until no excessive word remains.

With the orator intuition alone will never be enough. The great orator must attend to every detail. Only then is the mass easily bent to his will. Only then is submission total. The mass is not a person or even many persons. It is an animal, a creature without reason, a woman.

I have attended to every detail. I have deepened and strengthened my voice, squared my shoulders, changed the style of my hair and moustache until they created the most forceful image of leadership in the mind of the mass. But it is in the eyes that no grooming is possible. What is in the soul is to be seen in the eyes. It is in the eyes that vision is reflected. It is here that the soul's fire burns.

May 7th. The mass falls to the surest, the possessor of the greatest measure of inner certainty. It has no critical faculty, no rational inclination. It seeks to align itself with the man of power. It has no uncertainties and its hopes are of the simplest sort. It is as different from its leader as a mob is from a scholar. It seeks only strength and its only emotion is fear. It tolerates nothing that is in any way different to itself and no one that stands apart from itself.

He who would rule the mass must needs understand these things. He must know that it is only by its own fear that it will be subdued. He must know too that there is no room for the minority. To accommodate the outsider is a weakness the mass will never forgive. The true leader cannot even consider such a thing. The stranger should rather be purged, cut out, severed from the nation. And for this no harshness can be too great. Here the ultimate strength of spirit is needed.

The mass falls to the surest, and who is more sure than I?

May 9th. An election in less than two weeks. What a wonderful thing to be possessed of such certainty.

May 11th. Meeting after meeting, crowd after crowd, one no different to that which has gone before or to that which is to follow. I see the same eager empty faces, without thought or even memory, seeking only the moment of national ecstacy, wanting only that I should show them the way, that I should command them to follow. All that is needed is for me to decide which face it is that will seduce them most easily. Is it the national? Is it the sentimental? Could it be the social? Whichever they want I gladly give. All that I ask in return is that they follow without question.

May 12th. Logic plays no part. It is mystery and magic that compels. It is the power of the strong over the weak. It is the ancient tie of German to German, of spirit to spirit. It speaks through eyes and voice. It speaks through the vital forces that connect all true German souls to mine. It cannot be explained by science and it cannot be comprehended by him who is not the true German. It is a magic beyond their understanding and a destruction beyond their resisting.

There are those among my enemies who say that I am possessed of a deep insanity. They say that my actions are those of a madman. To them I say, "If I am mad, then the nation too possesses the madness."

May 21st, 1928. It cannot be. Such a thing cannot be. I asked Göring, how such a thing could be and he said, "My Führer, it cannot be." This is exactly what I feel.

I took pale and feeble Albert Rosenberg by the lapels and fixed my eyes upon his. "How? How? How?" I asked.

He became paler still and spoke so softly that I could scarcely hear him. "I do not believe it myself," he said.

I asked Goebbels and he said I should seek the blame with Strasser. As for Strasser, he said the blame must surely lie with Goebbels. Hanfstaengl said that that was life and Hess said that such a thing is a blot upon the nation.

How can such a thing be? I had taken every precaution. My style of hair, my moustache, the deepening of my voice, also the magic, the destiny and leadership. Nothing was left to chance. And yet we lost support in the election.

Not only is the mass without logic and irrational, it is also fickle, effeminate, cowardly, weak, vaccilating, treasonous and without true patriotism.

At least Goebbels had been returned to the Reichstag. For little Joseph it is a victory. I hope that he is happy in that silly debating chamber without his Führer.

May 22nd. What more could I have done? I looked the men in the eye as one man to another. I kissed the hands of the women. I even kissed the babies. I said to the communists, "Welcome workers, we are all socialists here . . ." I told them about my world vision. I explained to them that they need space to live and I will get it for them.

All this and what happens? They vote for the Social Democrats.

June 1st, 1928. The language of the body. This is what I lack. The body too can speak.

What would I do without my sweet Emil. Tonight he brought to me a party member by the name of Jan-Erik Genscher. This man is a seer. He looks into the future as easily as others look at the past. He looks deep into the soul of each one he meets.

As soon as he was introduced to me he said, "My Führer, I see that a glorious future awaits you. I see also the spirit of the prophet within you. I see the power of an orator of all orators." He was holding both of my hands clasped together in his. "But the body language," he said. "The body language does not speak at all."

From tomorrow he will be instructing me in this art. And the price he charges is truly reasonable. After all what is a few thousand marks to the party so that its Führer may learn the language of the body.

June 6th. Such a thing as this election can never be allowed to happen again. Now to the sweetness of my oratory is added the eloquence of an outstretched hand, the power of a clenched fist, the thrust of a belligerent chin. The language of the body will join the language of the voice. Now nothing can stop me.

June 16th. I am disgusted to learn that prostitutes, women of the night, such as Martha, understand the language of the body. Jan-Erik says their understanding is intuitive. He says they employ it as surely as if they had studied it for years.

I have doubts about the use of this form of language. It seems hardly to be a suitable medium for the use of a country's Führer. I shall have to give thought to the matter.

June 17th. I questioned Genscher further. This body language is employed intuitively, not only by prostitutes, but by other decadent individuals, actors and actresses, certain reactionary politicians, even Italian opera singers.

I asked about Bismarck, regarding the language of the body. "Did he use it?" I asked.

Jan-Erick Genscher shrugged. "I cannot say. Regarding Bismarck, it is impossible to say. However Enrico Caruso employs the language of the body with great elegance. Gertrude Lawrence also is an expert."

I shall have to be careful in my dealings with this Genscher.

June 20th. Enough of this body language. From now on I will appeal to the primitive and the uncivilized in the mob. This is the common denominator that holds them together. Gone is the rational word.

June 27th, 1928. Today is the happiest day of my life. At last I have a home of my own, a splendid little villa in the Obersalzberg. I have called it Haus Wachenveldt. Now I can flee from Munich when the torments of leadership become too great to bear.

Alone I wander along the mountain paths, bringing my inspiration from the same fountain as Wagner drew his. The wells of my genius will again brim to overflowing.

Also there is the matter of Geli.

July 1st. The important thing is to write the letter. Simply say, my dear Angela, it has come to my attention that your circumstances are difficult at the moment, largely because that worthless husband of yours did not provide suitably for you while he was alive. How much less is he capable of so doing now that he is ...

No. I should approach the matter without guile. A simple request is all that is required. My dear Angela, I should say, it is my brotherly duty to see that your needs are not neglected. For this reason I would like you to be my housekeeper at Obersalzberg. Bring Geli. The mountain air will do her good.

But perhaps Geli will be somewhere else. She wants to be a singer. She might be attending a college for opera singers.

My letter should say, dear Angela, your well-being is always uppermost in my mind, but so is Geli's. For this reason my offer must be conditional upon Geli coming with you.

Angela should also be told that I am now the head of the house. Poor Alois simply is of no importance. Perhaps I should write, Dear Angela, as the head of the family I require that you report to Obersalzberg to take up your new duties as my housekeeper. See that Geli accompanies you. Perhaps I should say that.

But what if Geli does not come?

July 3rd. This invitation is in the best interests of you both, is what the letter should say.

July 4th. And what of Germany? How can her future Führer survive if his own physical needs are neglected? And your charming daughter Geli is supremely well-equipped for the task . . .

No.

July 7th. I have asked Emil's advice on the matter. At first he did not seem to know to whom I was referring. But with a little help from myself he did remember her. Of course there is no reason he should have remembered her. She was simply a child who visited me while we were in Landsberg.

"Yes," he said "the one with the long brown hair and the narrow waist, also the legs, and such eyes . . . She must certainly come," he said. "The mountain air will be good for her. Also the old lady. There is no objection to the old lady coming."

July 8th. Emil has suggested that he go to Linz to approach the subject tactfully with Angela herself. He says that it will help if he speaks to her and lists all the advantages. Such a visit will also offer him the opportunity to persuade Geli, if persuasion is necessary.

Emil is a true friend. I wonder what method he intends using in order to persuade her.

July 11th. She is coming. My sweet Geli is coming, the dear child.

And Emil, what a friend he is. To go to Linz himself, simply

179

because he knows that this is important to his Führer, this is self-sacrifice. Such a man, one who places the cause of the nation above his own needs, such a one should be rewarded. Perhaps I will make him my secretary.

July 12th. Before the month is over I will have them safely installed in the Obersalzberg. It will be easy to slip away for a night or two. Also for the days in between.

The day draws closer. But what if a disgrace occurs, if the condition again asserts itself when next I see Geli? It is true that my will is even stronger now than it was then. It is also true that my mind is more than ever occupied by questions of national importance, and matters of the spirit. But what if there is a disgrace?

July 18th. I should discuss the matter with Emil. He will surely know. He is a man of great experience in the ways of women. He could advise me of some way in which the quickness might be controlled. Such a condition should only ensue when circumstances are suitable.

But to discuss it with Emil is impossible. A leader should never be humiliated in front of his men. They wanted me to join them in the playing of games while I was in Landsberg. But how could I allow myself to be beaten by my inferiors?

July 25th. Will power is all very well and mine is superhuman, but the day draws close and I had better speak to Emil.

July 26th. On the other hand he might not know a way.

July 27th. Today at my office I spoke to Emil. At first he did not seem to understand.

"But, my Führer," he said, "such a condition is desirable if one has a young lady in a suitable place and she might also be experiencing the same sort of feeling, even if she is one's niece . . ."

I silenced him with a word, and with great difficulty I explained the matter further, until eventually he seemed to understand. He looked at me with eyes that were round with the surprise he was feeling. "But, my Führer," he said, "such a thing is not a problem. When such a condition cannot be attained, this is a problem. If such a condition is attained too often or too soon it only shows the great

180

extent of my Führer's virility, which is something that will come as no surprise to any of his followers. Heil Hitler! And to get rid of it is the simplest matter of all. It only requires insertion . . ."

Again, with a word I stopped him. It was clear that he had not yet understood the extent of the complexities. With even greater difficulty than before I told him of the incidents that occurred in prison when Geli came to visit me. For just an instant I thought that I saw the beginning of amusement in Emil's face, but of course such disrespect could not be. When I looked more closely it was clear that I had been mistaken. "My Führer, this is a most unusual problem. I have never heard of this before and I have heard of almost everything with regard to affairs of this nature."

"But something must be done," I said.

"Of course," Emil said. "It would not do if we had a scandal. . ."

"It cannot be," I said.

"Especially in a public place. If the problem is obvious and . . ."

"Control," I said, "A measure of control . . ."

"Essential," Emil said. "If distress was caused to the young lady and she screamed, and one never can tell with young ladies. Their behaviour is usually erratic. Or if laughter was provoked in her and. . ."

"Let us not speculate any further," I said with great restraint. "I had thought that you might have a solution. Such speculation is without purpose. I had thought a man of your experience. . ."

At this point two SA officers who had been standing guard at the door, opened it quickly and rushed into the room. "Heil Hitler," one of them said. "Is everything in order, my Führer?"

"Of course," I said, the strength of my cold blue eyes fixed upon him.

"Excuse me, my Führer but we heard the shouting and. . ."

"Everything is in order. Return to your posts."

After they had left my attention returned to Emil. It returned to him sharply. He looked at me for a moment and then away, biting on his lip probably because of the anguish he felt at failing his leader. 'Well, there is something that they give you in prison. They didn't give it to us in Landsberg, but in ordinary prison . . ."

"You were in prison?"

"For a very short time, my Führer, just a few days really, hardly any time at all."

181

"For what?"

"A small matter, a thing of almost no significance . . . My Führer has experience of the sort of bourgeois attitudes one encounters in the courts. They are people without vision . . ."

"The name?" I said.

"The name, my Führer? Ravensbrück . . ."

"No, my Emil, what was it they gave you in the prison?"

"It is called saltpetre and it is given so that prisoners will not set upon each other or the guards or cooks or the prison psychiatrist for the relief of . . ."

"I understand why it is given," I said patiently. "How is it administered, by massage or simply poured on or . . ."

"With a spoon."

"With a spoon? How can it be applied with a spoon?"

"The saltpetre is placed in the spoon and the contents are then poured down the throat, and for a while all such feeling disappears, even in myself, and I can tell my Führer that in me such feeling is prodigious."

"Purchase a supply immediately," I said.

"Of course, my Führer."

August 1st. They are there. I met them at the station this morning personally in my red Mercedes and took them to the Obersalzberg. Before going I administered the saltpetre and as a result no scandal occurred. I have complete confidence that without it there would also not have been a scandal.

But, seeing Geli again, and watching her walk, the roundness of her buttocks like two kittens under a blanket and her bosom rising like bellows: seeing her in such a way again, perhaps the saltpetre was necessary.

I shall easily be able to make a brief visit and be back in Munich by mid morning. Geli blushed as soon as she saw Emil. Such innocence. Charming.

August 7th. This matter is quite ridiculous. Why should a twenty year old girl share her mother's bedroom It is true that they are new in Obersalzberg, but for a girl of her age to share her mother's bedroom is ridiculous beyond words.

August 9th. Today I went especially to visit Angela in order to put the matter clearly. "Angela," I said, "the house is large. There is no shortage of rooms. You may certainly have one for yourself and another for Geli. What manner of man do you consider me that I should not allow my niece her own room?"

"Thank you, Adolf," she said, "you are kindness itself."

At least that is sorted out. Now Geli will have her own room.

August 10th. I cannot understand the workings of my sister's mind. A room is made vacant. All is in order. The master of the house himself says, "Here is the room. Be happy in it." But still they share a room. This is extreme foolishness. My generosity is being rejected as if it was a thing of no value.

And saltpetre? Are there long term effects after the taking of so many doses?

August 11th. "And the saltpetre? What of the saltpetre?" I asked Emil.

"It can also be sprinkled on the food," he said, "until this matter of the bedrooms is straightened out."

August 12th. "An order," Emil said today. "An order must be issued. After all the old lady is only the housekeeper and my Führer is the master of the house. An order must be issued saying, the spare bedroom is for the girl. Her presence is required in the bed."

August 16th. I returned from Obersalzberg this morning. Angela was in the kitchen, peeling potatoes, when I approached her. "Angela," I said, "this problem regarding the bedrooms ..."

She left the potatoes and came towards me, smiling in a friendly manner. "My little Adolphus," she said. It was a surprise to hear her address me in this way. It is many years since I have heard it. "My sweet Adolphus, you are so kind to Geli and me. I do not know how to express my thanks." She looked back over her shoulder at the stove. "But now the rice is boiling over," she said, "and I must attend to it. We will talk again later."

The rice did not seem to be boiling over, but of course I am not knowledgeable regarding cooking. No doubt it was boiling over.

August 20th. I have decided to form a new troop, the *Schutzstaffel.* We will call it the SS. Their duty will be to protect their Führer. It can easily happen that the SA becomes too strong. There is no need to involve my faithful Ernst in this matter.

November, 1928. Such a cold winter. I am alone and Geli sleeps in her mother's bedroom. Soon there will be snow at Berchtesgaden and the cold will be enough to freeze the blood in a man's veins.

We held a successful rally in Berlin. At last our influence in the north grows. The mass comes to hear and recognizes its master and submits. It cannot be otherwise.

But this cold. There is a fire in my room, but nothing dissipates the cold.

All is not well within me. That Gutenberg was a fraud. I have kept exactly to the vegetarian diet since I was in Landsberg, but the disease remains. When I am alone in the world of my thoughts, and my only conversation is the dialogue with the voice: at such a time I feel it within me. I feel it reaching upwards from the affected area into every part of my body.

I have been to see Doctor Pittinger, but he says there is nothing wrong. German medicine is in a state of decay. When we come to power this too will have to be remedied. When the Führer approaches a doctor for relief of the venereal disease that is killing him, cannot have him reply that there is no disease. I have not forgotten little Joseph Goebbels's idea regarding these concentration camps of British invention. They will be useful in time to come. Of course the British are of Aryan stock. There is no hiding of good breeding.

But this winter. If only the cold were less intense.

March, 1929. We are the National Socialist German Workers' Party and we never forget that we are also socialists. We are for the German worker. Did I not tell them that in Berlin, and in Nuremberg? In the new Germany I personally will make the decisions and the worker will have precisely the same rights as everyone else. Of course the Poles, Czechs and such cannot be seen as workers. Work is alien to their nature.

Nevertheless, we are also moderates. There is no sense in ignoring the capitalists, just because you are a socialist. For this reason I have been holding confidential talks with the great men of capital explaining the system by which contracts will be awarded after we have come to power, also the way in which our friends will be treated, and by contrast the way we will treat our enemies.

This broadminded programme has had as its result a great improvement in the party's financial position. There is the new party headquarters on Briennerstrasse, also my apartment which covers one entire floor in 16 Prinzregentplatz, the villa at Berchtesgaden and of course the red Mercedes. In due course there will be state funds, but in the meantime the needs of the moment must be attended.

April 20th, 1929. Tonight I sleep in my bed in Berchtesgaden, under circumstances in which destiny has once again taken a firm grip. I brought Emil and Amman with me for my birthday celebration. I chose to hold only a small gathering with a few beloved colleagues. I can imagine the sort of celebration the party would have arranged for the Führer's fortieth birthday, but I naturally turn aside from such ostentation.

It was while we were gathered in the parlour, a small and joyous group, that this matter of singular significance occurred. Angela had put candles on my cake, one for each year since I became leader of the party. Max Amman had made a speech in which he spoke about our comradeship during the war, and Emil had sung *O Tannenbaum,* reaching all the high notes in a hopeless falsetto.

Everything was perfect. We were all smiling and friendly when Geli added her piece of goodwill to the party. "Uncle Dolf," she said, "I also have a surprise for you." She had risen to her feet before speaking and all eyes were directed at her.

I rose too and spread my arms wide. "Just your presence gives me pleasure enough, my dear child," I said. "And of course the presence of your dear mother."

"Uncle Dolf, I have decided to study singing in Munich."

"So?" I said. This was a matter of great interest. Angela would have to remain at Berchtesgaden if Geli came to live in a hostel in Munich.

"So?" Angela said, but the sound of her saying it was different to the sound of my saying it.

"So?" Emil said and the sound of his saying it was more like mine than Angela's, as if the breath had been knocked out of him.

"Of course," I said, "there are fine hostels. . ."

"Hostels, Uncle Dolf?" In a moment she looked so sad and unbelieving that I could not bear it. "I thought my Uncle Dolf might have a room in his beautiful new apartment for his little Geli . . ."

What a wave of guilt swept over me. How could I have been so thoughtless? The poor child was coming to me at last and I had almost turned her away. "My child . . . certainly . . . naturally . . ."

"Let us not have naturally," Angela said. "There is too much of naturally around here already. Geli, this is the first I hear of this. Why suddenly studies in singing? Why does your mother not hear first?"

"Oh, Mama," she said. She was smiling out of the corners of her eyes at me while she spoke. "I just thought I would tell Mama and Uncle Dolf at the same time. What is to be found wrong with that?"

"And when is this to take place, if I may ask?"

"Tomorrow. I return to Munich with Uncle Dolf tomorrow, if Uncle Dolf doesn't mind. Do you, Uncle Dolf?"

"Well, naturally, naturally . . ."

"Adolf," Angela screamed, "you stop this about naturally. And you, Geli, now you've spoilt the whole party. Why? Why? Your mother asks why?"

"Because I want to complete my studies. Also I want my own bedroom and my own bed."

"Your own bed? And what are you going to be doing in it?"

There was a moment of silence while Angela looked from one face in the room to the next. I was Emil who spoke. "Sleeping?" he suggested.

"Sleeping," I said.

Geli nodded firmly. "Sleeping."

I turned to look at Emil and was in time to see his nose twitch in the manner that it would twitch when hunting girls in the Munich cafés. This did not seem to be a suitable time for such twitching.

May 5th. Sleeping! That is all she does in that bed. Two weeks she has been here now and the door is locked every night. Oh, she is so sweet to her uncle Dolf. She smiles, she flaps up and down her eyelids. She says, Oh my dear Uncle Dolf, and, my kind Uncle Dolf, and, I love my Uncle Dolf. But at night when the day's work is over and all is quiet, the party members have gone and there is a little stillness, a time for human warmth and touching and holding tight, also feeling

186

exploring and the knowing of each other: at such times when only the sound of an occasional car can be heard from the road or perhaps the hooves of the horse that pulls the milk wagon, or the sound that the doves make, very softly, where they nest under the roof, perhaps a door opening and closing in the distance, a few footsteps of some young loafer on his way home after seducing some equally stupid slut: at such a time when everything is ripe for one such as Geli to be with her uncle Dolf, perhaps caressing and holding and causing the darkness to retreat: at such a time instead she is in bed and the door is locked.

May 7th. Emil says that Geli is unhappy. He says that perhaps he should move into the apartment too. In this way he would serve the purposes both of guarding his Führer and perhaps amusing the girl. He says that an escort is needed, someone who can be trusted just so that the girl does not go mad. He says that being confined to the apartment is not suiting her personality well.

"Would you have me hand this innocent child over to some seducer, some adventurer, some swindler?" I asked.

"No, my Führer," he said. "For this reason someone trustworthy is needed, someone who has the girl's interests at heart, someone like myself."

I am giving this matter consideration.

May 16th, 1929. She has her studies. Once a week I take her either to the theatre or to a restaurant. Once a month I go shopping with her, allowing a generous amount for her clothing which is something all young girls like, and next year I will allow her to go to the Shrovetide ball if I can find a suitable chaperone.

Other than that she has her Uncle Dolf and a visit to her mother every month or so. What more could a young girl want?

May 20th. If this is what she wants, if hardness of heart is all she will show to her sweet Uncle Dolferl, then I too can be hard of heart. This is not in my nature, but I can react to ill will, if I must. If she thinks I am going to allow her to wander around Munich without an escort of whom I approve, no, two escorts of whom I approve (one to take note of the activities of the other): if she thinks that, she is completely mistaken. Her dear Uncle Dolferl thinks too highly of her to allow

187

her to be seduced by any passing vagabond.

June 1st. Today we went for a walk in the park, Geli and I. It was pleasant weather and the grass was soft underfoot. The trees were dense with green and Geli's eyes were unfathomable with reflections and glowing shafts and deepness upon deepness. We sat down on a bench near the fountain and she said, "Can we not be happy, Uncle Dolf?"

"Of course, my child," I said gently, nodding with the wisdom of experience and compassion.

"But can we not be happy now?" she said. She is a very stubborn child.

"But we are happy, my Geli," I said. "Look at the world. Look at the June sunshine. Look at the ripples on the water."

"I see them Uncle Dolf. The sunshine looks happy and so do the ripples on the pond. The trees look happy and even the moss on the old church's bell tower. They all look happy. But we are not happy, Uncle Dolf, you and I. Why are we not happy?"

June 6th. I have visited a Doctor Schwanenvelder, regarding the disease. He is a party member, a man of intelligence. "My Führer, I might be wrong," he said, "but there is no sign of the disease you mention."

"Perhaps it is still dormant," I said.

"Perhaps. But if it is dormant, my Führer would feel nothing. The region in which the problem occurs, was there an accident or has it always been so?"

I looked directly at him "Nothing abnormal is there?"

"Of course not, my Führer. Abnormal is not a word that I would use in this context. Unusual perhaps, but abnormal ... not that normality is such a wonderful state. My Führer is super-normal one might say, in the sense ..."

"There has been no accident," I said.

"Ah," he said. "My Führer, there is a time in the life of every man even the great, perhaps especially the great, when outside help is needed, for the calming of the soul, so to speak."

I fixed the intensity of my stare upon this Schwanenvelder, a small man, considerably shorter than I, and without the impressive width of shoulder that I possess. "Speak plainly, Herr Doctor," I said.

188

"A psychiatrist is sometimes needful, even for the most brilliant. There is in Vienna a Herr Doctor Freud, a man of unparalleled excellence."

"This Herr Doctor Freud. I believe he is a Jew."

"A small blemish," this Schwanenvelder said," in an otherwise impressive character."

June 8th. There is no need, no need at all. Let them bring their psychiatrists to those who need them. As for this Doctor Freud he had better not think that Vienna is beyond my reach.

August 3rd. I have discovered what it is that is needed. I have considered the matter and after much deliberation I have come to the logical conclusion. The problem is one of pathology. My body is being attacked by an evil force and to counteract this a positive force is needed. Where evil now seeks to be dominant within my body, the opposite is needed.

And what could be more opposite to the disease that slowly devours me than Geli herself.

Last night I waited until she had entered her bedroom. I heard the door close. I came quietly into the passage and could hear her moving around her room. I could hear the gentle movement of clothing, one garment rubbing against another as she undressed. I could see the thin blade of light striking through the darkness from below the door. Then her dressing-table stool moved and immediately I imagined her sitting before the mirror, combing her curling brown hair as it hung in a disarray of locks around her head. For a long time I heard nothing and I was sure that she must already be in bed, but then I heard her move again, the springs of the bed creaking, and the light went out.

I crept slowly closer. My hand reached out and rested lightly on the door handle. Would it be locked? To turn the handle and discover this for myself was a greater act of courage than any that I have ever before accomplished. Compared to this the braving of the French shelling in the trenches was nothing. Marching against von Kahr's guns in our heroic *Putsch* was a small thing, not even worthy of mention.

I turned the handle and the door opened soundlessly. With a quick but silent tread I stepped into the room and waited. Listening carefully I could hear Geli's breath racing. "Uncle Dolf?" her voice came to me out of the darkness.

"Geli" My own voice croaked hoarsely.

"Uncle Dolf, your breathing sounds like a steam engine. Is something wrong?"

Uncertainly in the darkness, the outline of her form was visible beneath the blankets. Ever since Geli had come to stay with me in Munich I had not used the saltpetre. Now I stood just one step inside her bedroom door and waited for the condition to appear. Clearly the condition is needed before any action of a certain nature can be undertaken.

Her form made smooth mounds beneath the blanket. I could see this in the faint light entering the room through the window. Her hair was a dark patch on the white pillow, loose and scattered. The smoothness of her skin and her softness beneath the touch of my hand were real, as if I was already next to her on the bed, between the smoothness of the sheets, my hands reaching out. But the condition would not appear.

What would the expression of her face be and the sound of her voice? Would she say anything at that moment? Would there be gasps or groans? And the power that would be mine when she yielded to my will, the stronger conquering the weaker, male strength exhilarating in female submission. On the previous occasions with Martha the circumstances had been unfortunate and I was not aware of her sounds or the look on her face. But Geli, what tender ecstacy, what soft reception of my savage assault.

But still there was no condition.

The light came on. Geli was sitting up in bed. The frown on her face could have been of anger. "Uncle Dolf, what are you doing?"

"Geli." The one word held within it the passion of all my genius.

"No, Uncle Dolf, I thought that by this time it was clear that I have no intention of becoming your mistress. I thought that by this time it was clear beyond all doubting."

"Geli." Now the word carried the anguish of a thousand unfulfilled desires.

"No, Uncle Dolf, no."

"But you are a young woman . . ." I appealed to her reason ". . . in need of a . . ."

"In need of a young man," Geli said. It was impossible to imagine.

but I thought I heard the sound of bitterness in her voice. "Instead all I have is a prison . . ."

"Geli, how can you say . . ."

"A prison, a prison, a prison. I said it three times."

There is a time when womanly resistance must be overcome by strength. The female need to be dominated, crushed by her mate, must be accommodated. The muscles of my body tensed for the moment when I would thrust myself upon her, pressing home my advantage. But there was still no condition. And without the condition such an assault would become a thing for mockery. Concentration. Concentration of the will was what was needed. Only with concentration . . .

"Uncle Adolf? Here I am. You have not forgotten me, have you?" Geli was saying something that I did not altogether follow. The intensity of my concentration removed her words from my mind. She spoke again and her voice continued, coming to me from afar, a soft murmur, jumbled and unintelligible. The concentration was intense, but the condition was absent, a limp appendage hanging sadly earthwards.

Geli was standing in front of me, looking into my face. "Uncle Adolf? Is something wrong?"

"No, no . . ."

She reached up and touched my face with her hands. "My poor Uncle Dolferl, you are sick. Something is wrong. Why did you not say so? And I suspected you . . . oh. . ." She took my arm and led me out of the room and down the passage towards the kitchen. "A little coffee and a little schnapps and you will feel much better. But why did you not tell me? You should have said something."

October. It is as well. A leader's energies must be directed towards the battle of his life. To waste them on a mere empty-headed child would be a criminal act. It is better so.

But it is right that I direct her activities and apply a small measure of discipline to her life. In later years she will thank me.

October 13th. She may yet change. With a little more experience of life, with growing maturity . . . She is not yet ready. She is not fit for the task of being mistress to the leader of her people. At this age maturity comes quickly. Perhaps in a year, possibly sooner, perhaps even a month.

October 26th. Far-sightedness is very important in a leader. I can see now that I need to plan for the day when Geli will be mine. She is mine already, of course, but I must plan for the day in which she will be mine in that sense in which she is not yet mine.

In this respect a certain strategy is needed with regard to social relations. There are those who are unable to see the clear differences between common incest and the passion of a great leader for his niece. To argue with such people is futile. Bourgeois mediocrity would have us believe that there must be something wrong with a forty year old man who is not married. How are they to know that all of my energy is directed towards my life's work?

To these problems a common approach will suffice. A woman is needed, a young woman who can be seen by all to be my mistress. Such a one will stop all unnecessary talk.

A girl who is perfectly suited to the task works in Heinrich Hoffman's shop. She is young, probably twenty or thereabouts, pretty but not extravagantly so, and lacking in any real intelligence. For my purposes this is an important attribute. Naturallly she is very impressed with me. Tomorrow I shall approach her to attend the theatre with me. Her name is Eva Braun.

November 3rd. A pleasant enough girl, this young Eva. After the theatre she said that she had never been inside my apartment and would be most interested to see how someone like myself lived. Such a thing did not seem necessary to me. There were a number of leading party members at the theatre and we were seen by all of them. This is enough for the time being. I took her home.

December 1st, 1929, Today I discussed a matter of moderate importance with Emil. I explained that Geli was not yet ready for matters of a carnal nature.

"What sort of nature?" he asked.

"A carnal nature. She is not yet ready for matters of the body."

My poor Emil is not a man of very quick mind or very great intelligence. He looked puzzled for more than just a moment. Then he smiled. "I understand. She is not ready for love. I am sure that this is true." He nodded seriously. "After all she is little more than a child.

"Quite so. For this reason, my Emil, something else is needed."

"Something instead of love? There is nothing like it, my Führer."

At times his understanding is exceedingly slow. "No," I said. "Something to replace Geli, in a manner of speaking."

"Another niece?"

"Another woman."

"My Führer wants a woman?"

"Just so, my Emil," I said carelessly, glancing away as I said it. It is important not to appear too eager in such matters.

"I will give it my immediate attention," Emil said quickly. "Also I think Geli is not of my Führer's stature in such matters. She is no more than a girl. Perhaps a woman of greater knowledge and experience would be more appropriate. It is a question of stature."

This is something to consider. It is pleasing for a leader to have his followers look to his interests in this way. "See to it," I said.

"Heil Hitler," Emil said.

December 3rd. Employing great subtlety, I questioned Emil regarding progress that he might have made with respect to a subject of a certain importance. "Perhaps you have something to tell me," I suggested.

He understood immediately. "Not yet, my Führer. I am proceeding with caution in the matter of selection. A mistake cannot be made. Also it is tiring work. I have visited a great many establishments of a certain nature in order to procure the most suitable person. I have only a few more to approach, before a final choice can be made."

December 4th. Caution is good. I have no argument with caution, but excessive caution is also not suitable.

December 5th. I summoned Emil early today. He looked pale and tired. "Enough of caution," I said. "No more caution."

December 6th. Emil sent a message this morning, requesting my attention on a matter of urgency. "I have found her, my Führer. A person of knowledge and maturity, also immense skill and a kind and generous nature. I have examined her qualifications in every respect," he said on entering my office.

193

"Excellent," I said. And yet there was no point in rushing matters.

"The lady is ready, my Führer." Emil's right hand shot forward in a brief salute.

"Fine work," But I know from experience that too much haste is also the cause of difficulties at times. Haste breeds anxiety, and anxiety works adversely on the condition.

"Shall a time be arranged?"

This woman of experience, might she not expect an equivalent degree of experience? There might be demands. The demands of such as she might be fairly severe. There might be a measure of ridicule if such demands were not met.

"A rendezvous, my Führer, might such an arrangement be made? The lady has indicated her eagerness. And her qualifications are beyond dispute. I am a man who understands such matters and she will prove extremely pleasing . . ."

Eagerness? Too much eagerness can sometimes take on the form of vulgarity. "I will issue the order in due course."

"But, my Führer, the lady . . ."

"Enough of this eagerness and experience. I shall issue the order after further consideration."

December 8th. Too much haste is never healthy.

December 9th. The man of wisdom moves with care.

December 10th. I should never have agreed to this thing of the chaperones. I told Max Amman and Emil that she must be home by eleven. And here I am, the time almost five past, and they are not yet home, "A ball," she said. "I must go to a ball. I have never been to a ball."

"That's ridiculous," I said. "How can the party Führer be seen prancing around the dance floor like a goat?"

"The Führer can prance at home. It is not the Führer who is going to the ball. I am going to the ball. The Führer can keep himself company for one evening." I thought about it briefly. "Scowling at me like that will not help," she shrilled.

"Max Amman and Emil Maurice will escort you," I declared, holding up my right hand to indicate that no further argument would be permitted.

"Two old men," she screamed.

But she went anyway. And now, with the clock at almost ten past eleven they are not yet back.

The dress: I had not seen the dress. It was a deception. I understood that she would be wearing the blue one I had chosen for her.

Instead when she came down the stairs she was wearing a dress I had never seen before, red as blood, her shoulders naked and in the centre of her bosom, right in the valley of all ecstacy, she wore a large white rose as if to draw attention to that part of her body.

Emil and Amman leapt to their feet like two trained apes, their faces covered with idiotic grimaces of pleasure. "Chaperones, attention," I commmanded. The smiles left their faces and their heels clicked together. "Remember your duty."

"Yes, our Führer," they said as one man, but their eyes were on Geli.

They returned at quarter past eleven, a full fifteen minutes late. "All this waltzing and waltzing . . ." My attention was with Max and Emil. ". . . and late on top of it."

"The young lady," Max said, "there were young officers . . ."

"Young officers?" Max had moved. He was standing at the end of a long fiery red tunnel. "What was she doing with the young officers?"

"The waltz. She was doing the waltz."

"What else? What else was she doing?"

Max was staring at me like a fool, seeming to be unable to answer, but I heard Emil's voice. "The polka," he said. "With the young officers she was doing the polka as well as the waltz."

Max had moved further and the walls of the red tunnel had become darker, but I heard Geli. She was crying and I could hear her footsteps as she ran, then the closing of her bedroom door.

The tunnel was gone. Max was gone. Emil too was no longer with me and I was trying Geli's bedroom door, but it was locked. "Geli," I called "Geli."

December 12th. Today I took Geli shopping for clothes. She enjoyed herself immensely. There are a few things for which old Uncle Dolf is still useful. Afterwards we visited a café. As soon as we sat down she noticed a young man in a grey English-style suit. The way she kept glancing at him caused me intense pain. I told her plainly that this

195

sort of behaviour displeases me, but she paid no attention. Of course I had no alternative, but to leave immediately.

December 14th. Perhaps the time has come to issue an order to this woman of experience. Perhaps Emil should be instructed accordingly. After all Geli is no more than a child and without appreciation. This is clear now. I shall consider the matter.

December 15th. I made another of my regular appearances among the party leaders with young Eva Braun. On the way home in the red Mercedes she said that she would rather not come with me in future. "Why ever not *liebchen*?" I asked, smiling at her through eyes that were halfway closed. I am a possessor of Austrian charm, but I only apply it on occasion.

She looked down at her hands which were fastening and unfastening the clasp of her bag. "Well, Herr Hitler, I am flattered that you take me out to cafés and to meetings with your friends and also to the theatre. I am a simple girl and you are an important man." I nodded in sympathy. "And I am happy to know that my company pleases someone like yourself, but . . ."

Here she became silent. I felt the need to encourage her. "I am older than you," I said. "You are concerned because I am older than you?"

She shook her head. "No. I don't think that is important. It is such an honour for me, especially as Herr Hitler has such beautiful blue eyes and such a sweet little moustache. I am sure that if Herr Hitler was to kiss one it would feel like being tickled under the nose with a tiny paint brush. That Herr Hitler is older is not a matter that bothers someone like myself."

I might have known. All they think about is kissing, and soon kissing is not enough. They will be wanting more, and then there is torment and humiliation.

We were sitting in the back seat and Emil was driving. For a moment my eyes found his in the rear-view mirror. He had the audacity to wink at me. "Shall I take my Führer and the young lady to my Führer's residence?"

"Eyes front, driver," I ordered. "We shall take the young lady home."

"Heil Hitler," Emil said, trying to salute at the same time, his outstretched finger tips colliding with the windscreen and the car careering briefly from one side of the road to the other.

I did not speak to Eva the rest of the way home.

December 17th. "Of course there is always young Eva, if my Führer prefers to sample innocence, not complete innocence of course, and ignorance, rather than enjoying the benefits of skill and experience." This Emil is full of ideas of every sort. This too bears consideration.

December 19th. "The lady does not understand the delay, my Führer."

"It is not for her to understand. It is for her only to obey."

"Heil Hitler," Emil said. "Perhaps she is a party member."

December 21st. Today I was visited by Herr Kirdof. He was accompanied by his Director of Accounts, his personal secretary, his business secretary and his Director of Managing. "Such a noble and suitable policy cannot but be successful," he said. "Also it will do much for German industry, regarding armament supplies and matters of this nature."

"This is not a policy that should be good for German industry," I told him. "It is German industry that should be good for the policy."

"Of course, Führer," he said. He was smiling humbly and nodding his head lower and lower as if bowing to me. His spectacles had thick lenses and his lips were wet, his great width being the result of excessive eating of the flesh of animals; not a leader of the new Germany, but one to be used and kept or discarded according to the needs of the moment, not a man of permanent worth. "My companies make equipment of all sorts that will be of great value in time to come, items with military and civilian uses, electrical switches, wire and other items such as gas ovens and so on. . . . While the New Germany will probably not have use for gas ovens, there is much else that could be awarded according to contract to those who are numbered among the faithful adherents of so sublime a policy . . ."

At least this Herr Kirdof has an understanding of policy matters. "For the awarding of future contracts a relationship needs to exist," I said. "The party must survive."

Herr Kirdof nodded more vigorously than before, also the Director of Accounts, the Director of Managing and the secretaries of personal and business. "We thought perhaps a million Deutsch-marks a year until such time as the state funds are available. Führer, it might also be of value to consider the Herren Wolf, Thyssen, von Schroeder and various others. My department of marketing could make a list."

I looked sternly at this factory owner, a man of such rotund dimensions that the breathing comes with difficulty. "The list is an excellent idea. And I think one and a half million Deutschmarks will be in order."

He swallowed although he had not been eating, looked quickly at the Directors and the secretaries, but there was no help to be found among them. "Of course, Führer," he said at last. "It shall be as you say."

In time everything shall be as I say.

December 24th. I attended the party's Christmas dinner with Eva Braun. Rosenberg made an excellent speech in which he proved conclusively that Jesus was a National Socialist.

On the way home in the car Eva started crying again while Emil stretched his neck to see her in the rear view mirror. The female body is a structure that possesses extraordinary qualities. Within seconds her eyes were red and swollen to the size of small apples, giving her the appearance of a broken-hearted chameleon. I watched her crying for a while, the tears running down the sides of her nose to join with others that were leaking out of her nostrils. It was a disgusting sight. I turned to look out of the window.

From the front seat Emil added his own form of wisdom. "Excuse me, my Führer, but the young lady is crying."

"Is that so, my Emil?" I said. "I had not noticed." The sharpness of my wit is proverbial.

"I can see it clearly in the mirror," Emil said, "also the sobs, sniffles and so forth are audible."

At this the volume of Eva's crying grew still louder, causing people passing in the street to turn and look at the car. I leant across and patted her knee in a fatherly fashion. "Be quiet, you stupid child," I said. "You are making a spectacle of us."

"I want to die," she said, between the sobs. "I want to die because I do not please you."

I allowed my hand to rest on her knee. "My muddle-headed little pumpkin," I said.

In an instant she had moved close against me. "Oh, Herr Hitler, you do like me," she said. Her thigh was against mine, her shoulder against my chest, and her hair that smelt like the flowers of the Prater on a spring day was brushing against my face. "You do like me. I was wrong. I'm so glad I was wrong."

Emil's neck was stretching so far that dislocation had become a possibility. "Shall I drop the young lady at my Führer's apartment tonight?"

"You shall stop making suggestions. If I want suggestions I shall ask for them."

The car lurched as Emil removed his foot from the accelerator pedal in order to click his heels together. "I apologize for the suggestion, my Führer," he said.

"The apology is accepted."

"It is simply that the young lady seems to be in a condition of . . ."

"The young lady's condition is not the concern of the driver. The driver drives, the Führer leads and the young lady snivels. And that is the end of it."

"Yes, my Führer," Emil said smartly. There is no substitute for military training.

Eva was still crying softly, her shoulders shivering in a tremor of childish passion every hundred metres or so. "I thought that I pleased you when you called me your little muddle-headed pumpkin," she said. Her voice was muffled as if her mouth was filled with cotton wool. "Now I can see that I don't."

All that I wanted was for the stupid child to remain silent. Is it right for a Führer to have this sort of thing to deal with? Did Julius Caesar have stupid crying females upsetting his thoughts? Could Hannibal have crossed the Alps with a simple-minded country girl clinging to him and complaining that he did not find her pleasing? What about Bonaparte and Alexander? Did they have their Evas too? I cannot believe it.

"If I may be so bold, my Führer. . ." Emil began.

"Boldness involves certain dangers, my Emil," I said in a statesmanlike way.

"Yes, my Führer, but as my Führer is well known to be a man of mercy. . ." I could not deny the truth of this so I let him continue. "I thought that as the young lady is not pleasing my Führer tonight I should drop my Führer at his apartment before taking the young lady home."

At this Eva stopped crying and looked first at Emil, then at me. With her handkerchief she quickly wiped away the remaining tears. "An excellent idea," I said. I turned to the girl and spoke in kindly fashion. "Never mind, my dear, you are not responsible for your limitations. The German people need patriots of every type, the great and the humble, the wise and the ignorant. Let Emil escort you home and be happy." The kindness of my words and the gentleness of my manner calmed her immediately. She stopped crying and sat looking at Emil the rest of the way back to the apartment.

The apartment was in darkness so I tip-toed quietly to Geli's room. My hand had reached the door handle when I heard that she too was crying.

It is ridiculous. The whole thing is without precedent in the affairs of men. They ignore my explicit commands. A Führer should say to his subjects, be happy, and there should be no tears. Germany needs to learn discipline.

December 25th. "Perhaps the lady I mentioned would be a suitable Christmas present," Emil has suggested. "Clearly Eva is unsuitable in this respect."

"Clearly," I said. "Perhaps a new year's gift will be in order."

December 26th. I have held a conversation with Eva that has helped her to understand her position in the life of her Führer. "My child," I said, "I have many demands upon my time and energy. For this reason I cannot have a demanding or intelligent companion. I need a simple woman, not one who will wonder what she can get from her Führer, but one who will ask what she may give to him. Someone of your small intellectual capacity is ideal. You must also learn not to make demands of any other sort."

"I understand, Herr Hitler," she said seriously. She really is a charming girl.

"I cannot have someone with whom I have to reason or explain or anything else demanding ... do you follow?"

"Yes, Herr Hitler," she said. The appreciation of a person's own limitations is a noble trait, especially in a woman. In this gender it is rare and therefore the more to be admired when it does appear.

200

Since this conversation, whenever I have her accompany me Emil drops me at the apartment first and himself accompanies her home. She has adjusted so well to the arrangement that there is a new shine in her eyes. It is as well that I have such an understanding of women.

December 28th. Perhaps not early in the new year. Only fools rush in. The wise man understands patience.

January 25th, 1930. And so the martyrs of the National Socialist revolution are made to suffer. A young boy, little more than a child, a being of exquisite innocence, has been murdered by the communists. He was a person of immense talent and spiritual worth who had written an anthem for the movement. Swarthy little Joseph Goebbels says that we should sing it at every rally. He says that the mass loves a martyr.

Of course the communists have tried to destroy everything, but the truth will prevail. Their stories that he was a pimp and in bed with one of his sluts will not stand up to the harsh light of history. Anyone could have removed his clothing after he was shot, and placed him in the bed of the woman, and who could possibly give credence to a woman of that sort? To all true Germans Horst Wessel will always be a saint.

February 1930. Geli attends her classes regularly. She is a little pale and does not talk very much, but in time she will thank her Uncle Dolf. She will be glad that I did not allow any vagabond to lure her into his bed. Her attitude remains a little cold, but this will pass.

March 7th. Geli will know in time that I was right. But perhaps in the interval other arrangements will be in order.

March 10th. The time is right. A strong will is important in a leader, but the life of a monk is not necessary. It is clear that the will can be exercised in other ways also.

Tomorrow I shall consult with Emil.

March 11th. "This woman," I said, "she is a person of patriotic inclinations?"

"Woman?" Emil asked.

"The woman we discussed, my Emil." I spoke sharply. "Kindly

bring your mind to bear on the subject."

"Oh, the woman we discussed in December? A true patriot, a woman of the soil, of the earth, the loins . . ."

"I follow. There is no need to expand in this extravagant fashion. You are sure that she is favourably disposed?"

"Favourably disposed?" Emil's knowledge of the use of words remains poor. I once reprimanded him for this.

I know enough to ask the question, he replied. "My Führer means willing. Is the lady willing? She is more than willing. To be not willing is impossible. She is a professional person."

"Professional?"

"But only of the highest possible standard."

"And this professional woman, what is her name?"

"My Führer she is the sensation of Munich. She is the favourite of the wealthy and the upper classes. Her girls are the most beautiful . . ."

"My Emil, I scarcely believe my ears. Are you recommending a common . . ."

"No, no." Emil raised both hands, as if begging a favour, or imploring forgiveness, or pleading for mercy, perhaps the latter. "No, my Führer, not common, not common at all. And in my Führer's case one of the girls will not be used. This mistress of physical skill, this artist of love will attend the Führer herself. Fräulein Martha . . ."

"Fräulein Martha?" It was the voice that spoke. Emil had been standing before my desk. He took a leap in the direction of the door. "Fräulein Martha?" This time it was I.

He shrugged and one eye twitched. "Fräulein Martha is Fräulein Martha. I don't know who she is more than that."

"Describe her."

"Describe?" He glanced towards the door then back at me. "She is kind and honest, also patriotic and intelligent, at least with relation to her profession . . ."

"What does she look like, my little Emil? Describe her appearance."

"Ah, her appearance." He pressed the points of the fingers of one hand against the other. "She appears to have long dark hair with such curls, and such . . ." He demonstrated the nature of the curls with his hands. "Also a pale skin, like milk or snow, more like milk, and long lean arms, with legs as straight as two arrows."

"The chest, what of the chest?"

"Ah, the chest . . . the chest is of splendid proportions and a certain roundness, an exceptional roundness . . ."

I could restrain the question no longer "This Martha, have you mentioned my name to her?"

Little Emil's eyes grew round with the horror that now confronted him. He was a man accused of treason. "My Führer, how can my Führer ask such a thing of me? I am the very heart of discretion . . ."

"The soul . . ." I corrected him.

"The heart of the soul," he said. "I said only that this meeting was to be with a person of unparalleled importance."

"I see . . ." He was now closer to the door than to the desk. "My Emil, go to this Martha and mention my name. Proceed with subtlety. Do not mention it in connection with the other matter. Just speak of me in casual conversation. And report her reactions to me."

March 13th. Emil has been to see her again. "She is a woman of unfathomable insight, my Führer," he said. "I mentioned your name casually as you said I must. I simply said Adolf Hitler is a fine person, don't you agree? And immediately she said, so this is your client. And she started laughing, very loud and long. When she had finished she said, tell Adolf that he's welcome any time. Tell him I will do anything for an old friend."

March 14th. She is a woman of evil ways. She would heap more humiliation upon me. Such are her devices.

March 15th. But she says that she will do anything for an old friend. Perhaps there will be a degree of patience, a measure of gentleness. Is it too much to ask that there should be a little understanding?

March 16th. No. Such a thing will be madness.

March 20th. I must ask Emil to point out the location of her establishment. It would not be in excessively bad taste to drive past occasionally.

March 29th. No. I will put it behind me. The seeds of my destruction are within that woman.

Today Emil said, "Perhaps my Führer still bears in mind his old friend who is willing to do anything for her old friend."

"Do not talk, Emil," I said. "I am in the process of thinking." People of humble stature, such as Emil, have respect for the thoughts of the great. He said nothing after that.

April 15th. "A deal is a deal," Herr Kirdof said. "Also an agreement is an agreement. And you, Herr Führer, have broken yours." His friends, others of similar type, sat in a row on either side of him with arms folded and faces that said that there would be no more money.

"It is a small thing," I said, "of little significance. I am sure in time. . ." He did not even demonstrate the good manners to allow me to finish.

"No, Herr Hitler, it is not a small thing. It is not of little significance, and we do not have time. My company is paying one and a half million Deutschmarks a year and the companies of my esteemed colleagues are also paying large amounts."

"Three quarters of a million," one of the others said, a thin man with hollow cheeks and temples.

"One and a quarter," another voice joined the chorus.

Then all were speaking, with no apologies or by your leave or after you, my good sir. The unseemly rush was evidence of the poor manners of these capitalists. "Half a million."

"One million, six hundred thousands."

"Three hundred thousands."

"Eight hundred and seventy five thousands, and also not tax deductible."

I held up a hand for silence. "The tax deductible contributions will come as soon as. . ."

Despite my raised hand this Kirdof interrupted me. "We have not come to talk about tax deductible contributions." His head was bobbing up and down as a result of agitation and indignation. His little pig eyes seemed to form points in the centre and his damp lips were pressed tightly together in a hard moist rosebud. "We have come to talk about the strike. There is a strike and who is in favour? The National Socialist Party. It seems that the word socialist in the party's name is to be taken seriously. But this is not what Herr Hitler said to me. Herr Hitler said, never, Herr Kirdof, as long as the

National Socialists have anything to do with it will there be the wastage and anarchy of the strike. It cannot happen, Herr Hitler said. But what does Herr Strasser say? Herr Strasser supports the metal-workers strike. Herr Strasser says, strike and the National Socialist Party supports you. So they strike, and so there is no production and where will the one and a half million Deutschmarks come from then? Also the contributions of my esteemed colleagues, the half million, three hundred thousands and so forth? And furthermore who is the Führer, Herr Hitler or Herr Strasser?"

April 16th. This Kirdof is a fool and a madman. But even a fool has his moments of wisdom and the madman his moments of sanity.

If Strasser continues the support of the strike we shall soon be down to the pfennigs the workers themselves contribute. That is surely no way to build the party. Millions of Deutschmarks down the drain. And dare I ask who will pay for the party headquarters and the apartment, the red Mercedes and the villa in the Obersalzberg? I shall go to Berlin and put these questions to him directly. We will see what answers he has for my logic.

April 30th. Such leanness and paleness as I see in Geli is not necessarily a sign of ill health. The weeping is probably just the natural outpourings of a passionate nature.

May 1st. Even Martha is preferable to all this weeping. I am sure that Emil still remembers the address.

May 2nd. It would be better if he forgot it.

May 7th, 1930. Strasser is even crazier than I thought. He says the party's money will come from the workers. So I said that the workers have no money. They are poor. He answered that is the root of evil. The workers should have money. So I said that in the meantime while this problem is as yet unresolved we must take money from the capitalists who have much money. No, he said, this is a mistake. The money must come from the workers, he said. And I retort that the workers are poor...

So we went, round and round, my logic and Strasser's irrational meanderings. Finally I said, "This is enough. I am the party leader.

We have passed the point of reason. Now we have reached the point of discipline. The strike can no longer be supported. This is an order from Führer to follower."

"Follower?" Strasser said. "Indeed," he added after a pause.

Afterwards I saw little Joseph Goebbels of the sallow complexion. "Explain again of these concentration camps of British invention," I said. "A noble Nordic race, the British. Then after the explanations are finished clean out the Berlin party for me. Complete ruthlessness must be shown in dealing with the likes of this Strasser, as well as the other Bolsheviks, democrats and such. We must show the men of capital, worms that they are, who is running the party."

May 15th. A charming fellow, this Kirdof. "Such strong leadership, Führer, who can deny it? To say that this Strasser fellow got what he deserves does not put it too strongly." These were his words when we met this morning. "Naturally there is no problem regarding the contributions now. And remember we are not against the worker. His tax contributions are vital to the running of the state. Another thing, Führer, the young lady, Braun, a fine choice, much better than appearing in public with one's niece continually. Possessors of filthy minds, the communists and such, will always think the worst."

June 1st. Emil, my sweet Emil, what a fine fellow. His first thought is always for Führer and party. Only then does he think of himself. Today he again suggested that he move into the apartment to occupy the little closet at the back. "My Führer leaves Geli alone so often and servants are not to be trusted. I know it would break my Führer's heart if she was seduced by some reckless adventurer. But with me there my Führer's mind would be at ease. Also I could amuse her with games of scat and so forth."

An excellent fellow, my Emil. Of course I agreed immediately. It is a pity that his excellence did not encompass the procuring of a more suitable woman than Martha.

June 6th. Today I told Geli that Emil was coming to stay with us. She has been rebellious and ill-mannered lately so I employed my sternest aspect. "You are alone far too often," I said. "A chaperone is needed."

My heart ached at the bitterness I heard in her voice when she replied. "And who is the fine lady?"

"One is required who can combine the task of chaperone with other duties. I have chosen Emil Maurice."

"Emil?" She threw up her hands, then laughed loudly, and vulgarly and at great length. "He is the chaperone?"

The spirit of rebellion and ingratitude is clearly still thriving within her. "Do not think I will weaken," I said. "From now on you have someone to look after you. You have brought this on yourself."

"So my dear Uncle Dolf has chosen Emil Maurice to see that I do not get seduced."

"This is no way for a niece to talk to her uncle. And do not think that you can resist my will in this matter."

Before I left her I think that she was beginning to see the wisdom and justice in my actions. Her attitude was not without a degree of admiration. Her last words to me were, "A fascinating choice."

June 8th. What a time in which to live! A time of joy, a time of freedom. What exhilaration for the soul. The country is seized by depression. Three million Germans are without work. Everywhere the communists cause fighting in the streets and our boys in the S.A., young heroes scarcely more than children, have to restore order. Everything is chaos, poverty and misery. What excitement! What stimulation!

Germany is in need and who better to fill the need than the leader of the National Socialist German Workers Party? Every disaster further undermines the traitors of Weimar and the Communist and Social Democrat fools. And the mass falls into hands of the strong.

For everyone we have something to offer. For the unemployed we offer work and the knowledge that he will not be at the bottom of society. For this we have the Jews. For the farmer we have tax rebates, also Poland when the time comes. For the idealist we have a religion. For the student we have philosophy. For the patriot we offer a national presence, borders halfway to Moscow and all the way to the Mediterranean. For the military we have the promise of war, and for the dissident these excellent concentration camps of English invention.

For all we have slogans: *To victory with our leader! The leader is always right! Leader, we thank you!* What a time to be alive.

June 10th. A party member has registered the patent on a patriotic invention of undoubted significance. It consists of a catapult capable of scattering 10,000 leaflets over a distance of two kilometres. In this way leaflets can be spread over an entire city in half an hour.

June 12th, 1930. The elections are three months away and already we have been campaigning since March. Little Joseph Goebbels of the club foot and the sallow complexion should never have been put in charge of party organization. He is boasting that by the time of the election he will have organized ten thousand meetings and, by the appearance of matters to this point, it would seem that his Führer will have addressed most of them.

It must be his complexion that drives little Joseph to all this activity, also his Jewish nose. How he must envy my blue eyes. Nevertheless it is said that he has documentary proof of his ancestry for seven generations. Before that time it is not likely that a Jew could have crept in anywhere.

Young Eva travels with me to most meetings and, in accordance with Emil's excellent arrangement, he takes me to the apartment before escorting her home.

June 14th. Emil has been with us for three days now. Already Geli is looking happier. She senses that her Uncle Dolferl is only doing what is right for her.

June 17th. The meetings exhaust me. If it was just preparing to speak and then speaking, even speaking with intensity, I would be able to deal with it. There would be no difficulty.

I have tried calmness and softness of sound. Restraint, I have been the very soul of restraint. I have tried concentration and meditation. Nothing helps.

All is quiet within my soul when I rise to speak. The first words are those of reason and logic. Each phrase is carefully enunciated, each word weighed.

Before starting I wait a while, ten seconds, twenty, thirty. I can feel the audience growing restless. They are anxious to submit themselves. My voice is soft, every nuance studied. A hand is raised, a finger points, the language of the body is allowed to speak.

Then amidst the calmness with my words barely reaching the back

209

of the hall the stirrings come. Long before the audience I feel it growing and building. I try to contain it. I try even to ignore it. But from the first moment that it moves I know that it cannot be avoided. It grows, unbidden, somewhere in the depths of my soul. For a while it is hidden. My speech proceeds quietly and with dignity, but I can feel the storm growing. It rises to my chest, stretching, expanding, struggling to break free. By this time there is little more than a whisper until eventually I stop altogether. Then the voice shatters its cage. It is a torrent. "National Socialists, compatriots, people of Germany." It fills the hall. My body grows tense with the strain of it and the mass is gripped, pulled irrevocably into the vortex of my will.

When it is over the soul has been drawn from me and I am weak beyond all imaginable weakness. Only the weakness brought upon me by that evil woman, Martha, bears comparison. I sink down into my seat. Once last month I had to be helped from the hall. In Berlin I vomited in the rest room. The voice is too much for my body, weak and disease-ridden as it is. I should possess the voice, but it possesses me.

June 19th. Emil wants a motorcycle with a side car. I have told him clearly that party funds do not stretch to cover such extravagances.

June 21st. This little Joseph. I ask myself if he would have been so industrious if he had my blue eyes or my fairness of skin. This matter of seven generations of pure German ancestry is also to be doubted. I shall have Hans Frank investigate. The club foot is also a problem, but that needs no investigation. The colouring of skin, the narrowness of forehead and the shape of nose are all causes for suspicion. He would not be welcome in the SS, this dark Joseph.

June 24th, 1930. Now Geli can speak of nothing but the motorcycle with the side car. It will help as regards journeys to and from college, she says. It will also help as far as the running of errands is concerned. My time that is so precious for the party and the nation cannot be wasted on trivia. The future of Germany depends on the motorcycle and side car, she says.

July 1st. "No Jews in little Joseph's ancestry," Hans Frank says.
"There must be something," I told him. "What about a Turk, a

Spaniard, a Portuguese, a Greek?"

"Is that a German skin?" I asked. "Is that a German physique? The nose and the forehead, are these Aryan characteristics? Find the coolie among the forefathers," I said. "We cannot have deceit of this sort in the circles of the inner party."

My own hair was blond as a child. It is only with middle age that it has discoloured. In reality I am a blond person.

July 7th. She will weep. She will pine away. I will drive her into the bed of some reckless adventurer, a Jewish one. The motorcycle with the side car is necessary for the continuance of life, she says.

I discussed the matter with Emil. "What do you feel, regarding the seriousness of this matter?" I asked.

"It would be well not to underestimate a young girl's frustration, my Führer," he said. "No good will come of it. I am concerned for her condition of spirit, especially with regard to this Jewish adventurer."

"Such a thing is not possible with a niece of mine. It cannot be."

"Nevertheless, why take chances? In terms of the image necessary for Germany's Führer of the years ahead, such a thing would create a scandal of horrifying dimensions, worse even than Herr Goebbels's Turkish forefather."

It is a small matter this motorcycle and side car. Today I gave orders for their purchase. "Red," I instructed old Nothnagel who is responsible for purchases on behalf of the party. "This machine must be red."

"Red, my Führer?" he asked.

"Certainly," I said, "the brightest red that is available."

At least peace will now return to the apartment. Geli will be in possession of her red motorcycle with side car. This will enable Emil to tend her needs more completely. Everything is in order.

Geli will now be happy. Never mind her poor Uncle Dolferl's misery. She seeks only her own happiness.

July 13th. It is as I thought in the case of little Joseph. But I am a man of mercy and compassion. I summoned the sallow Joseph to my office. "The matter of the ancestry has come to my attention," I said. "It was not necessary to take note as far as seven generations. Far fewer than that provided the information, the concealed information, one might say." I enunciated the words with great care in order that the elegance of phrasing should not be lost. Despite his antecedents (this word means that which has gone before), despite these he is a man of culture who appreciates wit and the power of words. Whatever his shortcomings regarding the gypsy heritage it is clear that the clean German blood has all but cancelled out the other.

"I have taken note of the impurity," I said.

The yellow of little Joseph's skin was now a paler yellow. "I work hard for the party," he said. His voice was hurried, as if he was being pursued by not one but a band of gypsies. "No one works harder for the party, no one. With respect, with deep respect and in a manner not at all challenging to my Führer, I submit that not even the Führer himself works harder for the party."

"My Joseph," I said, my voice rich with magnanimity (perhaps a footnote should be introduced where there are difficult words). "My Joseph, this is a matter for forgiveness. At heart you are as pure an Aryan as I am. Deep in your heart this is true."

"In my soul, Führer."

"In your being, my Joseph."

"My spirit."

"Precisely. Such things are to be forgiven and never mentioned. The party is an instrument of mercy to those who deserve mercy. And who is more worthy than yourself?"

"Only my Führer," he said. He is noted everywhere for his clearsightedness.

"Except that I do not need it." I smiled benignly at him. "Such a thing is on the level of other minor imperfections such as the club foot. National Socialism aims at perfection, but we are not perfect yet. This is agreed by all."

"My devotion is absolute, beyond living, beyond dying." Little club-footed Joseph's face was that of a saint beseeching the Almighty.

"This is what is required, my Joseph. Devotion beyond devotion. Absolute surpassing absolute. If the party has this all else may be forgotten, but this the party must have. Always."

He is a man of intelligence, this Joseph. The devotion we have seen so far is but a small thing compared to what we shall see in future.

July 14th. There is too much of reason in the speeches in this election.

Too little of the blood and the instinct. This is a situation to be rectified in due course. The time will come when reason will play no part in Germany. Thinking will be the province of the Führer alone.

July 16th. The red motor cycle (the one with the side car) is in itself not a bad thing, perhaps. But now Geli is here, there and everywhere. It is true that Emil is always with her and that she could not be in better hands, but now the driver is hers, not mine. Whenever Emil is needed what do I find? I find old Nothnagel coming in, rubbing his hands together. "The Fräulein is out, my Führer. I heard the motor-cycle leave, Emil driving of course." I point my finger and speak loudly in anger but all I get is, "Jawohl, my Führer. Sofort, my Führer. But I cannot prevail with Emil. And Emil cannot prevail with the Fräulein."

August 1930. There is panic amongst these Communists. What else could be behind it? A meeting there must be. A neutral place must be chosen. Not the Hofbräuhaus, oh no. Everyone knows that this is Nazi territory. The meeting might just as well be held at the National Socialist offices.

A neutral meeting place was needed. Office of the Trade Unions would be suitable, they told us. Office of the Trade Unions, a place seething with every sort of Bolshevist and anarchist.

The Burgerbräukelder was suggested in a spirit of reasonableness. "Such a place," they said, "the scene of the so-called *Putsch*."

"So called?" I said, a finger pointing in commanding fashion.

"No offence meant, Herr Hitler, but a neutral venue is essential. What about the office of the Metal Workers Federation?"

"Why not Moscow?" Little Joseph suggested. "The Kremlin itself. What an excellent neutral place."

"You are not serious," they said. "We should stick together. After all we are all revolutionaries. We want to remove the existing order. You want to remove the existing order. You are socialists. It says so in the name of your party. We are socialists. After the election perhaps there can be a coalition, something of the sort." They paused to breathe: the one who had spoken. He paused to breathe. They were deep indignant breaths, as of one who has fought a battle or one who has been wronged. "The office of *Arbeid*," he said. "This will be an excellent venue."

213

"Perfect," Joseph said. "That Bolshevist rag. Why not the *Völkischer Beobachter?*"

"That Nazi cesspool."

"Better than an anarchist brothel," Joseph said.

"Rather an anarchist brothel than a fascist dung heap."

"Why not the premises of an excellent lady of my acquaintance," Emil suggested. For once the red motorcycle was in the garage, side car and all. "The lady's name ..."

Before the name could be mentioned I interrupted: "The public library will do excellently."

"Agreed," the communists said.

August 12th. They sat there with their pale faces and their principles and their envy. They would like to hold Germany's future in their hands. "We are all revolutionaries," they said, "as you are."

"Common ground," they said again and again, "there is much common ground."

"Violence." They hold up their hands in protest. "We too understand violence. But we are wasting our violence. We strike against you. You strike against us. We should strike together. In this way the régime could not survive a month, not even a week. Together we can establish our dictatorship."

We asked who would the dictator be and they said, "The proletariate. But of course the proletariate must be led. They cannot be left to do things in any disorderly way just as they choose. A leader is necessary. There is no problem. The proletariate is the dictator, but we must guide such a dictator."

"Only the problem of who is to be the guide for this dictator remains," little Joseph said.

The hands rose still higher, protesting to the heavens. "A small matter," they said, "A matter for negotiation, a matter for consultation, a matter for mutual agreement, a minor matter."

"Agreement is reached," I told them. "We are comrades forever."

August 13th. Ernst Röhm must by now have realized his mistake. Putting down rebellions amongst Red Indians for a gang of swarthy Spaniards is no work for a German officer.

A message must be sent to bring him home. The SA needs leadership of the right sort. In three weeks there is the election and afterwards these Communists will have to be dealt with firmly and finally. A man of suitable calibre is needed, a bold and immature man, one who does not require explanations, but enjoys the cracking of skulls, one who would rather conduct a revolution than celebrate it.

My sweet Ernst must come back at once. There is work such as will provide him with enjoyment and fulfilment of the soul. Also food for thought for the Communists.

August 14th. Too many meetings. The price to be paid is too great. The weakness is beyond bearing. What are the Communists and their deceitfulness or the Social Democrats and their mendacity compared to possession of the voice.

I have spoken to young Joseph again, concerning the number of meetings. "No one else has the effect, my Führer," he said. "Only my Führer's voice carries the authority."

Whose voice?

August 16th. With the voice it is terrible, the draining of strength from my body is unbearable, but without it there is nothing.

This dark club-footed little gypsy, this Joseph shows extreme devotion, but perhaps more than mere devotion is necessary. I have given express orders that such a thing should not be repeated. He should have known better. Such an arrangement, to address four members of the Bavarian Parliament, was a terrible mistake. For such a small gathering the voice will not appear.

I spoke softly at first, with restraint and caution, expecting it to rise suddenly within me, as always. But the inner tension was absent, the pressure of the spirit gone. There were only my own words, potent in themselves but without the power of the voice. At first I waited in expectation, then in anxiety, finally realizing that there was no choice but to stumble on alone.

Never again will there be a small audience, never.

August 17th. "And who is the Führer, the Führer himself or the Führer's niece?" This is the question I put to Emil, my own driver and now the motorcycle driver of my niece. (This is called irony, the use of irony. It is not something that can be employed by just anyone. A measure of skill is required.)

"The Führer. Heil Hitler," Emil said.

"I am pleased to know that you recognize this," I said. This too is irony. I shall employ it from time to time in the writing of these notes, as artistic necessity dictates.

"Always, my Führer. Such a thing I will always recognize."

"I am pleased, my Emil. Explain to me then how it is that the Führer no longer has a driver, despite the party salary that is being paid for the driver. But the niece has the driver. I am reduced to searching among young members of the SS for a driver. Once even old Nothnagel has been used as a driver. Do you realize what effect this has upon the nervous zones of the body. This is no cause for amusement. Kindly stop smiling and treat this as matter requiring serious attention."

"It was not a smile, my Führer. Just a nervous twitch."

"Ah, my poor Emil, I hope you are not ill. Perhaps all this motorcycle travelling does not agree with you. Perhaps from now on you will heed the command of your Führer and be ready when called."

"I always listen carefully to my Führer's commands." Emil was standing smartly at attention at this point in the interview. He would fit into the SS moderately well. "My Führer's command was to take the young . . . er . . . niece wherever she wanted to go. Well, the truth is that she wants to go quite often. Perhaps, with respect, my Führer will speak to the niece in question."

August 20th. Certainly I shall speak to her. Why should I not speak to her?

August 21st. Two weeks to the election. There is no reason at all that I should not speak to her.

August 23rd. It is a matter of domestic discipline that I should speak to her. This matter weighs heavily on the mind.

August 24th. Amidst all my problems young Eva Braun has the excessive audacity to say that she would like to attend all political meetings with me. She says that she would like to understand such matters. I am not sure that this girl was a sound choice. Again I was forced to explain in the greatest detail that if I had wanted an intelligent companion who would take an interest in politics and so

216

forth I would surely have selected one. It is precisely the feebleness of her intellect that makes her such restful company. I trust that this time she understood and will remember.

August 28th. Today I spoke to Geli regarding the motorcycle and the driver of the motorcycle whose true function it is to be the driver of the Mercedes. Perhaps I am wrong. Perhaps I have treated her cruelly.

She wept at great length and of a loudness to bring the SS guards up the stairs, their feet only touching perhaps a quarter of them in their haste to reach the source of the disturbance. There followed boisterous, almost continuous protestations along these lines: "You do not love me. You have never loved me. You do not want me to have fun at all. Also you do not care about my education or my well-being. For all you care I could starve to death or remain illiterate or never be able to reach top C. What do you care? Perhaps it is this Eva who has taken your affections away from your Geli. Perhaps since this loose woman entered the life of my Uncle Dolferl he is too involved with pleasures of a coarser sort to be concerned about a dull little thing like his Geli."

September 1st. I have definitely been cruel to poor Geli. An instruction has been issued that an SS man be put at her disposal to drive her wherever she desires. This at last frees Emil for his more important duties. I told him this and I could see that he concealed his delight with difficulty. "Is that not excellent?" I asked.

"As my Führer says," he agreed.

September 2nd. How am I to understand her? Her own driver, the red motorcycle, everything she wanted, but still she weeps. "Who is this youth?" she asks. "How do I know that he is able to protect me from reckless adventurers?"

"A member of the SS?" I replied.

"A man with experience is needed, a man with knowledge of the world," she says. "Emil Maurice."

The election is in two days. And still there are meetings. Between little Geli and little Joseph I am being driven mad.

September 3rd. Tonight is the last meeting.

217

At last Geli is content again. I have compromised on the matter of Emil. She is quite grateful to her Uncle Dolferl. I can see clearly in this the awakening of a new warmth, and as gratitude grows to warmth, so warmth will surely grow to passion. I can tell. I have knowledge of this. The waiting has not been in vain.

September 4th, 1930. The voting is over and in an hour I must appear at the election centre. Geli is in her room. The motorcycle only came in an hour ago and she went quietly up to bed without first saying goodnight to her Uncle Dolf.

When she first came to Munich I made the mistake of too anxious an advance. I pressed my suit with too much fervour. This time I shall respond to her growing warmth with greater gentleness. I tapped softly on the door.

"O Saviour, Uncle Dolf," I heard her say softly, below her breath so to speak.

"It is I, my child." My voice was soft with the softness of wisdom and understanding.

From the other side of the door there was a scurrying back and forth as if a party was being held within. "A moment, Uncle Dolf, a moment," I heard her say. She is a sweet child, wanting that everything should be in perfect order before allowing her Uncle Dolferl in. "Oh Saviour," she said again, very softly as before but in the quiet of the house I could hear it clearly. "Don't move," she whispered.

"Don't move? Of course, I will not move, my sweet."

"Yes, don't move, Uncle Dolf. I'll be there is a moment." The door opened no more than a hand's breadth and Geli looked out. She was wearing the pink night-dress that I had bought for her. Her eyes were hard and bright, like the brightness of two burning coals. "Oh, Uncle Dolf, I'm so sleepy," she said. "You don't want me for anything, do you?"

Apart from the brightness in her eyes there was a redness in her cheeks that I had not noticed before. The poor child, I thought, perhaps she has a fever. Perhaps she is studying too hard or straining the voice with too many high Cs. "I simply came to see that all is well with my Geli. That is understandable, is it not?"

"Of course. I hope that the election results are everything that could be wished and more besides. But I am so sleepy. The excitement has worn me out." Her eyes were two bright beads, round and

218

wide, without a trace of sleep. The need for sleep must have been within, deep within.

"My poor child, are you well?"

The door was still open no more than a crack. But the poor child was tired. Also clearly not well. "I am fine, Uncle, as fine as can be. Only tired," she said. She is not without courage, this fine Geli of mine.

"Sleep, my child. Perhaps a visit to Doctor Schwanenvelder tomorrow will be in order."

"Good night, Uncle Dolf."

September 5th. The election is over, the speeches are over, the many visits to Berlin with its dull Wilhelminian buildings are over, and the Communist's fright has turned to panic. The most extreme panic is still to come. If one hundred and seven National Socialist seats in the Reichstag frighten them, let them wait till my Ernst returns from Bolivia. Then we shall see some cause for panic.

October 14th, 1930. What a splendid sight: one hundred and seven National Socialist deputies, each wearing his brown shirt of the SA, each answering the call of the roll with the stirring words, "Present, Heil Hitler." Also other splendid sights were to be seen, a measure of broken glass along the fronts of the shops of Jews, a smouldering synagogue or two, a few Communist offices in ruins, here and there a trade unionist who is no longer in the best of health (the use of irony will be noted), generally a fine and exuberant performance by my sweet Ernst and his young men of the SA. Let there be no doubt that we are on the march.

October 21st. So good to have Ernst back. So fine to have a man of simplicity, a man lacking in unnecessary complications. Today at my special invitation he reported to the office. "Fine work, my Ernst," I said. "The signs of your activities are everywhere."

"It was truly a pleasure, my Führer, doubly so as it was my Führer's wish."

He seemed to have added a little weight, this Ernst of mine, his neck bulges over his shirt collar. He seems also to have added an extra scar while he was away, altogether an excellent fellow.

"Bolivia seems to have been good for you."

219

"Except for the Spaniards, Indians, cockroaches and other lower forms of life: except for these it is an excellent place. It also lacks a National Socialist Party and a Führer of suitable stamp. But in other respects it is in order. Brutality is respected in Bolivia as it is in Germany."

I added to the truth of his observation. "Also in Holland, France, Russia and Poland," I said, "particularly Poland."

"I can see that there are exciting times ahead, my Führer."

"Understandably," I said. "A revolution needs room in which to breathe, Poland, Czechoslovakia, Holland and so forth, for instance. But first we have a little more business with our own trade unions."

"Ah," Ernst said, his eyes gleaming with pleasure at the idea. "The secretary of the steelworkers, a little blond fellow of no more than twenty-two, perhaps I could take him into custody myself . . ."

October 25th. Geli remains in her room day and night and will speak to no one. She says that everyone hates her, myself especially, and that we conspire cruelly to bring misery into her life.

The motorcycle is faulty and is with the mechanics who are effecting repairs. They say that it has travelled a considerable distance for so new a machine.

November 1st. "A visit to your mother is in order," I said to Geli at breakfast this morning.

She cocked her head a little to one side like a small bird. "With the motorcycle newly repaired?" she said. "Surely you jest, Uncle."

"What about the wind," I said, "the continual blowing of the wind on the vocal chords? What of the effect? And where is high C?"

"Above B," she said, her eyelids going up and down like the pulse of a Communist in the election. "Bye bye. Emil is waiting." Before I could say anything, before I could do anything, before I could assert my authority she was gone. This is the influence on the young of rulers such as the Social Democrats.

November 4th. The election is over. Ernst is back. Geli is happy again. But the Führer. No one cares for the Führer's happiness.

I shall speak to Emil regarding a matter of some importance.

November 5th. We were on our way to a meeting with Herr Kirdo and his fellows regarding the party finances when I spoke. "You might recall," I said, "that we raised the subject of a Fräulein Martha. You might remember this."

"In precise detail," Emil said. "Also the precise detail of Fräulein Martha."

"I simply asked if you recall ..."

"As if it was five minutes ago, my Führer, less, two minutes, perhaps only ..."

"Then perhaps it will be possible for us to drive past the premises from which she conducts her business. You could point to such premises for the sake of my edification."

So Emil drove to a part of the city that, with my present status, I seldom find necessary to visit. It is to the south of Westbahnhof not far from where I once lived. This is a shocking discovery. "Emil, surely this woman has not been operating her profession in this part of Munich for long?" I asked.

"I think she's new," he said. "But service is so good there that I think the established ladies will have to conduct business in a more enthusiastic fashion. No more reading the *Munich Zeitung* while the client is sweating his guts out ..."

"Established ladies? There are others?"

"Well, of course, my Führer. This is the national recreation, so to speak. More popular even than the beer hall."

"Perhaps a new national recreation will be in order. Perhaps marching to the beat of a military drum will be an improvement."

Emil, being a man of slow wit, did not notice the intense coldness of my voice. "Oh no, my Führer," he replied. "Marching to a drum beat is the national obsession. Sowing the wild oats is the national recreation."

"I see," I said, employing a certain accentuation in order to indicate the use of extreme irony. This too was lost. It is pointless to employ such fine wit when dealing with Emil.

The building from which Martha conducted her business was old, grey and unpainted. It had an aspect of decay and dissolution, not very different to those who made use of it. "But inside, my Führer," Emil said, "inside is luxury upon luxury. And the girls that possess charms upon further charms. It cannot be imagined without a visit."

"Such a visit," I said, "might be noticed. A report might appear in some filthy rag. I think particularly of *Arbeid*."

"I will fetch her. I will bring her to the apartment with extreme discretion."

"There is also the matter of dignity . . ."

"The Mercedes will be used. No greater degree of dignity is possible."

We left the street where this place of business occupies premises and turned back to our meeting with Herr Kirdof. "I will give instructions regarding this matter in due course."

"Perhaps it will not be too long, my Führer."

"Perhaps not," I said.

November 6th. No sooner are the great perceived to be great than the vultures appear, trying to seize some advantage for themselves. Today Alois came. The fool in charge of the guard allowed him in without being announced, thinking this was in order because of family ties and so forth. I am a kind and generous man. For this reason I did not have him immediately reduced to the rank of private. "Alois," I said.

He stood in front of me, near the door, just as before, holding his hat in both hands and rotating it round and round like a top. "Adolf, my beloved brother," he said, showing care to remain at a safe distance while speaking. "I would like it to be known that all the members of the family, myself included . . ." He paused a moment to arrange his thoughts. "Nay, let me say myself especially, I am particularly proud of the immense success. . ."

I was about to interrupt him when Geli came in to pay one of her rare visits to her beloved uncle. Naturally no door is ever barred to my Geli. "Uncle Alois," she cried. If I had not known better I would have thought that I heard joy in her voice. She ran to him and coiled her arms around his neck as if she was trying to suffocate him. She is a kind person and tries even to make a miserable sort of person like Alois happy. "I am so happy to see you, Uncle," she said.

"No need to go that far, child," I said.

"But look at Uncle Alois. Isn't it wonderful to see him again." She still had her arms around his neck while he stood there grinning as if nothing more wonderful had ever happened to him. "Aren't you glad to see him again?"

"What do you want this time, Alois?"

But Geli did not let him answer. "Uncle Adolf, how can you speak to him that way? Uncle Alois will think that you don't want him here." She pressed the side of her head against his shoulder. The lengths to which her kindness extends goes beyond my comprehension. And my comprehension is considerable at all times. If only such kindness could extend to her dear uncle Dolf.

"Uncle Alois knows how I feel about him," I said. "Well Alois? Before you start please bear in mind that the guard had no business letting just anyone in here, and also that you have only a few minutes."

"Uncle Adolf, how can you be so unkind. Don't you remember Uncle Alois?"

"Perfectly," I said. "I remember him perfectly. Speak, Alois."

"Uncle Dolf?" Geli had Alois by the arm and was trying to draw him closer as if this would help me to recognize him. Alois, for his part, had taken hold of the door frame in order not to approach any further. "Uncle Dolf, I can't believe this."

"Speak, Alois," I said.

"Now that you are a great man, Adolf. . ."

I silenced him with a wave of my hand. "This is well known. Why are you here?"

"Adolf, I came because I have knowledge that I am sure might be of interest to you, intelligence, so to speak . . . a matter of some importance." His eyes were like little beads, resembling those of a rat.

"Perhaps you would be so good as to inform me regarding this matter," I said, smiling. "This is the use of irony," I explained.

"Excuse me Adolf," he said. "I am not accustomed to talking to people of your rank. I did not understand that."

I smiled knowingly. "I suppose it cannot be expected," I said. "Tell me what you want from me."

"He's come to visit." Geli, the sweet child, cannot be expected to understand the depths of depravity of my brother's soul. "Uncle Alois knows that he is welcome in our little home. Is it not true, Uncle?" I was not sure to which uncle the last question was addressed.

Alois grinned at me, the grin of the coward before the firing squad, von Khar during the *Putsch* or Harrer when I deposed him as head of the party, such a grin. "I had a letter from William Patrick," he said.

"Who is William Patrick?" My voice was light with unconcern.

"William Patrick Hitler, your nephew."

"I have no nephew." Alois and I were alone in a narrow corridor, the sides of which were heaving with the pulsing I felt in my temples.

"My son," Alois said from far away, "my son."

The voice spoke. It roared suddenly from me to fill the room. "Your son of the English wife, the fruit of your traitorous seed, the produce of your worthless loins."

I was alone in the room. Alois had gone. I looked for him in the passage and in the street outside, but there were only the SS guards. They were young men and looked at me out of eyes large and apprehensive with respect. I went to the door of Geli's room and placed my hand on the handle of the door, but through the closed door I heard again the sound of her weeping. What has he done, this Alois, to upset her so?

December 3rd. There is nothing wrong with a walk, a little stroll through the old section of the town. In this way the leader keeps contact with the people. And if such a walk should by chance lead past the building from which a certain lady conducts business, this does not indicate a weakening of the will.

December 7th. Such walks as I have started taking through the city are both good for the health and relaxing for the mind. Of this there can be no doubt.

December 11th. Inside there is luxury, Emil said. But outside it has the appearance of depravity. It is difficult to believe that the interior is as he describes it. Perhaps he is mistaken, regarding the address.

December 14th. "Mistaken?" Emil said today when I raised the subject. "I? Have not I been through those door many times in the past few months?" His nose twitched quickly a few times at the memory. "No, my Führer, I am not mistaken. No, indeed."

December 21st. Today for the first time I saw one of the young women leave the building. She was so covered in furs as protection against the cold that it was impossible to get even a vague idea of her appearance. She also passed out of the door so quickly that it was equally impossible to get even a momentary view of the building's interior.

These walks are proving to be very health-giving. I think I shall continue with them.

December 22nd. "It is the result of all these walks," Frau Hoffman, the housekeeper, keeps saying. "In this weather everyone should stay inside where it is warm. No wonder Herr Hitler has the flu."

She always say Herr Hitler, never my Führer. It is probably just her age. She does not understand these things. "The walks are for the requirements of good health," I explained to her.

"That is very interesting," she said. "Does Herr Hitler feel so healthy at the moment?"

December 29th. Another week in bed, Doctor Schwanenvelder says. How can I waste so much precious time? I need my walks.

If it had been summer the girl would not have been so covered in furs. I would have had a clear view. Also the door would have stayed open longer and I would have seen inside. If Martha had been near the door I might have seen her too.

If I allow my mind to think back about this Martha, I realize that she is a true patriot. Was she not at the front lines in the war, assisting the soldiers in distress, administering her gentle message of hope?

Perhaps she is not suitable to be the consort of the Führer, but as an occasional source of satisfaction, who can doubt her worth?

Another week the Doctor says.

January 7th, 1931. The flu is gone, but the weather is worse than ever. "No walks," Frau Hoffman says. "No walks for your own sake, for my sake, for the party's sake, for Germany's sake." Who can argue?

January 15th. Holding interviews with the newspapers, that is what he is doing, this William Patrick Hitler. Taking time off from his work to give interviews about his father who is the brother of Germany's next leader. Insights, they say. Read all about insights into the Führer of National Socialism.

"Send me Nothnagel," I said to Emil. "My friend," I said to the clerk, "air tickets are required."

"The Führer is going by air?"

"No. A young man with insights is coming to us by air."

January 17th, 1931. Insights, we shall see about insights.

January 19th. A walk would improve my health, but Frau Hoffman is a problem.

January 23rd. The weekend at Obersalzberg did me much good. I took young Eva Braun. Angela was very pleased to see her. "You have a young woman, Adolf," she said. "Excellent, excellent. Much better than being seen around and about with a member of your own family, much better." She put us together in one room with a double bed. Fortunately there was also a small couch in the room. Eva slept there. She is younger than I, also a dancer and therefore quite supple and accustomed to uncomfortable positions. Furthermore I am leader of the National Socialist Party and to sleep on such a little couch would impair my dignity.

January 24th. Angela was a great nuisance on the weekend. "It is wonderful, Adolf, truly wonderful that Alois's boy is coming. It is not right for one of ours to be living across the sea in a distant land. It is too far away for a Hitler. He should be here with us. William Patrick, what happy names. William is Wilhelm. Do you think they named him for the Kaiser. That would have been nice."

"Perhaps they named him for Wilhelm the Conqueror," I suggested.

"I don't know him, I'm afraid." She was knitting as she spoke and she conducted the conversation in the same way as she knitted. And the way in which she did both was without thinking.

"Wilhelm the Conqueror was an invader of the Nordic racial type who landed in England and subdued the populace who were no more than savages at the time. The English were a worthless horde until we injected a Nordic component into their blood."

"It must have been before my time, Adolf. I don't remember it." The needles clacked away together like things with a life of their own. "Don't get the idea that you are going to have William Patrick all to yourself. We are going to have a family meeting and he is going to meet all his German relatives. There will be no sending him back to England until he has met his Tante Angela and his cousin Geli . . ."

"I want them chaperoned," I said sternly. "There's no trusting the English."

February 3rd, 1931. They are here and have gone directly to Obersalzberg and Geli with them. I have given strict instructions that Geli and this William Patrick are to go nowhere alone. It must be borne in mind that he is the son of Alois. I will go in three or four days' time.

February 4th. It is all very well these English invading other peoples' countries, but they cannot expect us to be happy. The Obersalzberg is a big and lonely place. Anything could be happening up there. Only two or three days before I go.

But are they following my instructions? Is there a chaperone? And is this person someone of suitable vigilance? I go in the morning.

And what are the sleeping arrangements? Which bed is to be occupied by whom? Is Angela giving this matter sufficient thought? I must send for Emil. We leave immediately.

February 5th. On the way in the car I spoke to Emil. "I would not have suspected such a thing of Geli," I said, "this infatuation with the Englishman."

Emil's control of the car faltered for a moment, almost causing us to collide with the back of a hay wagon. "Is the Führer sure?" His voice sounded as if an obstruction existed in his throat.

"Do I speak without first possessing absolute certainty?"

"Of course not, my Führer."

"Drive quickly, my Emil."

"My Führer, we will surely be there as fast as German engineering can arrange it."

And such a meeting when we reached the Obersalzberg. The pale Englishman had brought his mother with him and they were being treated like family members, family members that cannot even speak German. Alois was sitting in the middle, translating what was said, and bearing on his face a smile that showed what importance he felt. Geli was looking at the young Englishman with eyes such as no German woman should turn towards an enemy of her country. As for Angela she was waddling back and forth to the kitchen, appearing with loads of strudel and coffee. In her life Angela has alone made enough strudel to feed Europe west of the Oder River, for months perhaps.

"I will not have it," I told them, "the interviews, the newspaper articles, the riding to glory on the back of the one who is gaining some

227

measure of importance, a not inconsiderable measure of importance. . ."

"Great importance, very great importance," Emil added.

Alois translated. Angela clucked along the following lines: "So loud is not necessary, Adolf. We can all hear perfectly. Also to behave this way before the foreign family. The family is accustomed, but the foreign family . . ."

"And the seducing of innocent German girls . . ." I said.

"An important point," Emil added.

Alois stopped translating. "Who?" he asked.

"Who?" my eye fell upon the Englishman.

"Wilhelm," Emil said.

"Wilhelm?" Alois asked. It is a matter for astonishment that one brother is so fast of understanding and the other so slow.

"Tell him," I said, "no more stories, no more riding to glory on the back of Germany's future *Reichsführer,* nothing of that sort, no scandals . . . tell him."

Angela's clucking was without pause: "After all, we are all family, and so loud is not necessary, and family is family, whether near or far . . ." and so forth.

Alois translated, the young English son of my worthless brother replied at great length and Alois translated again. "He says it is a matter of the money. The money is needful. He says that only a few personal matters are being mentioned in the articles, nothing of any consequence . . ."

At this point the Englishwoman interrupted him, pointing a long thin finger and speaking with a voice, the edges of which possessed a sharpness that Alois had felt before. He stopped speaking, his eyes assumed a hunted aspect, he swallowed the saliva of the born coward, himself raised a quivering finger which he tried to point at her and started yelling himself, his voice almost pitched as high as hers. "Translate, translate," I ordered, but neither heard. They continued shouting and pointing, their eyes bulging and the veins in Alois's neck growing thicker and redder. It is a cause of endless amazement that Alois and I grew up in the same house. Of course we had different mothers. Ultimately it is in the blood. It is clear that Alois's mother introduced the morbidity of corrupted blood into her offspring. For this reason he is excluded from the brotherhood of the pure and noble. Understandably I have always suspected this. One

228

only has to know Alois to suspect something of the sort. "Translate, translate, translate." I slammed my hand down on the table. They stopped speaking and stared at each other, their chests heaving and their eyes bulging.

Geli spoke. "I am not sure but I think *Tante* said the money is only necessary because some men do not look after their families, and Uncle said some wives do not obey their husbands' commands. And *Tante* said Uncle must consider also the bigamous marriage and bear in mind who is still the legal wife, and jail is probably as unpleasant in Germany as in England . . ."

"Bigamous marriage?" I looked at Alois.

He looked first at the floor, then the ceiling, then his hands which he raised pleadingly towards heaven. "Not exactly, not exactly. One was an English marriage and the other a German one. It is not exactly bigamy."

"Scandal," I said. "Scandal upon scandal. How can the leader of Germany have such scandals in his family? There must be no press, no interviews. I do not intend that these scandals should circulate throughout the world."

William Patrick, of the pale face and English mother, spoke. Alois translated, the veins in his neck subsiding. "William offers the assurance that there will be nothing of bigamous marriages or any sort of scandals. He would only like a few details regarding the Jewish grandfather. In this aspect there seems to be intense interest . . ."

February 6th. It must be in the female nature to cry much. I am continually surrounded by weeping and depressed women. It was not I that wanted a happy family reunion. It was not I that suggested bringing foreigners into so intimate a group. I did not suggest Alois either for that matter.

It was all the work of others and now they look at me with red eyes and flushed cheeks, I who am completely innocent in this matter. It is not my responsibility that there is so much unhappiness. Happiness itself is of little importance to the man of destiny.

For my brother's foreign seed a generous solution was found. "Here," I said. "A cheque for two thousand dollars, American dollars, to cover expenses in Germany. There will be a substantial amount left for other purposes, such as resisting the temptations offered by the Hearst newspapers." I held out the cheque and

William Patrick stepped forward, but Alois was faster. "Wait, wait," he said. "I will settle all expenses on their behalf and send the rest by mail. It is much safer so, much safer."

February 7th. Alois came to the car when we left. "You have always had everything," he said. "And I nothing. Father preferred you to me. You had a mother and I had no mother. You are a war hero and I a coward. Now you are a great man and I am still nothing. When you die all will revere you while I am forgotten. It is not fair. I want to be loved and respected as you are."

I looked at this snivelling man, wondering how we could have come from the seed of the same father. "Such love and respect must be earned," I said. Without another word I closed the car's window and Emil drove off. Geli, naturally, was safe in the seat next to me.

February 14th. It cannot be. I know that it is not so. I could not be as I am, if it were.

February 18th. If it were so, there would not be the strength of character that is so obvious. There would not be the blue eyes or the squareness of shoulder. There would also not be the vision, the use of logic, the knowledge of words, the elegance of phrasing. It cannot be.

February 19th. This weariness is beyond bearing. I have scarcely slept since Obersalzberg. I spend the nights seated at the desk in the study considering this matter that is beyond all consideration, thinking about the unthinkable. I know it is not so. I feel the Germanness within me. I have always instinctively known that I am what I am, and cannot be otherwise.

February 21st. Today I summoned Hans Frank. "You, Frank" I said. "You are the party lawyer. You are a man of wisdom and discretion. You are one to whom a mission of the utmost delicacy can be entrusted with safety. You are my friend. Furthermore, you are under orders ... There is a small matter of ancestry to be investigated, something of little significance, so minor that perhaps you will be surprised that I sent for you. Nevertheless, I want you to go the Leonding in Austria immediately. Even I must sleep."

230

February 22nd. "A little relaxation is what my Führer needs," Emil said. "Allow me to complete the arrangements." But who can think of such matters at a time like this.

February 26th. The SA intelligence office says that Alois has recently purchased a small inn. The report says that he now has all the airs of a property owner. My brother is rising in the world since the visit of his ill-born son.

March 5th. "But why, Uncle? Why?" Geli is an intelligent woman, but one must never lose sight of the fact that she is a woman. Their grasp of rational matters has severe limitations. "Why?" she asked me as I sat at my desk. "Why?"

"Why?" I replied today. I can suffer it no longer. "Why? Because the blood is everything. That is the reason why. Do you realise that the Nordic-Germanic race is God's only perfect creation in the human sphere? That is you and I, my child, we are the ultimate point of God's creation."

The child looked at me with her soft brown eyes, softer than the softest velvet. "Is this a reason not to sleep? Do you stay awake because we are perfect?"

"I am awake because of the lies, the young Englishman's lies."

"What lies? He is also a perfect Nordic-Germanic type, is he not?"

"The lies, the despicable lies concerning the grandfather. Regarding the type, there must be something from the side of Uncle Alois's mother."

"Perhaps a Turk?" Geli said.

It seemed that understanding was growing. "Certainly," I said. "Perhaps a Turk."

"Or an Arab?"

"I do not think an Arab."

"What about a Chinese or a Negro?"

I gave her the full force of my eyes. "This is a serious matter, child."

"I know what it is, Uncle. It's a Jew, the great grandfather." Her head pitched backward and she began to laugh, a high laugh, ringing like the bells of Hades. "Dear uncle Dolferl, it comes from us. We are not the perfect Nordic-Germanic types. We have a Jew in the family cupboard."

231

I leapt to my feet. "Lies, lies," I cried. "My eyes are blue. My hair was blond as a child. You do not know what you are saying. You do not know. . ."

Geli touched my forehead with her right hand, the tips of the fingers brushing gently against my hair. The early morning light was shining in at the window. I could see the ceiling above me and there was a throbbing at the back of my head.

Geli was on her knees next to me. "There, there, Uncle Dolf," she said "Having a Jewish grandfather is not the end of the world."

March 8th. Again I summoned Hans Frank. "The report," I said. "Where is the report?"

"It is not easy." He opened his eyes wide and raised his eyebrows to give an appearance of innocence. "The records are old. The references must be referred to other references and these must be cross referred to still other references which must be referred back to the original references before the truth can be the truth beyond all doubt. But, after all, the urgency is surely not great. The dead are dead, so to speak."

I spoke in measured tones, tones of reason and persuasion such as have a calming effect on the soul. "The dead are dead, Herr Frank. But if I do not have the result of your investigation soon some of the living will join them."

Frank sat back in his chair as if having been driven there by a great wind. He slowly withdrew his hands from his ears. He rose quickly to his feet, dropping his brief case and spilling its contents. Immediately he fell to his hands and knees to shove the mess of papers, pens, pencils and notebooks back. "Heil Hitler," he said and scrambled for the door.

March 10th. I should never have agreed to a meeting with this little policeman. I agreed to giving him the leadership of the SS and what do I get for it? Scientific suggestions. From this former chicken farmer scientific suggestions are offered to the Führer. He is a cruel and vicious man and of a sort with whom I would not normally associate. Such men may be used, but the Führer does not have to extend the hand of friendship.

"You wished an audience?"

"If it pleases my Führer. I know that I am not one my Führer's

232

inner circle such as Joseph Goebbels or Captain Göring or Eckhart or Hanfstaengl or Hess. I know that my Führer does not possess the same affection for me as for some of the others, but I wish to assure my Führer that he has no more devoted a man and also no more efficient a follower." I have never noticed it before today but Heinrich Himmler's face is pointed like the face of a rodent. There is a gleam in his spectacles that is reminiscent of the gleam in the eye of a rat. "This can be seen by the growth of the SS. When I took command our membership was three hundred. Now we have. . ."

"I am aware of the growth of the SS."

His little rat eyes grew moist behind the spectacles. "Of course, my Führer, excuse me. The Führer knows everything."

I made a gentle movement with one hand to put him at ease. "You said that you have a scientific suggestion to put to your Führer. Please speak."

"I have made a study of all my Führer's major speeches." He sat forward in his chair, the spectacles gleaming more intensely than ever.

"The result of much thinking has brought me to the knowledge that a race investigation office will be necessary. In this way we can list all half-breeds, those unfortunate semi-humans with one Jewish parent. I believe we should call them first-grade hybrids. But their children should be called second-grade hybrids, in other words those who have one Jewish grandparent."

"And what shall we do with these second-grade hybrids?"

He bobbed his head quickly from side to side and his thin-lipped little smile appeared. It is not correct that a person of my sensitivity should have to deal with one such as he. "Clearly they are not as repulsive as the first grade hybrids. They are far closer to being complete humans. They should nevertheless be viewed with a certain amount of suspicion. It should always be borne in mind that they are not completely human. They could be accorded the generosity one offers a favourite pet or a faithful horse."

I clapped my hands together sharply to show that the interview had ended. "This is indeed thinking of a very high order," I said. "A memorandum should be written. Set about this task without delay."

"My Führer." His hands were clasped in front of him, one massaging the other. "My Führer, this is the greatest honour that has ever befallen me. To be one of those to assist in forming the policy of the future National Socialist state, nothing could be more wonderful." The fool had not understood my gesture. "My Führer does me great honour, the more so since I have even more thoughts about the first- and second-grade hybrids that I would be honoured to lay before my Führer."

I rose and stretched out an arm in the direction of the door. This gesture did not have the subtlety of the previous one. "A memorandum will be in order," I said. "Mark it for the attention of the party leader."

He too rose, but the hands continued to massage each other and the mouth continued to speak. "I think that it would be in keeping with the stern and remorseless but also generous, truly Nordic character of our movement to make slaves of the first-grade hybrids, after they have been sterilized of course, while the second-grade hybrids could perhaps be allowed into the lower strata of the government service, clerks, messengers and so forth. They could even be allowed to reproduce themselves in a few selected cases where they have demonstrated their loyalty to Germany."

"An excellent idea," I said, my finger now pointing towards the door and waggling. "We would not want to seem to be lacking in mercy."

Even the waggling did not help. "Precisely my feeling. For this reason I felt that we should treat them according to what they are, beings that are not far below the fully human."

"A memorandum, a memorandum, a memorandum." I walked to the door and held it open.

"One more thing regarding the second-grade hybrids. . ."

"Enough of hybrids for today, my future Reichsführer SS. Place the one more thing in the memorandum." He left after much saluting and professing of loyalty and devotion, but no more talk of hybrids.

March 12th. This evening Geli was at my desk in the apartment when I came in. She was reading the memorandum of that fool Himmler. He did not even have the decency to wait a suitable period. Within hours of his speaking to me the memorandum was on my desk, delivered by an SS lieutenant. A lack of good breeding always shows. "Uncle Dolferl," Geli said, "you are my very favourite second-grade hybrid. If you show considerable loyalty to Germany I shall try to persuade future Reichsführer Himmler to allow you to reproduce yourself. He says here that such a thing is possible for the well-behaved. I must be a third-grade hybrid, but Herr Himmler does not mention us. Perhaps we are allowed to reproduce at will."

March 14th. Himmler again. He has more scientific suggestions. This time he has an idea that will prove very popular with the *Gauleiters.* He says that we are the creators of the master race, but our wives who were quite adequate in former years, are scarcely suitable for men such as ourselves. He says women should be trained, young and beautiful women, for the pleasure of the leadership of the masters. With these beautiful, young and well-trained women the old and worn-out wives will be replaced.

"My future *Reichsführer* SS," I addressed him, "I have no wife."

March 18th. Today Frank reported. I completely misread his character. I thought of him as a man of intelligence and integrity but, while I am normally an excellent judge of these matters, in this case I was completely mistaken. How one such as he can deliberately attack his Führer in this reckless and cold-blooded fashion is beyond understanding.

As for Geli, I had made the mistake of discussing the matter with her. After that she never stopped trying to persuade me to let her attend the meeting. "It is my family too, Uncle Dolf. The Jewish skeleton in the family closet is my skeleton too. Of course in my case its influence is only half what it is in yours, but nonetheless . . ." She seemed excited, out of breath, her breath coming and going with voluptuous eagerness as she spoke, the extremities of her bosom vibrating slightly at each exhalation. At length I yielded. This too was a mistake.

I pointed to a chair and Frank sat down. Then I went to the door and told the guard to retire twenty-five paces and not come closer until he received my personal instruction. Geli drew a chair to my side of the desk and sat next to me. "Proceed," I said.

"With all haste," Geli said. "Our Nordic hearts want to know if they are pumping a small measure of alien blood."

Frank opened his case and took out enough papers and files to trace the history of the entire German nation. "Well," he said, patting the top of the pile, "it's not so bad."

"Proceed, Herr Frank," I said again, this time tapping the point of one finger meaningfully on the desk.

"Also do it quickly," Geli added. "I am very anxious to know whether or not I am a third-degree hybrid," she said, lifting her nose, "which is better than being a second-degree hybrid. I can see by your surprise, Herr Frank, that you have a very poor knowledge of the party's theories of policy. Allow me to commend you to Herr Himmler's memorandum. He knows it all."

Frank looked at Geli and nodded slowly. "Of course, Fräulein," he said. "I shall contact Herr Himmler immediately."

"First the report," I suggested, now tapping my flat hand on the desk.

"Of course, my Führer," Frank said. "A service of this nature is something I see as being of special necessity to my country, its Führer, at least its future Führer and all with a deep attachment to and knowledge of . . ."

"Herr Frank!" It was the voice. It had not come for a long time, except in public meetings. Now it left me feeling weak and trembling.

"Oh, Uncle Dolf," Geli said.

Frank started talking very quickly. "My Führer, I have discovered that your father, a man of estimable character, a customs officer in the service of the state, respected by all and valued as . . ."

"He was a man of worthless character," I told him. "The creation of one such as I is a miracle of German history, a history that is replete, I say replete (I wanted him to note the knowledge of words, something that is obvious to the reader of these notes), replete with miracles. That I should be the offspring of so worthless a man shows clearly that the blood is passed on by the mother. This is a scientific finding of which there can be no doubt."

"Quite so, my Führer." Frank's eyes took on a sudden eagerness. "The gypsy in little Joseph Goebbels' line was a woman, I think. Perhaps this bears investigation."

"Perhaps." I waved a hand to show that little Joseph was of no importance in such matters. "Proceed immediately to the grandfather."

"Quite so. Quite so. It seems that my Führer's estimable father, excuse me, my Führer . . . My Führer's worthless father was the son of a true woman of the German soil, a soul of the earth, a person of the village of Graz at present part of Austria, but soon to be part of

236

Greater Germany in accordance with my Führer's wishes, and also . . ."

The patience of Hans Frank's Führer, who is normally a patient man, was being reduced to a fragment, a small and quickly withering fragment. "The grandfather," the voice said. "The grandfather."

"Uncle Dolf," Geli said.

"My Führer, my Führer . . ." Frank spoke still more quickly, but it seemed that nothing could change his manner of speaking. "My Führer's estimable grandmother, a woman of rare personal qualities and virtuous character, and bearing the name Maria Anna Schikl-gruber, had the misfortune at the sexually ripe, even over-ripe, perhaps I should say sexually mature age of forty-two, had the misfortune I say, to be employed by a Jewish family by the name of Frankenberger. Now it is well known to all scholars of human behaviour that the Jew is skilled beyond natural measure in the arts of seduction, especially when the victim of such seduction is a pure blonde virgin of unblemished Aryan origin, this being true even of Jews of a very young age such as the son of the Frankenberger family, no doubt a young man of excessively lascivious nature, something that is altogether common among men belonging to his race and religion. It is also rumoured, regarding the sexual prowess of men of this type that they are unusually fertile, a single insertion almost always . . ."

"Silence," the voice commanded. "How do you pretend to know such a thing? Were you there? When do you suggest this monstrous act took place?"

Frank sat rigidly back in his chair as if nailed to it. Then one hand reached out and softly patted the pile of paper. "I regret, my Führer, that for fourteen years the Frankenbergers paid a paternity allo-wance to my Führer's grandmother."

I looked at Geli. She was looking at me with large brown eyes. It is not fair that one of so few years should have to face this horror. "Thank the Saviour that I am only a third-degree," she said.

March 19th. Of course the truth of the matter is clear to me now. It is clear that my grandfather was a poor man and that he employed my grandmother to retrieve money stolen from him by the Jewish Frankenbergers. This is the obvious answer. I am surprised that Frank did not see it immediately.

237

I have summoned Frank and explained the matter to him. He followed the logic of my argument and all doubts are now settled beyond dispute.

March 21st. I am happy that this matter is settled beyond doubt. I am happy and at peace with my soul.

March 28th. Nothing can compare with the peace of soul possessed by the man who spends his life well, in the service of the Fatherland.

March 30th. It is as well that this little town of Graz holds no secrets. It is as well for the inhabitants.

April 2nd. Graz, what a cursed name.

April 7th. The time will come. Graz will be no more. It will be destroyed, every structure and every soul, by the troops of the victorious Wehrmacht of the future Germany.

The necessity of this came to me last night. I was in bed, first having ascertained the situation regarding the door of Geli's room. It is true that it was locked again, but it is clear that she cannot forever ignore the passion that she feels. I had switched off the light and was lying still in the darkness, concentrating to try to hear through the wall the sound of her breathing, when it came, softly at first as if from a long way off, blurred but growing in strength and clarity. The inner voice spoke and the message could not be mistaken. Graz must be destroyed. No trace must remain.

VOLUME XII

May 15th, 1931. Geli is warming towards me at last. I can sense it. At last I see the first gleamings of light in the darkness of my soul.

The walks are also no longer necessary. It is clear that because of my genius the baser part of nature can be more easily ignored. It is understandable that one such as I should be less plagued by these matters than would be the case with an ordinary man, even an ordinary Aryan.

With the door of my bedroom locked and a guard on duty I conducted a careful examination. Everything seemed to be in order. It fits well into its sack, without any sign of tension. Within the sack it seems to be of elliptical shape and of substantial size. Although I have no experience of this I sense that it is of larger than average size, in this way compensating for the absence of its partner. It is in every way an organ that should be a source of respect and admiration. Of its power there can be no doubt.

May 18th. Such a life as I have been leading cannot go on indefinitely. A rest was needed, a chance to gather strength and achieve a mature stability. After all it is now thirteen years since I was drawn into that trap in the officers' brothel in France and four years since the assault upon my will in Landsberg. A suitable period has elapsed and I am now ready to resume affairs of that nature.

Even in the great a time comes when these instincts must be allowed their natural role. Even the greatest of men are nevertheless men.

This evening I conducted a second examination. The organ has a certain full roundness of shape that it did not have before, as well as greater size and strength of an unequivocal nature. It is clear that one such is easily the equal of two or more of ordinary dimensions and capacity. I shall use it with pride and purpose. Also there is no problem as far as the need to work in unison is concerned. Where there is only one it works with a more singular purpose and a more admirable intensity. I have always been an individualist.

May 19th. Of course an object of passion is needed. I have not yet approached Geli with this in mind, but difficulties are not antici-pated. There is no arguing with destiny.

May 20th. What better time to pursue such matters. Perhaps a visit to Obersalzberg can be arranged. The trees are in bloom. The scent of the flowers fills the air, altogether a fitting background for activities of this nature.

May 21st. A suitable moment must be chosen, illumination must be allowed time to dispel all darkness. In a moment Geli will know where her destiny lies. Suddenly it will be like a flash of lightning and all will be resolved.

May 22nd. It is not beyond the man of talent to seek advice from the specialist. For this reason I called in Emil Maurice. I explained to him the matter of Geli's destiny. "A method of approach is required," I said. "I am sure that you will be of assistance in this respect. Your wide knowledge of these matters must surely be of use."

Emil cleared his throat and his eyes achieved an expression of unusual fixity. "My Führer, with respect," he said. "Is my Führer sure of this?"

"You know me well, my Emil. How can you ask such a question?"

"Forgive me, my Führer. Who is little Emil to question the acts of his Führer? But it is true, with deepest humility and a knowledge of my own ignorance, it is true that my Führer is over forty and Geli is a girl of little over twenty." He swallowed with difficulty and raised one shaking finger to the sky before continuing. "I have noticed as a result of my own experiences that young women are generally of a very lively nature and require a great deal of this sort of activity. Perhaps a more mature woman, someone of greater restraint and smaller appetite might be more suitable. My Führer is no longer in his youth and young women can be very exhausting. Once they have acquired a taste for this sort of thing ... Perhaps the Fräulein Martha that we spoke of before might be more amenable."

"This is a good word — amenable." I congratulated him.

"I believe I heard my Führer use it. But regarding the purpose for which Geli . . . "

I smiled and waved a hand casually to dispel his fears. "My dear, Emil," I said, "you need have no concern for my health. I have personally conducted an examination and everything is in order."

"My Führer?"

"Everything is in order. There is no problem. Youth will not be an obstacle. Not even a sixteen year old will be too lively or exhausting for me."

"I see," he said. His eyes were round and his face seemed paler than usual. No doubt he was surprised by the knowledge of his Führer's potency.

"A method of approach is required. I would like to be advised in this regard."

"As my Führer says." Emil rubbed his hands together. The poor man looked truly anxious. If only he could understand that his anxiety is groundless. "Well, dinner with candle light in a private room, champagne and the music of a violin: these are always of some assistance. Then it is necessary to pay careful heed to each word of the lady's frivolous conversation. No matter what one truly feels in this regard, each word should receive the sort of attention one would give to a Goethe or a Wagner. A pretence must be created that what the lady has to say is of great, even unprecedented importance. Each word must be listened to as if it was a note in the most exquisite symphony. Then, one must look into the eyes in a way that suggests that never before has there been such good fortune to look upon this manner of beauty . . ."

I interrupted him. "But, my little Emil, surely this reflects a lack of dignity on the part of a national leader?"

"My Führer, I have no knowledge in this regard. I am simply explaining a system that works without fail whenever I use it." He paused and shrugged slightly. "Almost without fail," he said.

"And after the meal? What happens after the meal? Does one proceed directly to the apartment?"

"At this point a certain amount of judgement is required. By observing the young lady it is generally possible to decide on the next step. The state of the eyes must be most carefully observed. If a certain fogginess appears to cover them and she simply stares directly at my Führer's eyes, then all is well and it is possible to proceed to the apartment with all haste. A small parting of the lips is sometimes a

241

good sign. A sudden flush to the cheeks or a heaving of the chest as if she is in the middle of some strenuous exercise: these are also useful indications."

"And if none of these signs is apparent?"

Emil was not looking directly at me. His eyes again possessed the earlier fixed quality. He seemed to be thinking about something else while he spoke. "If none of these signs is apparent a walk through the moonlight might be useful. This might afford the opportunity of comparing the sparkling nature of her eyes to the stars or the moon or the reflection of either in the water, or the brightness of herself to the fountains. If the indications are still not present, a slow ride in a carriage, with hands clasped and pronouncements of love for ever, a deep intent look into the eyes and a slight pressure of ankle against ankle, should resolve the matter beyond any protestation."

"And this will work on Geli?"

The glassiness of his eyes became altogether opaque. "Why not, my Führer? She is a woman."

May 25th. This little Emil has misled me. Over a period of years, in many ways, he has led me to believe that he is an expert in such matters, but now when for the first time his Führer asks his advice on this simple matter and, in deep trust employs such advice, what happens? Nothing happens.

Everything was in order. The champagne was of a correct brand and year. I was assured of this by the proprietor himself. The music was soft and melodious, the music of a violin, and, despite the trivial nature of her conversation, I listened to every word as if these were the last words the earth would ever hear.

In fact, there were not many words. The child was unusually silent. "Speak, child," I said.

"Concerning what, Uncle?" she replied.

"Concerning anything, no matter of how little consequence. It is the sound of your voice I wish to hear."

"You want me to sing, Uncle?"

"Simply to speak."

"In order to hear the sound of my voice?"

"That is correct."

"Why?"

"Because each word is the most exquisite symphony. I listen to you

242

as if you were Wagner or Goethe."

The eyes developed no fogginess, there was no parting of the lips, no heaving of the chest or flush of cheeks, nothing to produce even a small fragment of hope in the seducer's breast.

I noticed what seemed to be this fogginess in Geli's eyes, but she was not looking directly at me. She was looking past me as if she could not bear the intensity of emotion she was feeling. "Excuse me, Uncle Dolf," she said. "You were saying something?"

"I said that each word is the most exquisite symphony, and also that I listen to everything you say as if you were Goethe or Wagner."

Beyond all question the fogginess was present in her eyes, but she was still looking past me in the same fashion. "I also admire Goethe and Wagner," she said.

Her lips parted slightly and a flush appeared on her cheeks. "It is not Goethe and Wagner I admire. It is you." I was trying to look directly into her eyes in the manner described by Emil, but this was impossible because she was not looking at me.

"You do not admire Goethe and Wagner?" she asked.

At this point the persistent nature of her stare caused me to turn round in time to see a young officer sitting alone at the next table smile and bow in my direction, or to describe his action more clearly he was bowing in Geli's direction. I turned back to her. She too was smiling and the flush on her cheeks had deepened. "Exchange places," I said.

"Uncle?"

"Exchange places."

"But I like this place. I am happy here." This time it pleased her to look at her poor uncle.

I rose and started moving around the table. "Exchange places," I said.

With poor grace and a sullen expression she rose and exchanged places with me. The young officer, a man whose blond hair and fine Nordic features conflicted with his extremely poor manners, was looking very disappointed. But I am a man of determination and so I proceeded. Geli was giving me her full attention by this time. "I want you to speak so that I may hear your voice which has the sound of the most exquisite of symphonies and is more pleasing to the ear than Goethe or Wagner."

"That is very interesting, Uncle Dolf," she said in a voice that

243

wounded me because of its coldness of tone. "But I must point out that Goethe was not a composer. Perhaps you were thinking of Bach."

"That sentimental religious nonsense," I said.

"Or Liszt?"

"Romantic trivia." The conversation was not proceeding according to the correct pattern. It seemed that a suitable opportunity for comparing the brightness of her eyes to that of the moon or stars was not likely to come about. I also did not think that the carriage ride would be of great help.

"Please proceed, Uncle Dolf," she said smiling in a manner that suggested a greater warmth. "Perhaps you were going to mention something about the brightness of my eyes."

"How did you know that?"

"Perhaps we have the same friends."

I have an alert mind and this reference was not lost on me. But why should Emil explain these matters to Geli. Clearly she will not be intending to seduce any young ladies. "I can kill him," Geli said.

This time the reference was too obscure. I was about to demand clarification when another voice interrupted our conversation. "Dear sir, dear Fräulein, kindly allow me to present myself. Lieutenant Moltke of the Munich militia, at your service." He was smiling and bowing, in a way that only the militia can manage.

Geli's eyes began to sparkle like the moon and stars or the fountains to which Emil referred. "The pleasure is ours, Lieutenant. My name is Geli. This is Herr Hitler, leader of the National Socialist German Workers' Party."

It seemed that this Moltke was not a bad fellow after all. His heels clicked together and his arm shot out in salute. "Heil Hitler," he said. But this was an unfortunate illusion. Immediately he cleared his throat and while remaining at attention, he spoke in the following manner: "Exalted Führer, I have never before had the privilege of meeting with you. I also had no idea that my Führer, whom I so love and adore, could have a daughter of such beauty. I therefore ask, with greatest respect and in all humility, that I be allowed to visit my Führer's beautiful daughter within the sight and under the control of her family with the aim of gaining a deeper knowledge of her, and with the ultimate aim of matrimony. My Führer's daughter is clearly a pearl of rare quality."

Only old Alois, that cursed name, or the younger Alois, equally cursed, could have conceived an insult of this nature. I raised a threatening finger and pointed it at him, but before I could speak I heard Geli's voice. She was laughing. I turned to observe the cause of her merriment, but she had closed both eyes, and tears of laughter were squeezing between her eyelids. Her laughter always comes at the most inopportune moments. It was the Lieutenant of the militia who was next to speak. "My Führer, I believe that I have made a mistake, a very serious mistake. A word is sought with my Führer in private. But first my apologies, of course."

"Go with him. Go with him," Geli gasped between the tears. "He is a man of honour. Anyone can see it."

I accompanied the young Lieutenant to the men's room. "My Führer, forgive me," he said. "I misunderstood everything. For my ignorance and my poor powers of perception I grieve beyond words. Of course my Führer's being here tonight with this young woman only indicates my Führer's immense potency, a matter that surprises no one, least of all the humble Lieutenant Moltke of the Munich militia. Naturally there is nothing wrong with the party Führer being seen in a public place with a beautiful young courtesan. An attitude that suggested anything out of place in this would be bourgeois in the extreme."

May 26th. Emil is nowhere to be found. He has not reported for duty and is not in his room. He will not easily avoid me.

May 27th. During the night Geli too has vanished. I have sent for Ernst Röhm.

8am. "My dear Ernst, a catastrophe of national proportions, a disaster of terrifying consequences."

"Goebbels has defected to the Communists?"

"No, my Ernst. A matter concerning the Führer's dignity." I told him of the treachery I had suffered.

"Rest at ease, my Führer. The men of the SA shall find them. I'll keep Maurice (he has a merry smile) and hand the girl to my Führer."

11am. Where is Röhm? It is hours since he left, but there is still no sign of them.

Noon. What is the punishment for one who brings such humiliation upon the head of his leader? He was trusted, treated like a favoured friend, but behind the back of the one who trusted him he was acting the part of the bully and thug, pushing his way forward, employing two of which his Führer only has one, and using these to unfair advantage. What punishment is enough?

4pm. A message from Röhm. "Hold fast. We shall not fail. Heil Hitler."

8pm. Another messenger. "There is no place on earth where they can hide and I cannot find them. Heil Hitler."

May 28th, 1am. I have sent Frank to find Röhm.

2am. There is an arrogance amongst those with two, a contempt that they feel for others. Given the opportunity they will exert a harsh dictatorship over the rest of us. It cannot be. Never again will I accept a subordinate position to any man who is endowed in this way.

3.50am. There is nothing wrong with one. Geli would have found satisfaction with just one. If the one in question is of sufficient power no woman can be dissatisfied. She does not know what she has missed, this girl. To prefer the disorganization and disunity, the conflicting pressures of two operating in unhappy discord, is ridiculous.

7am. Göring found Frank who has received a message by hand from Röhm. "Strike hard. The honour of the Fatherland is at stake."

10am. Geli is back, picked up at the railway station trying to board a train for Paris but Emil Maurice is still free.

May 30th. She will not leave her room. She will not eat. She will not talk. She does not smile. Her skin has a pallor it did not possess four days ago. Her hands shake. She also does not sleep.
  She will get over it. The disappointment of failing her uncle cannot last forever.

May 31st. Emil Maurice has been seen in France, en route to South America, it is said. He has not considered the future with care. Who knows how far the borders of the Reich will reach eventually? Bolivia might not be far enough.

June 1st. She is a child, no more than that. I have been a fool to waste the power of my genius on one so immature. She was not worthy of me. It surprises me that I have taken so long to realize this.

Today I took a walk to the old part of town again. The weather was warm, the afternoon sun pleasant and bright. On the top floor of a certain building some of the windows were open and I could hear the meaningless chatter of female voices.

June 2nd. Standing outside Martha's place of business for a moment, no more than that, purely a passing chance, I was recognized by an admirer, a boy of no more than twenty-three or twenty-four years. He grasped my hand and shook it with such fury that it seemed as if his intention was to break it off competely. "Herr Führer, Herr Führer," he said, "to meet you yourself unexpectedly like this. What a joy! What a pleasure."

"In this way, passing amongst the ordinary people, I measure the pulse of the nation," I explained to him. "I am at one with all."

"I knew it," he said. "My friend across the road there said that you were looking at Fräulein Martha's place, but I knew that could not be, not someone like yourself."

June 5th. The evenings are warm and pleasant and by far the best times for taking a walk to the old part of the town. Also there is little chance of an admirer recognizing me.

"Such long walks," Frau Hoffman said when I came in this evening. "Excercise is well, but too much exercise is also not a good thing. It can cause strain of the heart, fallen arches and the giddiness that results from too much fresh air."

"This does not apply to me," I explained. "I am a person of a very vigorous nature.

June 6th. More trouble with the SA. They are always cracking skulls. Still, this is their purpose. Also there is jealousy between these ruffians and the SS, my pure and unblemished SS. For this reason I

247

held a meeting, bringing the warring parties together, all the Munich brownshirts and blackshirts together at the same time. Ernst Röhm sat on one side of me and Heinrich Himmler on the other. I stood silent for a full minute before I spoke. Not even the sound of breathing could be heard. From the first word it was the voice that spoke through me. "I am the SA and the SS. Each one of you is a member of the SA or SS, a part of the body, each fulfilling a given function, each one a part of me. I am within you in the SA and the SS, just as you are a part of me. In this way I am within all true Germans, and they are also part of me. But you, you are the heart, the core of my spirit. And I am the strength of yours.

"It is the miracle of our age that I have found you and you have found me among so many millions. That I have found you is Germany's good fortune."

For twenty minutes they stood and cheered, fifteen thousand men, each the possessor of two, whereas I just have one, and they stood and cheered for me.

June 8th. To just go inside, open the door and step quickly inside. It will not be so difficult. I can hold my cravat across the lower half of my face and I will not be recognized. Then in a hushed voice I can instruct the girl who opens the door to bring me Fräulein Martha. There will be no problems. In a matter of moments I will be rushed upstairs to a luxurious room that will be prepared and waiting for me. Everything will be as it should be. Martha has never disappointed me.

June 10th. Angela has become a foolish old woman. Instead of gaining in wisdom and experience she has taken to inventing strange stories. Today she came from Berchtesgaden with an old woman's witches brew of rumours. "Adolf," she said, "I hear there was trouble with Geli. I hear the child ran away from home."

"This story is foolishness," I assured her, the poor woman. "She could not be happier. She is here with me."

"But she looks so thin and pale. And she would hardly say anything to me, her own mother."

"She probably fears that you want to take her back to Berchtesgaden. Leave the child alone. She is happy. Why don't you be happy too? Here in Munich we are all happy."

June 11th. She has a very pale skin this delightful Martha of mine, narrow ankles that swell enticingly to soft and fleshy calves, thighs of a warmth and eagerness that go beyond imagination, a bosom of such formidable roundness that only the most potent dare approach it, also long dark hair that falls, in waves from crown to shoulders, and small of back and magnificence of bosom, in luxuriant splendour. I shall go tomorrow.

June 12th. Today was not possible, but soon. I shall go soon.

June 13th. On the other hand affairs of an especially weighty nature are occupying me at the present time.

June 15th. Last night in bed I thought of her again. My thoughts were of a pure, almost a spiritual nature, but despite this, unbidden, the condition ensued and remained with me all night, of astonishing hardness and increasing painfulness. Only my immense strength of will prevented me from committing that sordid deed that is unworthy of one of my character.

June 17th. Last night the condition appeared again, with an even greater anger than before. Tomorrow night. Tomorrow night I shall go.

Perhaps I should have Julius complete the arrangements. But if he sees Martha and arranges for such a time and such a place and possibly provides the driving to take me there, he could easily sit downstairs in the salon while I am led up the stairs like a criminal mounting the gallows. And to the girls he could be saying, "At this moment the Führer is doing such and such, and now he is losing this article of clothing, and now that one. Now he is in such a condition, and now such. Now he is ready to strike. Now all his power is being applied. And there could easily be undue merriment at such a description, and smiling faces, scarcely able to conceal their excessive amusement . . .

I shall go alone. Tomorrow night I shall go alone, with valour, but also with discretion.

June 19th. Tonight I went. Such a thing was a necessity. In such a manner is the steel of character tempered. It was my destiny, and if the destiny of the leader is to suffer, then there is no alternative. As could be expected I deported myself with dignity throughout the ordeal.

I stopped across the road from Martha's place of business. It was a busy night in her profession, the needs of the citizens of Munich apparently being considerable at this time of the year. Late summer is always a period of undue debauchery. The door was continually opening and closing with the coming and going of many patrons. Each time it opened the sounds of merriment, loud laughter, music, the tinkling of ice in buckets, all the evidence of dissolution and immoderate behaviour, reached me.

For some time, from the shadow of a doorway, I watched the ebb and flow of lascivious humanity through the door of Martha's establishment. I wore the leather hunting jacket given to me by little Joseph Goebbels, with a cravat wound tightly around my neck, its purpose being to provide something that I could use in the most natural manner possible to hide the lower half of my face.

My plan would have worked with exceptional smoothness except that as I reached the door it was thrown open suddenly and a man, by no means a young man, wearing evening dress and a top hat resting at an unplanned angle, came staggering out. One of the girls, a plump young women with much blond hair bunched upon the top of her head, was close behind him. "Will you get safely home, Herr Kirdof?" she called after him.

"Safely home? I will get safely down the road to Fräulein Edeltraut's residence," he shouted, throwing back his head for an instant to roar briefly in a manner that was supposed to suggest laughter. His face was in shadow and I stepped closer to examine it. His eyes met mine and the laughter stopped immediately. It was indeed Herr Kirdof, the chieftain of industry. With a further lurch that again almost threatened his uncertain equilibrium he tried to draw himself upright and click his heels together. His right arm shot forward in a salute that missed the point of my nose by no more than a centimetre. "Heil Hitler," he roared.

The girl hurried to me from the doorway, her mountainous bosom surging like the mid-Atlantic swell with each stride. "Herr Hitler?" she said. "Herr Adolf Hitler? You are coming to us? Come in. Come in." Taking me by the arm she dragged me through the door and into the house. "Madame Martha is going to be so pleased," she said.

"Everyone knows that you are an old friend of hers. She never stops talking . . ."

We had entered a short passage that ended in an arch, through which the figures of men in reclining chairs could be clearly seen, also the figures of girls, most of them seated on the laps of the men. It might perhaps be more accurately stated that they were enveloping the men, or perhaps spread over them, even wrapped around them. To say that they were seated does not truly reflect the positions they were occupying.

Close behind me a hoarse bass voice started singing the first verse of the Horst Wessel song. I looked back over my shoulder to see that Herr Kirdof was following us down the passage. He had removed his top hat and was waving it robustly back and forth trying to keep time with his singing. Neither singing nor waving hat followed any sort of regular rhythm though.

I tried to turn back, but Herr Kirdof filled the passage completely, top hat waving on one side and his free hand on the other. Also the girl was clinging to my arm like a leech and dragging me on. By the time we reached the entrance to the salon most eyes were turned towards us, drawn I am sure by Herr Kirdof's energetic and tuneless singing. As we stepped into the room the blond girl released my arm and began jumping up and down, her hands waving above her head and her bosom bouncing with a stately majesty. "Allow me to present Herr Adolf Hitler, leader of the German National Socialist Party," she screamed in a thin soprano. For his part, Herr Kirdof had squeezed into the room next to me and was singing as forcefully and with as little musical inclination as before, his right hand pointed straight ahead in a salute.

All over the room men were leaping, scrambling, staggering erect, coming to attention and saluting. The girls who had been spread over, enveloped or wrapped around them tumbled from their laps and took up positions of all sorts on the floor. Some landed on hands and knees, some on their backs, a position they perhaps occupied as a reflex, or sprawled in ungainly fashion, clothing disarrayed and surprise on their faces.

The men had scarcely reached their feet when they all joined Herr Kirdof's singing. The vigorous tunelessness was now compounded twenty-fold, but the expressions of face were stern and the salutes more or less unwavering. Some of the girls, still spread around the floor, started clapping their hands in time with the singing, an action that was difficult to achieve as each singer kept his own time. As for me, the only recourse was to stand to attention and return their salutes, my right arm stretched out, rigid as an iron bar, while at the top of the stairs that skirted one wall of the salon a group of girls had appeared, most of them wearing the small amount of clothing that was perhaps customary when entertaining their clients. I glanced in their direction for only a moment, less than a moment, but immediately I recognized the figure at the head of the group. It was Martha. She was wearing a scarlet robe that fell all the way to the floor, but compensated for any extravagance in the use of material in the lower half by employing very little in the upper half of the design. Her back and shoulders were naked and her immense bosom, although not as immense as that of the blonde girl, threatened to erupt from its tiny covering at the slightest movement.

As the fourth verse of the Horst Wessel song commenced and my right arm was starting to ache with the prolonged salute, I saw from the corner of my eye that Martha was coming slowly down the stairs, her gown trailing. In the theatre this is known as an entrance. I have a wide knowledge of such things. Noticing Martha's approach the blonde girl grabbed hold of my arm again and faced defiantly towards her Madame.

Martha reached the foot of the stairs as the fourth verse ended. She turned two furious eyes on the blonde girl. "Kriemhilde," she said and the word contained a more complete note of command than even General Ludendorff could ever have achieved.

"But I found him," she said. "It's not fair. You always do this when we get a special one."

"Kriemhilde," Martha said again.

The girl let go of my arm and took a step away as the men started the final verse. "It's not fair," she said. "It's always like this."

Martha approached slowly. She was wearing a perfume designed to confuse the senses and inflame the passions. The scent of it reached me first, followed immediately by the image of herself, drawing slowly closer. My eyes were fixed firmly on the far wall of the room, but despite this the vision of her shoulders and bosom flowed through my mind like a cataract.

Unbidden, and with no consideration for the circumstances, the baser side of my nature struck. The condition ensued with extreme

252

urgency. I heard Martha's voice, soft as a bed of down. "Oh, Adolf, what a compliment," she said. Then reaching out she rested a hand on my outstretched arm and gently lowered it. "There, there," she said. "We cannot have everything pointing forward."

Without another word she led me to the stairs, then up towards the bedrooms above. From down below there were shouts of Heil Hitler. Then someone began counting the stairs as we ascended. "...three, four, five, six..." In a few moments every voice in the salon had taken up the count. There were thirty-two stairs. We reached the landing and a voice that sounded like Herr Kirdof's made itself heard. "Tonight you feel the power of the new Germany, Martha."

A few men from the bedrooms, some of them wearing only shirts, had reached the landing, coming to investigate the cause of the disturbance. Most of them seemed surprised to see me, then turned and went back to the rooms in a sullen and moody way. As Martha led me along the passage one of them stopped in an open doorway and said, "This is not fair, Martha. It's our half of the evening. Fair is fair."

"Ach, Karl," she replied, "he is an old friend and this is a special occasion. It will not happen often. I'll do the same for you one day." To me she whispered, "They're Communists. We have the Communists in the early session and the National Socialists in the late one. The boys downstairs are all your friends. We keep the National Socialists for the late session because their appetites are larger."

"Appetites?"

"For food and beer, so while they are kept waiting they consume more than the Communists would have. The Communists have never got much money. Also the National Socialists have a greater appetite for the girls. If we let them in first the Communists might never get a chance and who can tell what damage that might cause to our fragile political structure in Bavaria. We are very conscious of our responsibilities. After all, we provide a social service."

Martha's room was at the end of the passage. It was very large, but, apart from a few cupboards, it possessed only small articles of furniture ranged carefully along the walls, except for the bed which stood in the centre of the room and by its immense size and the fine quality of its covers compensated for the smallness of the other items of furniture. It was not difficult to assess which was the most important part of the room. "Adolf," she said, the scent of her perfume

253

floating around me like a cloud, "Adolf, it has been such a long time since Landsberg. Four years, I believe. That is the nature of our relationship. But you always return to your Martha." She unwound my cravat and slipped off my jacket. "I suppose that between our rendezvous there is an endless stream of sophisticated women. Munich is full of rumours regarding yourself and Hélène Hanfstaegl, Winifred Wagner, and plenty of others. It all shows that one good one can do the job equally as well as two." She pointed me to a chair and I sat down. "A glass of wine?" I nodded. I could not take my eyes off her. The long dark curls tumbled down to her shoulders, spilling in every direction, then cascading to her bosom, and such a bosom, held in place by such meagre restraints. It was clear that any sudden movement might reveal all. Even a small movement might. The condition was an instrument of fury, beyond all imagining. Her eyes rested on it for a moment and she smiled. "You were impatient as a young man too," she said. "There have also been stories about yourself and your niece. You've been so in demand that I was surprised when you sent little Emil the first time. By the way, what's happened to him? He was a nice fellow, such an intimate smile. He spent every night for a week here, trying out all the girls to see which one suited you best. This was the first time we've been paid with a party cheque. The little devil wanted to try me too. I said to him, little Emil, tell your Führer I will deal with him personally. Trials are not necessary."

She poured the wine and brought the glass to me. "No need to stare at me so, Adolf. I'm no stranger, you know. And you could say something, even if it is just good evening. I don't expect more than that. After all, in my profession, we are not often treated to verbal foreplay." She placed the wine glass in my hand. The condition was trembling with urgency, pulsating with an intensity caused by the months of being frustrated by Geli. My grip tightened on the wine glass and I was about to spring to my feet and seize her when Martha dropped to her knees in front of me and placed a hand on each of my thighs. "You've become so important, Adolf," she said. "One day you are going to be very powerful. I wonder what you are going to do with all that power." Her hands slid up my thighs and stopped where leg meets torso. The condition was a bow string, a quivering foil, a thrown knife vibrating in the trunk of a tree, Vesuvius an instant before the destruction of Pompeii. Her eyes passed quickly over it again and she turned her head to look at me out of the corners of her eyes. "I think we can find a place for that," she said, "a comfortable dark place, very comfortable, very dark."

Very dark? What in my life has been dark? Vienna was dark during those distant days. The Prater was dark on winter nights when my only shelter had been a wooden shed. The trenches had been dark before shelling, the clothing of a rabbi on the streets of Vienna, his grizzled beard and hair, the colour of the cursed Doctor Bloch's eyes before my gentle mother died: they had all been dark.

The condition had vanished. It had been an oak of the forest, a cavalry lance, the cross of a most passionate crucifixion. Now it was a limp extension of the foreskin, an empty gourd, nothing more than a hollow pretence. "Adolf?" Martha's voice held a profound accusation. "What happened?" She placed her hand at the point where the condition had been in evidence. "What happened?" Then she leapt to her feet. Her eyes too were dark, darker even than the streets of Vienna or the rabbi's beard. "Adolf, you fool," she said, her voice low, but passionate with menace. "With you there is always something, isn't there? You can't do it to a woman, so you'll probably do it to the country. Poor Germany, if you get hold of her."

"I must go."

"What else is there for you? What possible reason to stay here?" I leapt to my feet, but her anger was still pouring from her mouth in a vulgar undignified fashion "All this fury, Adolf, where does it go to?" She pointed to a certain definite area where the protrusion that had existed was now absent. "What happens before you actually use it? Where are you storing it?" Her words were a mere babble, without meaning. "What will happen to all of us when you finally release it?"

I rushed from the room and down the passage, but stopped at the head of the stairs. In the salon my followers were waiting for the Communists to finish. At my appearance above them they again struggled to their feet, more slowly this time, giving the girls time to alight. "Accomplished with all haste," Herr Kirdoff shouted. "One powerful thrust and this woman will never recover."

"Heil Hitler," the others shouted, and in a moment all hands were again raised in salute.

I squared my shoulders and returned their salutes before descending the stairs in majestic fashion. As I crossed the street I heard Martha's voice from one of the windows above. "Drop in again some time, Adolf. We're always open for business."

June 21st. Tonight the dream came again. It is the seventh time that I have suffered through it.

I was in the midst of a forest, and each tree was a man, while at the same time in some strange way remaining a tree. At the end of a long corridor among the trees I could see a fair young girl, completely naked, tied to a stake. The stake was thick and tall, reaching high above the head of the girl and shaped like the organ of a man, that most profane of all organs. I sensed immediately that the girl was in great danger and ran down the corridor towards her. But no matter how fast I ran I seemed to draw little closer. Slowly, as I strained towards her, I came to realize that the girl was Geli. I struggled on while round about the man-trees grew high above me on every side, their branches waving in agitation while they watched my struggle.

I ran and ran and I was drawing closer to Geli, but slowly, very slowly. Out of the forest there appeared a dark-skinned figure, naked, a Jew, and possessing two of the thing of which I have only one, and the two being of a huge and bulbous form.

I struggled on, but my progress was slow, achingly slow. The apparition approached her with the ease and stealth of a wild animal, reaching her bound figure while I was still far off. Then with ease, and with no resistance offered, he performed the deed with her, again and again while I ran vainly on. And, horror of all horrors, as I slowly drew closer, I saw that she was co-operating, matching him pressure for pressure, while still tied to the stake. I knew that if I had been able to reach her more quickly she would have been mine, instead of belonging to the ghastly figure whose body was still joined to hers.

At last I was drawing close. If I reached them I would kill him, then surely Geli would be mine. I lifted my hands to take hold of his neck. But at the last moment he drew away and his face turned towards me. It was a dark face, an ugly face. It was the face of the old Alois, and it was laughing at me.

It is he. He is the Jew. It is his father who was the Jew. And in my dreams he tears my Geli from me.

July 7th. The dream rarely leaves me to sleep through a night without rising to torment me. Last night it woke me in the early hours of the morning and as I lay awake, recovering from the horror that comes

256

with sleep I heard Geli's footsteps in her room. She was walking slowly back and forth.

In time to come she will realize that these restrictions were necessary. She will know then that it was love that governed my actions.

July 10th. Last night I accompanied her to the theatre, the Residenz. The play was a trivial work, one that I would normally have avoided, but my motive was one of kindness. The child does not have much excitement in her life.

But I am afraid that kindness was not repaid. All evening it seemed as if she could not sit still. She seemed to have no desire to follow what was happening on the stage. Only the other people in the audience were of interest to her. She continually turned in her seat to look back or to either side. Nevertheless, since she is no longer permitted to go out alone I must sacrifice an evening from time to time for the child's entertainment.

July 12th. All my natural instincts regarding Geli are vindicated. This evening after my usual meticulously prepared vegetarian meal she presented me with a gift, a gift of very special meaning to me. She also offered to taste the food before I placed myself at risk by eating it. She is a truly thoughtful child. "It's the least I can do, Uncle Dolf," she said.

But the gift, what a charming thought. It was beautifully framed in rose wood and printed in gold — my certificate of Aryan ancestry, and signed by Hans Frank. "There, that should put it beyond doubt," she said.

What a wonderful idea to have such a certificate. Perhaps in time we can make such a document legal. Every German shall have one. And those that do not have them shall not be Germans. We shall call such a certificate the *ahnenpass.* Her gesture shows clearly that I was right all along. It would please me if she smiled occasionally though.

August 1931. I have had a clear report from the SA on Emil Maurice. Ernst Röhm delivered it in person. It seems that a cousin of this little Emil told a waitress in the Café Heck that his uncle had mentioned that the fugitive was in Bolivia and starting a National Socialist league there.

"Currying favour, my Führer. He is doing nothing but currying favour to cover his disgraceful conduct." Ernst said. "He is obviously pro-Jew, anti-German, egotistical and corrupt as a Turk, also probably a draft-dodger, deserter and a profiteer. . ."

"A profiteer?" I asked.

"Certainly," he said. "There are many ways a man in favour with the Führer can profit from such favour. With women for instance. . ."

"Women?" This was something I had not considered.

"Certainly. Such an association with the Führer lends a man great prestige. My Führer must have noticed that Maurice was never short of women. . ."

"But he had a way, a technique. . ."

The corners of Ernst's mouth turned down in an expression of great scepticism. There was also a sardonic element. (The word sardonic means with the corners of the mouth turned down sharply and a bitter and knowing look in the eye. I often use it.) "These are his lies, my Führer. These women were attracted by the power and prestige of Ernst Röhm's Führer, nothing else. Such a man tries to appropriate for himself some of the Führer's success with our German womenfolk."

At last an explanation to satisfy the unremitting logic of my own mind. All this talk of technique, of hanging like a fool on the senseless babblings of a young girl, carriage rides and moonlight, champagne and eyes with an appearance of a Ruhr fog: within my soul I always knew that it was nonsense.

Ernst's right hand shot out in salute. "Saluting," he said, "and marching: these are the most meaningful forms of our profession of faith in National Socialism. And this Maurice, if my Führer recalls clearly, he could never march well, and a sloppier salute cannot be imagined. Such a man is not to be trusted. Also as far as young women, nieces and such; as far as they are concerned. As for me, I have no interest in women . . ."

"We are not all so fortunate, my Ernst," I said.

"But what of this Maurice?" Ernst's great neck bulged over his collar and quivered with the intensity of the indignation within him. "Let us send an emissary to Bolivia to deal with him. It's only a small country. Within a month we'll have him back here in a hat box."

"You are so loyal, my Ernst," I said, "but we need all our men here, for the Communists and so forth."

258

His chest puffed out like that of a pigeon outside the Munich town hall. "Heil Hitler," he said. "As I have said before, my Führer does not need to explain a political or military measure to his humble Ernst. My Führer only needs to say, be there, and our presence is assured. I am a man of fundamental habits and simple tastes who receives little pleasure from life, except the breaking of a few bones for the sake of the Party. Also the indulgence of a few young boys for the sake of a restless and promiscuous nature. It is surely not much to ask of the Fatherland."

August 21st. I knew that it would not be long. Already the brightness of youth is returning to Geli's eye and the colour of spring to her cheeks. Wisdom and discipline have triumphed as expected.

August 27th. She is still cool with her uncle, but I can see by her new cheerfulness of disposition that all will soon be normal.

September 1st. Hoffmann accompanied me to the rally in Frankfurt. He took more than two hundred photographs for distribution to the press, party offices, radio and foreign diplomats so that they should be aware of Germany's future leader, but none was usable. When the light was correct the striking gesture was absent. When the gesture was present the singular strength of purpose on the facial expression was not. And when the expression and the gesture were correct the face was in shadow. "Do we show this to Germany and the world?" I asked him. "Would you have your Führer shown to the world as a death's head or without a head at all?"

"Studio conditions," Hoffman said. "Studio conditions are required."

"I looked at him with disdain. Clearly the remark was unworthy. "Who makes a speech in a photographer's studio?"

"A speech does not have to be made," he said. "Only the expressions and the gestures."

September 2nd. Last night the Communists tried to break into the apartment.

Almost certainly this was an assassination attempt, but fortunately I was not at home and therefore not placed at risk. I knew that my assailant was not a Jew because the SS guard chased him for a kilometre, across the park and down Prinzregentenstrasse before he escaped, and he was blond.

I phoned young Himmler regarding this matter and he said that the guard would be doubled, trebled, quadrupled, but never again would anyone slip past. I also phoned the faithful Ernst. "My Führer," he said, "it is the fault of those softies of the SS. They should be at home with their Mamas. The brutality and bloodlust of the SA is required to explain matters to these Communists."

September 5th. I posed at length for Hoffmann today, concentrating on the expressions and gestures, the scowl of anger, the pointed finger of accusation, the raised fist of declaration, the chopping blow of exorcism: they should all have been there, but they were not. I cannot understand how this fool of a photographer cannot capture the grandeur, the glory... My patience is wearing thin.

September 6th. Hoffmann called with more miserable proofs. Proof of what? I would like to know.

September 9th. Last night I brought young Eva Braun home to the apartment for the first time. It was a mistake. She used the opportunity to try to take advantage of my good nature by sitting on my lap and kissing me. When I reprimanded her she started to cry, whimpering that she does not understand. I explained to her that there is much that she does not understand, but this is not a reason to be upset.

September 10th. I summoned Hoffmann to give account of himself and his unflattering photographs. He brought with him a beautiful young woman, a maker of motion pictures. "Leni will assist with the posing," he said quickly. "She has much talent."

I employed the charm I learnt in Vienna and she was suitably impressed. "Talent is always obvious to me," I said, smiling flirtatiously from the corner of the eyes in Viennese fashion. "I could see it immediately when you entered the room." She also has fine Nordic features and a narrow waist of great elegance.

"I did not expect such courtesy," she said. She did not know that I surprise everyone. She did not say, my Führer, but this is not something I insist on in a beautiful woman. I could see by her manner that she appreciated the difference in rank between herself and me.

A new appointment has been made and Leni Riefenstahl will assist with the gestures and so forth. Heinrich Hoffmann is a good National Socialist. It would be useful if he was more than just a good National Socialist. On the other hand too many clever and talented people will always be a problem. Let us rather have good National Socialists. I will provide the genius personally.

September 12th. This morning I summoned both Himmler and Röhm. "How can it be?" I demanded. "You," I pointed at Himmler. "You said that the guard would be doubled, trebled and so forth. And you . . ." My unwavering finger aimed at the centre point between Ernst Röhm's eyes. "You said that the Communists would be taught a lesson they would not forget. But what happens: that young Communist thug was in the apartment again last night, endangering the life of your Führer."

Ernst Röhm was the quickest to respond. "It is the ineffectiveness of the guards, my Führer. Now if my Führer's choice fell upon the strength and resilience of the SA, instead of the cream puffs of the SS . . ."

"And where is the object lesson?" young Heinrich Himmler asked in his soft voice. "Where is the SA's object lesson? We have no support, my Führer, none at all. Instead of giving us support the heads of the SA are in their bunks having carnal knowledge of their corporals."

"Corporals?" I could not believe my ears.

"Also privates, lance corporals, the occasional younger sergeant no doubt . . . Everyone except the nurses, prostitutes and such."

Ernst Röhm's face was turning the colour of the red background of the party flag. "Choose your weapons," he roared.

"Be at peace, Ernst," I said. "I will not have duelling between my right hand and my left." In this way I solved the problem. "But why the exception with regard to nurses and prostitutes?"

"They are female," young Himmler said softly, nodding.

"Ha!" Ernst roared. "Who salutes a swastika better than I? Who marches to the beat of the drum in a more military fashion? Who has cracked more Communist skulls? Who burnt the Augsburg synagogue to the ground in just fifteen minutes? Who?" He held a finger, the thickness of Ludendorff's baton, under Himmler's nose. "Who?" he asked again. "Ernst Röhm, that's who. I also know all the verses of the

Horst Wessel song and can sing it both in bass and baritone." He turned to me, his red face puffed up like a balloon. "These are the facets of loyalty, my Führer."

Young Himmler's face was without expression, except for a slight air of boredom. "Also the widening of the *arschbacken* of the younger and blonder storm troopers."

Ernst Röhm leapt to his feet. "Pistols at twenty paces, foils, sabres, the choice is yours."

Young Himmler remained seated. "For the SA clubs would be more appropriate. Foils are obviously out of the question. It would embarrass us both if you pointed the wrong end at me."

"Silence." It was the voice that spoke, and the silence was immediate. It had not spoken since the Hamburg rally and then it had appeared so late that the audience was becoming restive. "If the left hand fights the right, what is left to defend the body?" There was no answer. Ernst Röhm's little pig eyes were fixed on young Himmler, but Himmler looked only at me.

"While you are fighting among each other the Communists are murdering me."

"Permission to speak, my Führer." Himmler's voice was soft and polite. Some quality of its politeness made the hair on my back rise slightly and bristle gently as if disturbed by a Obersalzberg breeze. "Granted," I said. It was I, not the voice.

"There is more to this than is obvious to the keenest mind. Give me five hours to investigate and the matter will be cleared up."

"Hah!" Ernst Röhm said. "Naturally, to the SS all is possible. Even the impossible only takes five hours. Only protecting the Führer is impossible to the SS."

I raised my right hand in an imperious gesture. "Captain Röhm, I still decide on these matters." To Himmler, of the thin moustache, thin lips, narrow shoulders, narrow eyes and narrow mind, I said, "You have till morning."

"We may examine the apartment, within and without?"

"Within, without, above, below: set about it immediately." After he had gone I turned to Röhm. "No more corporals," I said.

"My Führer?"

"No more corporals. Make use of your privates if you must, but corporal is a certain rank and must be shown a degree of respect. No corporals under any circumstances. Only privates."

262

"Heil Hitler," Ernst Röhm said.

I shall have to look into this matter of corporals. My loyal Ernst might have to be chastised. Corporals should be treated with a measure of dignity.

September 13th. Today has been a day of revelations, revelation upon revelation, shock upon shock, infamy breeding infamy. My Geli, my Ernst, even my little *mütterchen,* Frau Hoffmann. Am I able to trust no one? Perhaps only little Heinrich Himmler, of the flaccid face and lifeless skin, perhaps only he.

I rose and went to my office early today. Not a good place to be, this office. The walls are too close and when the door is closed and I am alone there is cold and fear within.

When I arrived, Himmler and two of his officers were waiting for me. One of the officers was carrying a pair of old leather boots. "Well, my little Heinrich, you have an answer for me or only footwear."

He was already standing at attention. He thrust forward his chest. It is a chest of only modest dimensions and its forward thrust was of a proportionately modest nature. "As always, my Führer, we have all the answers."

I seated myself behind the great desk and allowed him to commence. "We have been deceived," he said.

"Who is included in the word, we?"

"The SS, National Socialism, the Führer himself: we have all been deceived."

I leapt to my feet. "I won't have it. This is the one thing I will not allow. I am a mild and tolerant man, but deception will not be allowed." Himmler was silent, as if expecting me to continue. Instead I slowly resumed my seat. "Sit down, Heinrich," I said, "but do not imagine that I have been deceived. I am never deceived. Now describe exactly what you have discovered, but first close the door. Your men may wait in the corridor."

Little Heinrich of the splay-footed gait and the steel-rimmed spectacles folded his hands in his lap and spoke with barely a movement of his lips. "The would-be assassin is in SS custody, my Führer. His name is Horst Junger. He is formerly a citizen of Austria and he gained entry to the apartment by posing as an assistant of Frau Hoffmann. In fact that kind lady supplied him with a kitchen uniform and he passed the guards in her company and carrying her parcels . . ."

I could feel my chest swelling and the voice welling within, rising closer to the surface. "This is a fairy tale, Heinrich. You are skating on thin ice and those who skate on thin ice often fall through. Kindly bear that in mind. Frau Hoffmann worships the ground I walk on: one footprint in the sand and she worships the spot."

Young Heinrich swallowed deeply and a little row of moisture appeared along the top of his forehead. "Everything can be corroborated, my Führer, everything. And as for Frau Hoffmann, she is innocent. She too was deceived. She only helped him enter because he is your niece's lover. She simply thought . . ."

"Heinrich!" This time it was the voice. He fell backwards off the chair and stared up at me from his new position on the carpet. "Lover?" the voice said. "Lover? Have you no respect for your life, young Himmler?"

"My Führer, my Führer, my Führer, my . . ." The words were punctuated by the chattering of his teeth.

The pressure within me fell away, the voice sank again to the depths it inhabits and I spoke. "You had better have proof, my little Heinrich."

"My Führer . . ." The teeth chattered less this time. "My Führer, everything is incontrovertible, everything is corroborated."

"Corroborate then. I am listening."

He resumed his former position on the chair, sitting close to its edge. "Frau Hoffmann, a lady who at this moment is suffering terrible assaults of conscience, has admitted smuggling the would-be assassin in, thinking that it had only to do with the extreme intimacy of his relationship with . . . well . . ." The voice rose, but Himmler paused and the rising paused with it. "We approached the young lady with much respect, unending respect, and she said, What of it? When approached about the young man who had been spending his nights . . . Of course, the Fraulein did not know that the young man was a Communist or what his real intentions were. She thought his intentions were, excuse me please, my Führer, of a carnal nature with marriage as the ultimate aim." Young Heinrich was speaking more and more quickly, like a man who can avoid an explosion only by the extreme rapidity of his pronouncements. "As for the perpetrator of the conspiracy, this Junger, he was, of course, misleading Fräulein

264

Geli as to the nature of his intentions and also Frau Hoffman. We took him into custody yesterday afternoon when he again appeared with Frau Hoffmann with the aim of furthering his liaison with Fräulein Geli and putting into effect his abominable plan which, Heil Hitler, has now been foiled by the intercession of the SS."

I spoke loudly in order to interrupt the intense gush of words coming from this Himmler. "This traitor, Junger, bring him to me."

Himmler's voice calmed and its tone became as soft as it had been when speaking to Röhm yesterday. "I would gladly, my Führer, but he resisted us and had to be forcibly interrogated. He is no longer in a condition to answer questions."

"And when do you anticipate that he will be in a suitable condition for the answering of questions."

"My Führer, he resisted with great vigour and had to be restrained with a fair degree of severity. I'm afraid he will never again be able to answer questions. But everything is in order. The chief of police was present and there will be no difficulties." He permitted himself a little smile of self-satisfaction. "Also we arrested two Communist party members who at first would not admit that Junger was a member, but after prolonged and intense interrogation they both confessed. Every aspect is corroborated." This young Himmler might yet be more useful than my trusted Ernst.

Geli, I thought. My pure precious Geli. Intentions of a carnal nature. "You are wrong about my niece," I said. "Such a thing is out of the question. Kindly do not mention it again. Everything else is correct."

"Of course, my Führer."

He sat looking at me out of the smooth emptiness of his face, this little policeman. He comes into my office like a snake to make insinuations about my Geli. But this Junger was a different matter. A conspiracy is a conspiracy. There is no doubting that. "Is there anything else, Herr Himmler?"

He smiled his little thin-lipped, putty-faced smile. "Such formality, my Führer. If you could see yourself free to call me Heinrich or little Heinrich or something of the sort . . ."

"Is there anything else?" I asked him. It is possible to make use of such a little soulless henchman, but to call him by his christian name, this is an abomination.

"Just one thing, my Führer. Let me call for the boots . . ." I made a graceful gesture of hand to indicate that I had no objection to boots. He scuttled over to the door and called into the corridor. "Gunter, the boots."

When he returned to his seat he was carrying a pair of muddied and much worn private's boots. He had the audacity to place them on the surface of my desk. "From Fräulein Geli's cupboard, to whom no guilt of any nature whatsoever is imputed." The slight trace of self-satisfaction was again present. "Clearly they were left there during Junger's hurried flight on the previous night. He left by the Fräulein's window at a time when she was no doubt innocently asleep in bed."

I spoke in tones of cold disinterest. "Conspiracies interest me, Himmler, not boots."

"Ah, but Führer, these are boots of unusual interest. They are the boots Junger was wearing. They are also the boots that are worn by the SA. Now it becomes clear who it is that is arranging conspiracies."

September 14th. I have told little Heinrich Himmler of the impoverished moustache and receding chin that an eye must be kept on Röhm, nothing else. Such a view of this conspiracy becomes believable in the light of this Captain Röhm's way of using his corporals.

The photographs were taken today with Leni Riefenstahl assisting. I was in excellent form, my gestures imperious and my eyes like steel. I could see that she was impressed. "No doubt many people will be fascinated," she said, "I'm sure there is a certain mentality these will appeal to."

September 15th. "I loved him," she said, screaming. If she could only know how this sort of uncontrolled behaviour disturbs her uncle. "I loved him, but this is an emotion my Uncle cannot understand. I loved him and you let that horrible little gangster murder him." And much more of a similar nature, most of her remarks showing a complete absence of sensitivity, concerning my feelings.

"What of the plot to murder your poor Uncle?" I demanded.

"What plot? What plot? What plot?" Her voice rose higher with each repetition. "The plot was to ride upon the body of your niece. That was the plot, the successfully executed plot."

She is temporarily deranged at the moment. She does not understand what she is saying. The strain of recent times has been too much for her. I have placed a guard on her bedroom door for her own safety. I will also not bother her further with knowledge of conspiracies. She cannot be expected to understand these things.

She is happy here. She has always been happy here. Her Uncle Dolf arranges it so. When the weeping stops and all is in order again I will allow the guard to accompany her out of doors. This will be a pleasant change.

September 16th. I allowed Eva Braun to come to the apartment today. I insisted that she wear the uniform of a servant woman, a wise precaution in these days when a scandal can so easily be set in motion. When I am chancellor such scandals will no longer be permissible. I also made it quite clear that no unwarranted familiarity would be permitted. She again asked if I do not find her attractive. This matter is becoming tedious. Still her company is a comfort in some way that cannot easily be explained. There is a certain charm to be found in the company of a feeble-minded woman.

September 17th. I am writing from the Deutscher Hotel in Nuremberg. Schreck, my new chauffeur, is driving me to Hamburg to address the Gauleiters. This is a matter of a fairly serious nature and you would think that someone in my position would be granted a degree of peace to deal with it, but no.

I had just completed my breakfast at home this morning and was about to leave when I was called to the telephone. Frau Blomhoff, Geli's singing teacher, was wanting to tell me that Geli had not attended lessons for two weeks. "And she has such a nice little talent too," she said.

I replaced the ear piece of the telephone and turned to leave only to find that the young lady herself had crept up behind me and was blocking my path. "So," I said. "Top C can never be achieved in this manner."

"I do not care for top C," she said. Her face was white, by no means its usual deep colour. "I also do not care for life here."

"In Munich?"

"In Munich, under this roof, under your dictatorship."

"Dictatorship?" I looked at her sternly and in horror. I wished it to be clear to what extent she had wounded her uncle. "I, a dictator? I am a leader. A dictator is a brutish unthinking creature."

"I am going to Vienna." She thrust her little chin forward as if the small power of her will could in any way compete with my own.

"I forbid it." The words echoed and re-echoed in the room. "I forbid it, I forbid it."

"Why do you scream?" she said. "Why always scream?" This is her way of trying to transfer blame to her uncle.

"I forbid it," I repeated. "The guards will receive instructions accordingly."

Vienna indeed. It cannot be permitted, to wander around that city of corruption, to have the flower of German womanhood sullied by Jews, Turks, Gypsies, Slavs and others of inferior blood. Such a thing will never be permitted.

September 18th. Everything was as it should be. Breakfast had been served in my rooms in the hotel by a waiter who bowed often and took a few backward paces when retiring from the table. The silverware and furnishings were of a high standard and the ornaments were of the traditional heroic type. The manager himself called to see that everything was to my satisfaction. Julius Schreck, of course, dined with the servants.

Everything was perfect. A new triumph awaited me in Hamburg, a chorus of approving voices, the admiring ladies, the men hoping to win my favour. And I, the centre of everything the final stage of German history, the true voice of providence. For me, all doors were open.

Then this.

Who is the pistol's owner? I want to know. This is the one fact I must have. Whose pistol is it that has brought this disgrace upon me? Just when power is within my grasp, at the moment when I am riding the high tide of German history, I am dragged to my knees in this way.

I will have the owner of this pistol.

September 19th. They blame me. The *Post*, that filthy socialist scandal sheet, will not be allowed to exist in the new Germany. They hint that I pulled the trigger. They say that we were always fighting, that there were reasons I would have preferred her dead. They say that I had the opportunity. Never mind that I spent the night in

Nuremberg. They say the pistol was mine.

September 20th. This is just one more instance of deception. I gave the child only love. How could she repay me in this way?

Now the gutter press is trying to destroy me. The scandalmongers suggest that my love for her was a perversion. They drag the most pure of passions through the filth of their pages. Is this what she wanted? Did she want to turn the whole world against her Uncle?

Now there is no more personal happiness, only national glory.

VOLUME XII

September 21st, 1931. To reach Vienna I changed to a smaller car. The Mercedes might have attracted attention. The present and temporary régime have seen fit to bar me from entering the land of my birth.

The city has not changed since I passed through it many years ago in the search for my identity. The motley rabble still throngs the streets, the wealthy Jews still subvert the nation for their own purposes, the pleasure seekers still crowd the Prater and the rooms of the women on the Spittelberggasse, but the Opera is there, and the hostel on Meldemannstrasse remains.

All were part of the process of refining and tempering, the scalding and purifying.

Throughout the journey the voice spoke within me, so that I should hear and learn. I know it at last. For the first time there is recognition beyond any doubt at all. The voice is the deep-rooted well of my own genius. It speaks to me, adding to my wisdom and strength, preparing me for my role in the future and triumphant Germany of which Vienna too will be a part, a reluctant part perhaps, but one which will also feel the purifying fire of my will.

The words they put on the stone are "Here sleeps Geli, our lovely ray of sunshine." I stood at the grave for a short time, while the voice moved within me. As I stood there the day grew dark with the approach of evening and I knew the air had grown cold because Frauenfeld and Schreck were waiting some distance away near the gate and they were wrapping their arms around their chests and walking up and down to keep warm. I felt neither the cold, nor the wind that was blowing from the mountains. When I turned to go I could not see Schreck and Frauenfeld for the intensity of the darkness.

She was the same as the others. When I needed them most they always left me. It was so with Mama and it is the same with Geli. There is always Eva. Poor stupid Eva. She will be there because she

270

does not dare to leave. She could not allow herself such impudence. She is not willful as Geli or Martha, and not stricken by fate as Mama was.

September 22nd. Before returning to Munich one more action had to be taken. I have never been one to turn away from problems. It has always been my way to approach them directly and deal with them decisively. A single stroke is my way. For this reason I had Frauenfeld arrange the meeting.

The notorious doctor was dark and bearded as would be expected in one of his race. He had the ill manners to light a cigar when I entered the room. I spoke briefly, with accuracy and no wastage of words and waited for his reaction. "As I understand this fascinating web of euphemisms and obfuscations with which you try to hide the meaning of your words, you are telling me that you have only one testicle? Is this correct?"

"Clearly," I said.

He inhaled from the cigar, then breathed a dense cloud of smoke into the room. This is something that is not easy to bear for one whose nature is as sensitive as mine. "Clearly is not the word I would have used. However, to answer your question, if it was a question (not even that is clear): the human male functions equally as well with one testicle as with two."

"Possibly even better in some cases," I suggested.

"Clearly not," he said, while further polluting the air with his cigar smoke. "Not in any cases at all, I shouldn't think. But performance should be quite adequate in order to lead a normal life."

"Then I have no problems." I slapped the palm of one hand down sharply on the surface of his desk.

"None of a physical nature," the dark and brooding doctor said.

"I knew it," I said with great confidence. "I knew it."

"Which does not mean that there are none at all." Through the cloud of cigar smoke a dark and impudent sneer could be seen. "We are not only physical creatures."

"There is the soul," I said with great authority. "No one needs to tell me that there is the soul. I am a man of the soul. I am a man of fire and earth."

"Of course," he said. "And one such as yourself must, I am sure, have had a remarkable father. Tell me about your father. I should

271

like to hear something about the father of one such as yourself."

"Hah." I pointed an accusing finger at him. "You are wrong, Herr Doctor. I knew that your knowledge was not perfect. From the beginning I knew." I sat back in the chair, looking directly into his eyes, to savour my triumph. "My father was a worthless individual, a person of no value whatever. I have attained a certain position in life purely through the strength of my own will and the power of my genius, nothing else. My father had nothing to do with it."

"I am consumed by interest," he said. "Tell about your mother. She surely must have been a remarkable person, if one considers the certain position in life that you have attained."

"Correct. This time you are correct, Herr Doctor. I am not one to deny the accuracy of your remarks when such accuracy exists. She was a person of exquisite gentleness, great beauty and goodness beyond all natural goodness."

"So you loved your mother and you hated your father. In your eyes she was a fine person, but he was worthless."

"Not in my eyes only." I was careful to make the point clear. "This was generally known to be so. There can be no doubt about it. He was well known for his barbaric ways and his brutal nature while she was looked upon as an angel by all."

"I see," this Herr Doctor said. His eyes were half closed and he seemed to be pointing the cigar at me, as if it was a weapon. "The world in which you live, Herr Hitler . . ."

I interrupted him. "Most people with whom I have contact call me Herr Führer."

He lifted the cigar to his lips before answering and looked at me through dark conspiratorial eyes. No Aryan can possibly imitate such an expression. This is the face of the Bolshevik revolutionary, the decadent writer, the impressionist painter, the prophet of weakness, the rabbi. "Herr Hitler will do in this case," he said. If such a thing had not been impossible, I might have taken his tone of voice to be one of boredom. "Herr Hitler, we live in a world that is filled with ghosts from the past. Your world has, I am sure, many threatening authoritarian figures, shadows of your father, and in your particular case each one has two testicles as well. As a child you felt that this man stood between yourself and your lovely and tender mother . . ."

This little Jewish doctor was not altogether a fool. "It was plain for all to see," I told him. "He was always doing it. He would take her by

272

the arm, lead her into the bedroom and close the door. He was a man of extreme vulgarity."

"Perhaps he also referred to your one testicle?"

"No!" The voice spoke for me. "He would never have dared."

This little doctor's eyes widened and he inhaled from his filthy black cigar. "As I was saying, your world is full of threatening authoritarian figures, the possessors of two testicles, and it is your intention to remove them by force, if not the testicles, at least the men. And in so doing you will prevent them from having knowledge of your mother." He sat looking at me through eyes that were again partly closed and through smoke that covered his face like a veil. What did he know of my mother? Did he not understand that she was taken from me many years ago. And who is he talking about? Papen, von Schleicher, Hindenburg? Each one will have to be dealt with. "Herr Hitler, you sit here, looking at me through those dreamy blue eyes, the eyes of a mystic . . ." This dark and bearded doctor was speaking again. "Tell me, why do you bring your problems to a Jewish doctor? Why do you not go to one that you trust? Your views are well known in Vienna, and regrettably, shared by a few."

"Not such a few."

"A minority. Why do you come to me for help?"

"Help?" It was the voice again. "Help? It is not I that needs help. It might be you that needs help, Herr Doctor. Do not assume that I need help." I had leapt to my feet and an arm was extended towards him, one finger pointing. "It is not I that needs help. The force of National Socialism will be felt in Vienna also. The fine ladies and gentlemen of the Viennese academies and Viennese society think that Germany's turmoil does not concern them. They are mistaken."

A door to the office opened and the head of a woman appeared, a young woman, of the same swarthy type as the doctor, but he waved to her, indicating that she should leave. Clearly he did not want to suffer his humiliation in public.

The voice withdrew and I sat down again, one hand resting against the desk to steady myself. The desk shook, but it was not of my doing. I think this doctor pushed against it at that instant to create the impression that my hand is unsteady. People such as he are capable of anything. "And the masses follow this?" He waved a hand in the air in a grotesque parody of my masterful gestures. "Despite the coarseness of it, your power comes from your oratory. Stop speaking

273

and your influence will immediately start to shrink." I said nothing, but looked sternly back at him. "Truly," he said. "The group is no more than a submissive herd that cannot live without a confident leader. If his will is strong they follow anywhere."

I laughed, a bold confident sound. "Anywhere," I said. "They follow the Führer anywhere. As you correctly said, it is a matter of the will."

He looked past me, as if not seeing anything.

"During normal times you would have been a noisy eccentric failure, but our time is not normal. Only now can you have this effect on men and women. How fortunate for you that the human group does not think. I fear that they will indeed follow you anywhere, without thought and without inhibition, but where will you lead them, Herr Hitler?" He is a strange man, this Doctor Freud. He asks the same question as Martha. Only his race prevents him from achieving true status. Of course this is a serious impediment.

September 23rd, 1931. Frauenfeld had the good grace to drive slowly past the Opera on the way out of Vienna. It was the scene of so much inspiration amidst the humiliations of those far-off days. In those days every Viennese gentleman with a coach and four treated Adolf Hitler as if he was dirt. Every well-fed café owner and his red-cheeked *hausfrau* were warm in bed at night while Adolf Hitler shivered through the cold nights without shelter. Every *Judenjungen* had money in his pocket, every Slav, every idle Italian, but not Adolf Hitler. The times have changed. And they will change with greater effect in the years to come. Life might not always be so comfortable for Vienna's well-fed gentlemen.

At my request Frauenfeld took us past the Prater as well. The shed where I had often sheltered on winter nights was gone, nothing of it remaining to provide a memory of my sufferings. But nevertheless I remember. Truly, Vienna, I remember you well.

Frauenfeld drove to Salzburg as quickly as his little car would allow. I told him and Julius Schreck that conversation would not be appropriate. There was too much of importance for conversation. For the first time in months my mind is clear. Everything is as it should be. Even this Jewish doctor is in agreement. The mass will follow the man of will without thought and without inhibition. There can be no doubt of it. And whose will is of greater potency than mine?

Who is more single minded?

"So, Gauleiter," I said to Frauenfeld. "Such times . . . " I said.

He nodded slowly. "Such times, my Führer," he said, "such sad times for my Führer . . ."

"Sad times?" I looked sharply at him. "My dear Gauleiter, there is nothing sad about these times. They are fine times, times to take hold of opportunities. In future years you will look back on these times and then you will agree that these were fine times . . ."

He glanced away from the road to examine my face, no doubt to read either pleasure or anger there. Such things are of great importance to the humble. His Führer's receiving or spurning of him is the simple difference between life and death. "I spoke of the girl, my Führer. I know of my Führer's deep attachment. I meant the girl . . ."

"Of course, of course," I said, patting him on the shoulder in a comradely fashion, "of course, the girl . . . it was unfortunate. But these are fine times, Frauenfeld. Remember my words. The loyal ones such as yourself will be well rewarded. We will have power not later than 1933 and Austria will be part of a great united Germany. You have my word on it."

"Heil Hitler," Julius Schreck said from the back seat. He is a man of fine reflexes, a National Socialist to the core.

"It is a wonderful thought, my Führer," Frauenfeld said, being careful this time to keep his eyes on the road.

After Salzburg we parted with Frauenfeld and changed to the comfort of the Mercedes. Schreck drove. "Slowly, my Julius," I said. "Drive slowly so that I can absorb every detail of our fair land."

"As my Führer says," the humble Julius answered. "There is no fairer upon earth."

"Spoken like a son of the German soil," I said. "And now the struggle for our soil is just beginning. Next year we will have the presidential election. A year later we take power in the Reichstag. From that day all will be ours. All problems will be solved with German diligence and German thoroughness."

"What will we do with Germany when we have it, my Führer?"

"What will we do? Ah, what will we do? Everyone asks this." What a question to ask of one such as I. In the fields and against the hillsides on either side of the car the trees were already showing the yellow and red shades of autumn, the sign that winter was not far off. But for me it is surely spring. Everything has changed. Bonds that were fettering my soul have been loosed and, deep within my being, I feel the stirring of the voice, a growing and strengthening presence, waiting for the moment that was almost upon us. "What will we do, my little Julius? First we will eradicate. All reactionary elements, all bearers of tainted blood, all who cling to outdated ways and beliefs, all who lack patriotism, who possess alien loyalties, all who lack true German intelligence: all such will be removed from among us. First our society itself will be cleansed. Some nights of purifying will be needed. We will move the Jews out of those big houses in Dahlem and such places, and reward the worthy.

"The crime that fills our streets and is the result of harbouring such elements will cease. Everything will be perfect.

"The Junkers that at present hold the strings of power have been trying to avoid me, but their days are past. I can no longer be ignored."

Julius turned a little in his seat. The imploring expression in his eyes was clear to see. "I hope my Führer will remember me in those future days. I have always been a loyal and true follower of my Führer and member of the party."

"Of course, my Julius," I said. "Of course I will remember you."

EPILOGUE

MY COUSIN MOHAMMED'S photographic studio was on the second floor of a building in Plein Street. He was not allowed to operate from there, but he paid fifty rands a month to a custodian. This was a title given themselves by a singular breed of white men who made a living as the front men for small black businesses trying to survive in white business areas.

I went up the stairs rather than trust my safety to a lift that rumbled and groaned as it came down the shaft in answer to my summons. The stairs were dark, the walls in need of painting, and Mohammed's door was made of steel that clanged like cymbals when opened or closed. As I came in he had a black woman and her two small children seated in front of a photograph of the Acropolis that covered one wall of his studio.

"Hullo, cousin," he said as I came in. He had not seen me in ten years, but he showed no surprise at all. He was like his father in many ways.

The woman looked from him to me and then back to him and shrugged. We do not look very much like cousins. "Hullo, Mohammed," I said.

"Smile," he said to the woman and her kids, "as if you were on holiday in Greece."

After they had finished smiling and having their picture taken and had gone away with Mohammed's assurance of how good they were going to look in the picture he pointed me to a seat at his desk. From an old padlocked wooden cabinet he brought out a bottle of whisky and two glasses. "You see this bottle," he said. "My old man left me a case. For use on special occasions, he said. He mentioned you by name. He said I should give you a drink whenever you came round."

"He was a generous man."

"We'll drink to him." He poured two fingers into each glass.

"To a real gentleman," I said.

"An adventurer," he said.

"A gentleman and an adventurer," I said.

"If we keep on trying to find titles for him, we aren't ever going to get this drunk," Mohammed said. So we stopped trying to describe him and drank the whiskey.

Outside it was getting dark. The concrete canyons between the buildings were in deep shadow and the daytime inhabitants of the city were hurrying homeward through the cold winter afternoon. "I'm sorry to keep you here after hours," I said.

"Keep me here, cousin?" His eyes looked amused. "Where do you think I sleep?"

"Not here surely?"

"Why not? It's better than going all the way out to Atlantis every night. I go home weekends."

"But the police?"

"I am quiet as a mouse." He raised his glass to me and took a slow mouthful, his slow cunning smile and his every gesture reminding me of his father. "You wanted to know about the diaries, I suppose?"

"Anything that you can tell me."

"Ah, you're too late, cousin. I know nothing about them. I knew the old man had these manuscripts but he never spoke about them. Will you believe that I did not even know whose they were?" He went round the room, pulling down the blinds. "My evening blackout. No sense in advertising. But, regarding the other thing, you're too late. You never met Auntie Martha, I think. She died last week. She seemed to know all about them. She was born in Germany, you know. She followed the old man out here a few years after the war. God, how Mama hated her. We had strict orders never to go near her place. But she was a great old dame and we all spent a lot of time with her. I don't think you ever met her, did you?"

Wessel Ebersohn
Johannesburg
June 1986